Bede
Griffiths

SUNY series in Religious Studies

Harold Coward, editor

Bede Griffiths

A Life in Dialogue

Judson B. Trapnell

Foreword by
Kenneth Cracknell

STATE UNIVERSITY OF NEW YORK PRESS

Published by
State University of New York Press, Albany

© 2001 State University of New York

All rights reserved

Printed in the United States of America

For information, address State University of New York Press,
90 State Street, Suite 700, Albany, NY 12207

Cover photo by Judson B. Trapnell

Production by Kristin Milavec
Marketing by Dana E. Yanulavich

Library of Congress Cataloging-in-Publication Data

Trapnell, Judson B., 1954–
    Bede Griffiths : a life in dialogue / Judson B. Trapnell ; foreword by
Kenneth Cracknell.
        p. cm. — (SUNY series in religious studies)
    Includes bibliographical references and index.
    ISBN 0-7914-4871-1 (alk. paper)—ISBN 0-7914-4872-X (pbk. : alk. paper)
    1. Griffiths, Bede, 1906– . 2. Camaldolese—India—Biography. 3.
Benedictines—India—Biography. 4. Benedictines—England—Biography.
5. Catholic Church—Clergy—Biography. I. Title. II. Series.

BX4705.G6226 T73 2001
271'.102—dc21
[B]   00–038767

10 9 8 7 6 5 4 3 2 1

For Fr. Bede Griffiths, OSB Cam.
and for the tradition of Christian *sannyāsis*
he represented

Contents

——

Foreword, Kenneth Cracknell   ix
Acknowledgments   xiii
A Chronology of Bede Griffiths's Life   xv

Introduction   1

Part I
God in Nature: 1906–1932

An Evening Walk   13
1   The Romantic Explorer of English Countryside   15
2   Reconciling Reason and Imagination   20
3   God through the Symbol of Nature   27
The Conditions for Dialogue   37

Part II
God in Christ and the Church: 1932–1968

Night of Conversion   43
4   The Benedictine in England and India   46
5   Faith as a Way of Knowing   56
6   God through the Symbols of Bible, Liturgy, and Prayer   71
Into Dialogue   101

Part III
Nonduality *(Advaita):* 1968–1993

The View from His Window   111

viii   *Contents*

7   The Guide of Shantivanam and Prophet of Dialogue   114
8   The Way of Intuitive Wisdom   128
9   God beyond the Symbols of the Religions   148
Through Dialogue   183

Conclusion   194

Notes   209
Bibliography   261
Index   271

Foreword

——

As we move into our new century, Christians, Hindus, and people of faith within all traditions continue to be perplexed and challenged by the interreligious encounters that are now part of everyday life. In this situation we reach out for guides and mentors to lead us through what some see as the pitfalls and some as the springboards of this new reality. Happily, in the past century giant figures have emerged within most communities of faith as pioneers of positive interreligious understanding. These people were acute theologians speaking with authenticity from within their own traditions and also, wonderfully, were empathetic interpreters of dimensions of religious commitment far different from their own. Such men and women have been voices in a swelling dawn-chorus of a new world-community in which we must all come to speak confidently about what God has been doing for all humanity. One such towering figure was the English Benedictine monk Bede Griffiths, who died in 1993. It is beyond doubt that the achievement of this devout Roman Catholic *sannyāsin* will be reflected upon, and built upon, throughout the twenty-first century. Many Christians, some of whom are as yet unborn, will be inspired to follow his example, and commit themselves to "the meeting of East and West" very much as Griffiths described that encounter. Many others will want to offer critiques of his vision and, very likely, to discover quite different paths to the one that he trod.

In this situation we need exactly the kind of judicious overview of Griffiths's work that is offered in this scholarly and finely crafted book. I think there are at least six kinds of readers who will be particularly touched and helped by this book.

In the first place because this is not a straightforward biography (there are already some excellent narrations of the Griffiths story), it gives us a perspective that sets Fr. Bede within the intellectual history of the twentieth century. Of particular importance is the awareness of the significance for Griffiths of Blake, Wordsworth, Coleridge and the post-First World War poets. This was the period of T. S. Eliot's "The Waste Land," which captured the deadly and depressing materialist cityscape of London, where Griffiths was to work in his midtwenties. Accurately assessing Griffiths's Romantic attachment to the English countryside, we see that it was no accident that he studied English literature at Oxford under the guidance of C. S. Lewis, his tutor and, later, his close friend. Lewis started Griffiths on a philosophical path that was to be marked by a search for an adequate relationship between reason and intuition. Throughout the twentieth century there lurked the unresolved conflict between "science" and "religion," between "ratiocination" and "imagination," and between "fact" and "faith." There is little wonder that Griffiths took to himself eagerly the Indian distinction between *vijñāna* (discriminative knowledge) and the "unitive wisdom" extolled in the Upanishads and in the Bhagavadgītā. Later he was to meld them into his own vision of the "new science," as expounded by such writers as Fritjof Capra, Ken Wilber, Rupert Sheldrake, and David Bohm. In the deeper background of Griffiths's intellectual pilgrimage lay, on the one hand, such figures as Susanne Langer and Paul Ricoeur and, on the other, Carl Jung and Teilhard de Chardin.

Part of the intellectual history of our century is its complex theological development, and this book explains those Catholic traditions that nurtured Griffiths and that made him open and confident in the face of *advaita* Hinduism. Protestant readers like myself will note the influence of Thomas Aquinas, Henri de Lubac, Pierre Johanns, Raissa and Jacques Maritain, and later Karl Rahner. But Catholics as well as Protestant thinkers will also find much to reflect upon in Griffiths's own idiosyncratic version of Logos theology.

A third class of readers will be formed by those who find Griffiths a stimulating Christian thinker but who may readily acknowledge that they are seriously limited in their knowledge of the Indian traditions. These will find this book to be a gentle and lucid guide that offers judicious and accurate comments on Hindu thinking, particularly of its *advaita*, nondualist aspects. Of great value, too, are the commentaries on such figures as Roberto de Nobili and Brahmabandhab Upadhyay, as well as Griffiths's immediate predecessors Jules Monchanin and Henri Le Saux (Swami Abhishiktānanda). This shows us that not even a pioneer like Griffiths is a missiological Melchizedek, "without father, without mother, without descent."

This book explores Griffiths's work as a "culture bearer" and indeed as a potential transformer of culture. Both scholars and general readers will be helped by the analysis of the subtleties involved in Griffiths's culture critique, in his epistemology, and in his mystical theology of symbols. It is suggested that the difference between a convert and a cultural bridge builder lies in the deliberate attempt of the former to sever continuities between the old and the new whereas the latter finds a way to use language and symbols that cross over two different sets of paradigms. Thus Griffiths worked on expressing a Christian *advaita* in which the traditional symbols of the Trinity and Christ, communion, love, and Logos are seen in the light of the contemplative vision of India. By these means the previous symbols are revived within a new religious paradigm in which intercultural and interreligious dialogue is accepted as a powerful method for disclosing what is true.

Those of us who teach missiology (a fifth class of readers) will find such discussions of the discontinuities and transformations of cultural and religious symbols an invaluable resource to which to direct both our students and colleagues. All students of Christian liturgy, for example, need to ponder Griffiths's efforts to incorporate elements of Hindu ritual into the celebration of the mass or his efforts to harmonize Hindu temple architecture and symbols with Christian themes in the ashram at Shantivanam.

But perhaps Griffiths's real legacy to the twenty-first century lies in his wholehearted embracing of the task set out by Henri de Lubac in words addressed to Jules Monchanin: "To rethink everything in terms of theology, and to rethink theology in terms of mysticism." This book demonstrates the interdependence of spiritual experience and theological reflection throughout Griffiths's life, and thereby throws a great light on Griffiths's actual conclusions about the *advaita* that lies at the heart of mystical experience, and therefore at the heart of all religious traditions. In his own person Griffiths united two great symbols of the life of prayer, devotion and surrender. The English Benedictine *sannyāsin* in his Indian ashram became for many people a living symbol, through which they could sense what it might mean for followers of different religious traditions to meet "in the cave of the heart."

To be sure Griffiths was no plaster saint, and one of the great merits of this book is that it neither hides nor glosses over the distress and ambiguity of his final months. Trapnell's close reading of all Griffiths's extant writings as well as the taped records of their many conversations disclose other inconsistencies, many of which are discussed in chapter 7. As

Raimundo Panikkar remarked at a memorial service in Chicago in 1993: "We can find fault with many of his ideas in which the presentation was not up to the point. That was not his forte. That was not his mission. The importance of Fr. Bede which we should never forget, for us, was his person . . . was his being there." Perhaps the most important aspect of this book is that it enables Fr. Bede to "be there," once again for us.

KENNETH CRACKNELL

Acknowledgments

With deep gratitude I acknowledge the colleagues, family members, friends, and teachers who have contributed in varied ways to this project. For their guidance in bringing this manuscript to publication, I am grateful to Harold Coward, Nancy Ellegate, Marilyn Silverman, and Kristin Milavec. For their generous support in gathering sources, I thank Sr. Pascaline Coff, OSB, Milo Coerper, Beatrice Bruteau, and especially Bro. Wayne Teasdale and Fr. Jesu Rajan. For their insightful responses to the written text, I am indebted to James Robertson Price III, Chester Gillis, and especially Fr. William Cenkner, OP, Fr. James Wiseman, OSB, and Victoria Urubshurow. In response to his gracious foreword and inspiration in Hindu-Christian dialogue, I thank Kenneth Cracknell. In return for their friendship and sharing of ideas, I am grateful to my past colleagues in the Theology Department of Georgetown University and in the Religion Department of Hampden-Sydney College. To my family I express my heartfelt thanks for their support, especially my grandfather, George Hann, my parents, Richard Trapnell and Jane Buck, my wife Rose, and my daughters Grace and Maria. Finally, to my teachers from "East" and "West," I offer gratitude, especially to Sri Sri Ravi Shankar for his graceful presence and to Fr. Bede Griffiths for his time and interest in this project and for his inspiring example, the impact of which has endured beyond his death.

A Chronology of Bede Griffiths's Life

1906	Born, Alan Richard Griffiths, December 17, at Walton-on-Thames, England.
1919	Enters Christ's Hospital, the "Blue-Coat school."
1924	Evening walk during which he experienced an awakening to God's presence in nature.
1925	Enters Oxford in the fall.
1927	Begins to study English literature with C. S. Lewis as tutor.
1929	Completes studies at Oxford. Lewis, by then Griffiths's close friend, experiences a first conversion to theism.
1930	Begins an "experiment in the common life" at Eastington in the Cotswolds with Hugh Waterman and Martyn Skinner. Serious study of the Bible, and Western and Eastern philosophy.
1931–1932	Returns home. Prepares for Holy Orders in the Church of England. Works with the poor in London. Undergoes powerful conversion experience. Returns to the Cotswolds as a hermit, then as a farm worker. Received into the Roman Catholic Church, December 24, 1932.
1933	Enters Prinknash Priory in January; begins a year-long postulancy.
1933	Clothed as a novice, December 20, taking the name "Bede."
1934	Simple profession, December 21.
1937	Solemn profession, December 21.

1940   Ordination to the priesthood, March 9.

1947   Appointed prior of St. Michael's Abbey, Farnborough, April 29.

1951   Transferred to Pluscarden Priory in Scotland as novice master, December 20.

1954   First autobiography, *The Golden String,* is published.

1955   Departs for India with Fr. Benedict Alapatt, March 9. Arrives in Bombay in April. With Fr. Alapatt, he attempts to establish a Benedictine monastery outside Bangalore.

1958   Founds Kurisumala Ashram with Fr. Francis Mahieu in Kerala.

1966   A collection of articles from 1953 to 1965 is published as *Christian Ashram,* later as *Christ in India: Essays Towards a Hindu-Christian Dialogue.*

1968   Accepts the challenge to revive a monastic community at Saccidananda Ashram, Shantivanam, near Tiruchirappalli in Tamil Nadu (founded in 1950 by Frs. Jules Monchanin and Henri Le Saux, OSB [Abhishiktānanda]).

1973   *Vedanta and Christian Faith* is published, based on lectures given at the University of Madras in 1968.

1976   *Return to the Center,* written in 1972, is published.

1980   Becomes formally affiliated with the Camaldolese order.

1982   Saccidananda Ashram is formally received into the Camaldolese community. Attends conference in Bombay on "East and West: Ancient Wisdom and Modern Science," significant for his encounter of the "new science" that would be integrated into his synthesis of Eastern and Western religions throughout the 1980s. *The Marriage of East and West: A Sequel to The Golden String* is published.

1983   *The Cosmic Revelation: The Hindu Way to God* is published, based on lectures given at Conception Abbey, MO, in 1979. Again travels to the United States and to Australia.

1986   Two monks from Saccidananda Ashram, Amaldas and Christudas, are ordained priests of the Roman Catholic Church in the Camaldolese order.

1987   *River of Compassion: A Christian Commentary on the Bhagavad Gītā* is published, based on talks given at his ashram.

1989   *A New Vision of Reality: Western Science, Eastern Mysticism and Christian Faith* is first published in England.

1990   Serious illness and accompanying spiritual awakening in January. Works to help found and support lay contemplative communities, especially during visit to North America.

1991   Delivers lectures at the John Main Seminar, New Harmony, IN. *Vedānta and Christian Faith* is republished.

1992   Final visits to Australia, the United States, and Europe. *The New Creation in Christ: Meditation and Community* is first published in England, based on lectures given at 1991 John Main Seminar. Bede Griffiths Trust is founded to oversee publications and continue work of contemplative renewal. Second debilitating stroke on December 20, only days after documentary *A Human Search* is filmed (an edited transcript of which is published in 1997).

1993   Dies at Shantivanam, May 13.

1994   *Universal Wisdom: A Journey through the Sacred Wisdom of the World* is published.

Introduction

———

This is not a *biography* of Bede Griffiths in the usual sense of the term, that is, a comprehensive account of significant life events and of personality development. Excellent biographies of him in this sense are already available.[1] In contrast, this book presents a highly structured interpretation of Griffiths's life and thought, shaped by categories that he himself suggested in later years as he reflected upon the paradigmatic quality of that life. These chapters, then, are guided less by concern for completeness in conveying events, character traits, and relationships than by attention to the trajectory of his self-understanding. In its method of examining Griffiths's life and thought, this book seeks to fulfill the conditions for "integral understanding" articulated by Joachim Wach in the mid-twentieth century, which included not only the accurate gathering of information but also "an engagement of feeling . . . or participation," a constructive orientation of will and experience in the broadest sense of the term.[2]

Griffiths thus not only lived a life, he created a work, a "text" whose literary shape and symbolic power he himself sought to understand and put into words. It is the intention of this book to disclose the contours of the life-as-symbol he thus discerned. In accord with the theory he articulated, his life-as-symbol intentionally points beyond itself to the divine mystery of which that symbol is an expression and communication.

To bring the symbolic shape of Griffiths's life into focus, we begin with the end, with the evening of a life that spanned most of the twentieth century.

1

His Final Months

In May in southern India, even in Shantivanam, the "Forest of Peace," it is oppressively hot. Shaded by tall palm and mango trees stand the thatched huts of the ashram. Inside one such hut, on a bed beneath a window, lies a long, frail figure, wrapped below the waist in the worn saffron cloth of a *sannyāsi*. In between his ragged, painful breaths are deep silences. Crows caw in the surrounding forest.

An American disciple appears in the always open doorway at the foot of the bed; the older man's blue eyes open, and he beckons. When the American comes to the bedside, the older man reaches out his right hand, grips the other's, kisses it, and then gently pulls the younger man into an embrace. As they converse, the older man cannot place some of their common American friends; his brow wrinkles with frustration. Then they pray together, still holding each other's right hands: "Hail Mary, full of grace. . . ." No wavering in the elderly Englishman's voice or spirit: "Sacred Heart of Jesus, have mercy on us all. Sacred Heart of Jesus, have mercy on us all. Sacred Heart of Jesus, have mercy on us all." Silence. Then: "Hail Mary. . . ."[3]

An Australian friend, taking his leave before dawn for what they both realize may be the last time, says quietly: "May we meet merrily in heaven." Whereupon the blue eyes open brightly as the older man lifts himself up on an elbow, raises one gnarled finger in recognition of the famous statement, and identifies its speaker playfully: "Thomas More! Thomas More!"

The friend lays him back down on his bed, embraces him, and then says in parting: "I will go now."

"No. You are only leaving my hut. You will never leave my heart."[4]

A few years before, shortly after a first stroke, he had felt the nearness of death. He had said all the usual prayers and waited. Eventually, he felt the inspiration to "surrender to the Mother," after which a kind of death did happen: "I'm being overwhelmed by love," he cried out.[5]

Almost three years later, only days before a second debilitating stroke, he interpreted this earlier experience of surrender in a filmed interview:

> I was very masculine and patriarchal and had been developing the animus, the left brain, all this time. Now the right brain—the feminine, the phonic power, the earth power—came and hit me. It opened up the whole dimension of the feminine, of the earth. . . . It

was very violent at first, like something hits you on the head; but then it is extremely loving. It comes and embraces you.[6]

Who is this "Mother" to whom he has surrendered? "[F]or me, 'mother' means Mother Nature, Mother Earth, mother of the living world and the human world, and my own mother. They all come together in the Virgin Mother, and it's very, very deep now."[7]

When doctors examined him shortly after his second stroke, they reported that his right brain had shrunk, that his left side was paralyzed, and that his heart had been irreparably damaged. For a time in the hospital, even the abiding sense of communion with God, deepened by the first stroke, was disrupted: "Suddenly the whole thing ceased. . . . I felt the absolute disappearance of God. It was a terrifying experience."[8]

❧

He sleeps much of the day and is awake much of the night. When awake he acknowledges pain; at times, in the physical agony of being moved, he screams out; in the distress of forgetting loved ones, he weeps. Nevertheless, there are moments when his blue eyes beneath white eyebrows seem to gaze beyond, or open for the eyes of others to glimpse through them what cannot be expressed.

The nights are still, dark, warm. An Indian monk, one of the first to join him at Shantivanam over twenty years ago, sits at the bedside. The white hair and beard of the teacher glow in the candlelight; occasionally the head turns and the old eyes catch the flame. With sudden animation, the older man begins to shout loud vowel sounds: "Christudas, pray with me! Lift up your voice to the Lord; shout to the Lord with all your heart." Then, from his depths: "Cry out to the Lord with all your heart."[9]

Another night, while the rest of the community sleeps, he speaks with the Indian disciple who would later take responsibility for guiding the younger monks: "I am waiting to come live here with you."

"We will be happy to have you here with us," Bro. John Martin replies.

"That is what I want." He continues, seeming to forget that the other of his first disciples, Amaldas, had died suddenly three years earlier: "I really want you and Christudas and Amaldas and me to be living as brothers in unity. That is what grace is in my life. Can we do that?"

"Yes, we can do that."[10] Not a movement of the surrounding palm fronds disturbs the silence.

Yet often as he rests in the stillness, the hand that has written so much and blessed so many in his life as a priest moves in circles before him while he prays the Hail Mary or whispers simply "Jesus" or "Bless you."[11]

He can no longer wash or relieve himself without the help of others. He suffers from pneumonia, an agonizing cough, fever, and the searing pain of a urinary tract infection. He is frequently confused, even delusional. Yet out of the disorienting slow dance of dying emerge moments of communion with those caring for him.

One day he says: "I feel that God has created a love and understanding in us that I have never experienced before and that has completed my life. It is a plan of total love, of total self-giving in love."

When he is asked if his time has come to go beyond, he replies: "I don't think so. In a sense I feel complete but something is growing all the time."[12] Yet to the same devoted friend, Russill, he later acknowledges that he is ready to die and then adds: "Would you die with me?"[13]

Continually he prays to Mary and to the Sacred Heart of Jesus; his meditation is upon the Gospel of John and upon the Upaniṣads, including these verses that he often asks Russill to chant at his bedside: "I know the Spirit supreme, radiant like the sun beyond darkness. Those who know him go beyond death, for he is the only path to life immortal. . . . Those who know him who is greater than all, beyond form and beyond pain, attain immortality."[14]

In the heat of a May afternoon, as he lies beneath the window in his hut, he quietly prays: "God the Father, God the Son, God the Holy Spirit, I surrender to you."[15] Then he sleeps. As he breathes out gently, the silence opens, unbroken, spreading wide.[16]

Surrender through Dialogue

We are inclined to suspicion about religious insight or spiritual transformation that accompanies serious illnesses such as a stroke or pneumonia. When a person's memory begins to fail or when they become prone to emotional excesses, we may regret that such persons are no longer themselves, that they are no longer in their right minds. Is this what we should conclude about Bede Griffiths's final months? An answer to this question is significant for a work that attempts to portray his journey; how we interpret the terminus ad quem will shape our view of all its prior details.

As his final illness exemplifies and as his final words reaffirm, Griffiths understood his life as a continuous act of surrender in love. Near the end of his 1954 autobiography, *The Golden String*, he writes:

> The divine mystery is ultimately a mystery of love, and it reveals itself to love alone. It is only if we are prepared to give ourselves totally in love that Love will give itself totally to us. . . . But it is a love which revealed itself in an agony of self-surrender on the Cross, and only makes itself known to those who are prepared to make the same surrender. For the love of God is not a mild benevolence; it is a consuming fire. To those who resist it it becomes an eternal torment; to those who are willing to face its demands, it becomes a fire that cleanses and purifies; those whom it has once penetrated, it transforms into itself.[17]

From this perspective, his final months take on poignancy and meaning in continuity with the eighty-six years that preceded it. To bring that continuity into focus, it is necessary to develop briefly some of the key principles of Griffiths's self-understanding—principles that are fundamental to the structure and content of this study of his life and work.

A few years before his death, Griffiths discerned three stages in his lifelong surrender: God in nature, God in Christ and the Church, and *advaita* or "nonduality."[18] Especially important to his understanding of these stages is the principle that when a new phase in individual or collective evolution occurs, the prior stage must not only be transcended but integrated as well.[19] Griffiths therefore did not perceive these three stages of his life as unrelated to one another; rather, each prior stage is found implicit within the latter, while the latter cumulatively explicates what was implicit from the beginning.[20] The three major parts of this book correspond to these three stages.

To grasp further how Griffiths perceived his own life and its method of inquiry, it is important to understand his view of the integral relationship between ideas and experience. In remembering how he sought through reading philosophy to understand his continuing experience of God in nature, he writes:

> It was the experience which came first and so it must always be. All our knowledge comes to us directly or indirectly from experience, from the vital experience of the senses and imagination. The philosopher can interpret our experience . . . , but ideas can never take the place of experience. An idea of God which had no relation to my own experience would have no interest for me.[21]

This claim for the primacy of sensory and imaginative experience over ideas or theory, written in 1954, remains normative and helps to explain his ambiguous relationships to external authorities as well as his interpretation of revelation and dogma.[22] As with other personal tendencies, Griffiths sees his own craving for the direct experience of spiritual truths as typical of his era; like himself, others in modern times in their "rediscovery of religion" have desired to base their religious convictions upon the authority of their own experience.[23] To reflect this predilection, each part of this study begins with his account of an experience that was formative for that period, and that he would strive to explain in continuity or at times necessarily in discontinuity with preexisting ideas.

Given the primacy of experience in his method of inquiry, surrender is, for Griffiths, not only an intellectual act; it is necessarily holistic, engaging body, mind or soul, and spirit—an anthropology he derived from the apostle Paul and from the early Fathers of the Church:

> Man has a body, a physical organism, a structure of energies, forming part of the physical universe. He has a psychological organism, consisting of appetites, senses, feelings, imagination, reason, and will, which forms his personality and is integrated with the physical organism. But beyond both body and soul, yet integrated with them, is the spirit, the *pneuma* of St. Paul, the *ātman* of Hindu thought. This spirit in man is the point of his communion with the universal spirit which rules and penetrates the whole universe. This is the point of human self-transcendence, the point at which the finite and the infinite, the temporal and the eternal, the many and the One, meet and touch.[24]

This threefold and integrated view, he believes, corrects the Aristotelian anthropology of body and soul—a reduction of the person that has had increasingly negative consequences in modern Western culture.

The schemata of body, mind, and spirit is used to structure each of the three, chronological parts of this book. In the first chapter of each part, key biographical events of the respective period are described to illustrate the interaction of cultural ideals constitutive of his self-understanding and view of history. In the second chapter of each part, his intellectual development and theory of mind are traced, focusing on the relationship between rational and nonrational ways of knowing. In the third chapter of each part, his spiritual journey in the respective period and his understanding of that journey are recounted, especially with reference to the key symbols that mediated his mystical experiences of God.

If surrender of body, mind, and spirit in love is how Griffiths experienced and conceived the general movement of his life, then dialogue is the praxis through which that surrender was fostered. This dialogue took many forms: intrapersonal, interpersonal, intercultural, interreligious, and cosmotheandric.[25] As will become apparent in this book, these multiple forms are simultaneous, interdependent processes within a greater dynamism. Griffiths's account of interreligious dialogue discloses the grammar of interrelationship common to the various forms of this dynamism:

> [D]ialogue, when properly understood, is not a compromise with error but a process of enrichment by which each religion opens itself to the truth to be found in the other religion, and the two parties grow together in the common search for truth. Each religion has to hold the fundamental truth in its own tradition and at the same time allow that tradition to grow, as it is exposed to other aspects of that truth. Thus we begin to realize that truth is one, but that it has many faces, and each religion, is, as it were, a face of the one Truth, which manifests itself under different signs and symbols in the different historical traditions.[26]

Clearly, dialogue in any form for Griffiths is not a process within which one's self is totally lost in the other—whether that "other" is another aspect of oneself, another person, a culture or religion different from one's own, or even the divine mystery. As this study will explicate, the interchange between self and other that is dialogue assumes and discloses the nondual relationship between them, an intimacy that is further reflected in the relation between the parts and the whole—self and other being two of the "faces" or facets of that whole. Dialogue, then, constitutes full engagement in mutuality as a means to surrender to a truth that is greater than and incorporates self and other.

To clarify how dialogue as a method matured throughout his life, each part of this study concludes with an account of how this method underlay the activities and insights of each period, with particular focus upon the development in his assessment of the religions.

The implications of such a view of dialogue include the insight from holographic theory that Griffiths was fond of repeating, that the whole is present in every part, that is, the interactive relationship between aspects of his psyche (rational and intuitive or masculine and feminine) corresponded to the dynamics of intercultural, interreligious, and global realities. Seen from this perspective, his life took on more than a private significance: "From the earliest time I can remember I have always had the conviction that what I was experiencing was being given not for me alone but for others, in a sense for humanity."[27] It was from this perspective as well that he would often say: "My monastery is the world."

Particularly paradigmatic in Griffiths's life was his turn East. After steeping himself in Western Christian culture for his first forty-eight years, he spent his final thirty-eight years bringing it into dialogue with India—an intercultural exchange now being replicated for many at a global level.[28] Griffiths thus plays the role of what Karl Joachim Weintraub has called a "culture bearer." Weintraub, citing Augustine as a clear example, describes those unique individuals in a society who through their upbringing and education fully "bear" the surrounding culture within them and yet "lose trust" in the very ideals of that culture. Such persons then experience a fundamental disorientation, no longer able to rely upon their culture to guide their life journey. In reorienting themselves by establishing an ideal that goes beyond yet integrates existing values, such individuals serve to transform the culture itself.[29] A particularly modern aspect of Griffiths's role as a culture bearer to be examined in this book is the fact that his reformulation of a cultural ideal is achieved in explicit dialogue with the civilizations of the East.

Griffiths thus also became a pioneering exemplar of what his early companion in India and lifelong friend and colleague in dialogue, Raimundo Panikkar, has called "multireligious experience":

> [H]e seriously attempts an existential incarnation of himself into another world—which obviously involves prayer, initiation, study and worship. He does this not by way of trial but rather with a spirit of faith in a truth that transcends us and a goodness that upholds us when we truly love our neighbor. . . . It is not experimentation but a genuine experience undergone within one's own faith.[30]

In his life, in fact, Griffiths anticipated and illumined an experience that is today becoming more common, achievable for many without needing to emigrate to a new culture.[31] He envisioned a "marriage of East and West" not only within himself but also in his ashram, in the church, and in the global community. By participating in dialogue at any one level, interrelationship at the other levels is nurtured.

The individual living in dialogue thus becomes a symbol of the collective—even, for Griffiths, a symbol of the divine, expressing and communicating God's nature and activity. For Griffiths, that divine nature and its activity are experienced as a communion in love, a dance of self and other that is reflected intrapersonally, interpersonally, interculturally, interreligiously, and cosmically *for* the person and *through* the person who surrenders to that love.

In the trajectory of Griffiths's self-understanding may be discerned what he provocatively suggested was the direction of civilization as a whole, a rediscovery of religious truths based upon experience that was at once mystical and dialogic. His intercultural explorations, his efforts to integrate rational and nonrational ways of knowing, and his interreligious mysticism—the three interrelated topics within each part of this study—raise questions with implications that reach beyond a single life: To what degree is it possible to translate oneself into and learn from another culture, with consequent benefit for one's own? How can one successfully negotiate the differences between the intellectual frameworks of two cultures and religions for the sake of a more holistic and dialogic approach to truth? How may one draw upon the riches of a foreign tradition, while remaining connected to one's religious roots, in order to foster a fuller mystical awakening?[32] Through posing such questions, the "text" of Griffiths's life in dialogue opens a "world" within which members of various traditions can recognize themselves and can interpret the challenges of contemporary religious life.

Surrender through dialogue, then, at its many simultaneous and interactive levels, is the context within which to interpret Griffiths's final months in all their apparent ambiguity of spiritual blessedness and physical pain, of emotional richness and loss of mental acuity, and of light and dark. Surrender through dialogue is an attentive participation in, and a humble acknowledgment of, the dynamic interaction of complementary values inherent to reality:

> God is not simply in the light, in the intelligible world, in the rational order. God is in the darkness, in the womb, in the Mother, in the chaos from which the order comes. So the chaos is in God, we could say, and that is why discovering the darkness is so important. We tend to reject it as evil and as negative and so on, but the darkness is the womb of life.[33]

Griffiths surrenders not only to the light, but to the darkness as well, as complementary aspects or "faces" of what is ultimately realized as whole:

> The hidden mystery behind all the pain and suffering and disaster of the world is a tremendous ocean of love. And I am sure that when we die we shall discover this ocean of love which is hidden from us now. . . .[34]

With this picture of his end now in mind, we may turn to his beginning.

PART I

God in Nature:
1906–1932

—

For I have learned
To look on nature, not as in the hour
Of thoughtless youth; but hearing oftentimes
The still, sad music of humanity,
Nor harsh nor grating, though of ample power
To chasten and subdue. And I have felt
A presence that disturbs me with the joy
Of elevated thoughts; a sense sublime
Of something far more deeply interfused
Whose dwelling is the light of setting suns,
And the round ocean and the living air,
And the blue sky, and in the mind of man:
A motion and a spirit, that impels
All thinking things, all objects of all thought,
And rolls through all things.
　　　—William Wordsworth, "Lines Composed
　　　　　a Few Miles Above Tintern Abbey"

An Evening Walk

In the early evening, a tall, slight youth walks alone, with unhurried determination, across the playing fields. The angled light defines his strong jaw; his lips are slightly parted; his eyes gaze reverently at the countryside before him. Although such walks have become almost a ritual, his blue eyes are brightly attentive, as though he is about to meet someone whom he might not recognize unless all of his senses are quietly alert. All around him weave the wing and song of birds.

His shadow lengthens gradually as it moves upon the grass—until he pauses. Before him are hawthorn trees laden with clusters of white blossoms. For minutes he stands still. Suddenly nearby a lark of sandy brown plumage rises, as if without effort, straight up into the evening sky, its trilled, warbling song mimicking its quickly alternating ascent, descent, and ascent. With the final falling of wing and song, the evening settles and darkens around him, the last traces of gold and red flaring in the western sky. For minutes more he remains still.

Almost thirty years later, having been a monk for over twenty of them, he would use a description of this experience to begin his autobiography, identifying this walk as "the beginning . . . of a long adventure," the end of a "golden string" that he would wind through his lifetime into a ball, leading to "heaven's gate":[1]

> I remember now the feeling of awe which came over me. I felt inclined to kneel on the ground, as though I had been standing in the presence of an angel; and I hardly dared to look on the face of the sky, because it seemed as though it was but a veil before the face of God.[2]

13

For months, even years after this experience, the young man spends a significant part of each day walking in the countryside of Sussex. He learns the names of the birds and flowers. He wanders through the hills and woods, sometimes sitting beside streams, simply watching the movement of life around him—seeing and waiting to see. At times he brings with him a book of verse, the words of those who also have seen. These walks, too, he would remember, and the quiet urgency behind them:

> I took no pleasure except in this mysterious communion with nature. I felt the presence of a spirit in nature, with which I longed to be united, and every form and aspect of nature spoke to me of an invisible presence.[3]

Only months before his death, his tall, slight frame now bowed with age, he still remembers and draws from these experiences:

> I recall that I went up into the hills and was completely alone, and a mist came over and I felt as if I was alone in the universe—a sort of total emptiness, and yet total bliss, was there. . . . [T]his was an awakening to the whole world; and in a curious way I still live back in that time. . . . It was a coming, I suppose, to maturity. I think you live out only what you experience, and then, through the rest of your life, in a way you bring out what was implicit from the beginning.[4]

While the countryside surrounding the ashram in South India is very different from that of Sussex in England—palms replacing hawthorns, crows more frequent than larks—nature remains for him a symbol of and "a veil before the face of God." Lying near death in a hut so far from the scene of his early awakening, he still waits upon the unfolding of "what was implicit from the beginning."

1

The Romantic Explorer of English Countryside

A lan Richard Griffiths was born on December 17, 1906 in Walton-on-Thames, England. The youngest of four children, he was christened and raised in the Church of England. After a financial crisis, the family moved to the country and near the sea to live what Griffiths remembers as "a wild, open-air life" that was for him a time "of almost unclouded happiness in spite of our poverty."[1] While his father remained a somewhat detached figure in Griffiths's life, he experienced unfailing support from, and "a relationship of total oneness" with, his mother.[2] Reflecting late in life upon the value of his family background, he says: "I realize more and more what a grace it was for me. I keep looking back on that and feel that the mother—and it's not only my mother, but 'the Mother'—is behind me all the time."[3]

As a boy and later as a youth in school, he spent much time outside, especially bicycling or walking through the countryside of Sussex. His experience of nature resonated strongly with the sensibility conveyed by the English Romantic poets he began to read, especially Swinburne, Shelley, Keats, and Wordsworth. Love of nature and of poetry, he would later recall, was "the whole heart of my religion," of far greater import to him than Christianity.[4]

Immersion in Western Culture

Griffiths was attracted at an early age to reading and to the life of ideas. His formal education was comprised of a preparatory school and then Christ's Hospital, the grammar school where one of his later poetic and intellectual inspirers, Samuel Taylor Coleridge, had studied. He describes his passionate reading of Dante, Shakespeare, and other classic

15

authors, as well as his early interest in socialism and Christian human-ism.[5] By the end of his secondary education, Griffiths considered him-self an ardent pacifist and socialist, clearly prejudiced against any dogma or imposed moral absolutes, and generally skeptical of Christianity. As he described the attitudes of his close friends and him-self some thirty years later: "we did not believe in any authority beyond our own reason."[6]

Griffiths's appreciation of nature, combined with his rejection of much that was modern in the society around him, prompted his first lengthy trip into the countryside, an action that he later understood as "symbolic," and indicative of "the course which my life was to follow." His further characterization of this trip illustrates his enduring self-orientation: "I was beginning to turn consciously to nature and to seek for a more primitive way of life than that of the modern world. . . . I had the sense of belonging to an immemorial past, in comparison with which modern civilization was only a temporary excrescence."[7] This identification with the past as well as his distrust of modernity become thematic in Griffiths's self-understanding throughout his life.

It was also near the end of his school years in 1924 when Griffiths ex-perienced his dramatic and formative opening to the presence of God in nature. What he saw and felt on his evening walk transformed his way of seeing the natural world around him and inspired a worshipful attitude toward it—a reverence that for a time would overshadow completely what then seemed like an "empty and meaningless" Christianity.[8] Of the enduring quality of this experience he writes:

> I experienced an overwhelming emotion in the presence of nature, especially at evening. It began to wear a kind of sacramental char-acter for me. I approached it with a sense of almost religious awe, and in the hush which comes before sunset, I felt again the pres-ence of an unfathomable mystery. The song of the birds, the shapes of the trees, the colours of the sunset, were so many signs of this presence, which seemed to be drawing me to itself.[9]

Significantly, this sacramental sense of nature and openness to the "un-fathomable mystery" endures, even after his later reassessment of orga-nized Christianity.

In interpreting his early experience of spiritual awakening, Griffiths speculates about the nature of the time in which he was then living. With many others during the years after the First World War, he shared a "sense of disillusionment at the apparent failure of our civilization."[10] He also identified with others of the previous century, such as Wordsworth and many of his contemporaries who, as a result of an experience of divine presence in nature, then abandoned organized religion. Left to themselves, such people like himself then had to meet the challenge "to work out one's religion for oneself."[11] Griffiths's further description of this challenge reveals his sense of his life's work:

> For many people the very idea of God has ceased to have any meaning. It is like the survival from a half-forgotten mythology. Before it can begin to have any meaning for them they have to experience his reality in their lives. They will not be converted by words or arguments, for God is not merely an idea or a concept in philosophy; he is the very ground of existence. We have to encounter him as a fact of our existence before we can really be persuaded to believe in him.[12]

It is significant that, writing as a Catholic monk and priest thirty years later, Griffiths upholds the value of what others might identify as a "pagan" experience of the divine in nature. It is also important that he claims for this experience the status of grace in its role not only in his own "long adventure" and but also in his Western Christian culture's "rediscovery of religion."[13] Griffiths thus clearly identifies his own situation with that of his culture as a whole.

Ambivalence toward Western Culture

After a reverent exploration of the English countryside, Griffiths began his studies at Oxford in the fall of 1925. His pessimism about the evident decay in the civilization around him grew, a feeling that he saw reflected in T. S. Eliot's famous poems of that period, "The Waste Land" and "The Hollow Men."[14] Griffiths was prompted to pursue socialist and pacifist activities further, as well as to propose a new religion founded on the prophetic examples of the Romantic poets and on the experience of the divine in nature. With the help of two close friends, Hugh Waterman and Martyn Skinner, he came to formulate a philosophy of life that accepted the ability of the "poetic imagination" to see into reality and that called into question the influence of the "scientific mind." As he objected to the divorce of reason from feeling and imagination, so he condemned what he perceived as the church's separation of morality from love, and of conscience from passion.[15] Thus, Griffiths's social critique, his philosophy of the mind and its faculties, and his sense of religion were all interrelated even at this early stage of their formation at Oxford.

It is not surprising that Griffiths's studies while at Oxford and just afterward informed the self-discovery and spiritual search he was experiencing at the time. With the guidance of his tutor and later close friend, C. S. Lewis, Griffiths explored the breadth of Western philosophy and literature, becoming not only deeply familiar with the heritage of thought contained therein, but also identifying with the struggles of each author.[16] As Griffiths later recognized in writing his autobiography, through his early philosophical studies he was searching for a rational explanation of what he had experienced, and was still experiencing, as a presence in nature.[17] Underlying his reading of Spinoza, Berkeley, Kant, and especially Coleridge, he came to realize, was his desire to reconcile, as it were, two sides of himself: the voracious student of ideas and the lover of nature, or, the philosopher and the romantic poet. It was also at this time that Griffiths first read some of the classic texts of Eastern philosophy, specifically, the Bhagavad Gītā, the Dhammapada, and the Tao Te Ching. These books, he would later reflect: "were to act as a secret ferment in my soul and to colour my thought without my knowing it."[18]

During his formative college period, Griffiths, again with his friends Waterman and Skinner, began to practice living in a community, set apart from the urban society whose values they had rejected. First during their vacations from Oxford and then as a full-time "experiment" beginning in 1930, the three lived in the countryside "a life primeval in its simplicity."[19] This experiment was undertaken in response to their deep disillusionment with their cultural milieu. Griffiths would later write that they had confronted "the disintegration of the human soul—of all human culture."[20]

The exploration of a spiritual order or rule, which included devotional reading and ascetic practices, especially fasting, became an important dimension of their common life. It was during this period of communal living that Griffiths also began his gradual rediscovery of Christianity and of the church. Through reading theologians such as Augustine and Aquinas, through experiencing the art of Bach, Dante, and Giotto, through his correspondence with Lewis,[21] and through a prayerful study of the Scriptures, Griffiths began to reassess his own religious heritage and its potential role in his life, to the point of considering ordination.

The "experiment" of living in the countryside became a time when he not only practiced the values and spirituality he had formulated at Oxford, but also began to look beyond them, not only building upon that initial revelatory experience in nature, but also recognizing its limits.[22] Prophetically, Lewis had advised him to cease trying to recover the experience of the evening walk when God in nature was so apparent:

"You always want to recover that paradisal experience, but you cannot. You have to go forward through the struggle, the pain, to something beyond."[23] After less than a year, the three friends disbanded their communal life, each pursuing divergent interests. Griffiths's path first took him home, where he began regular church attendance with his mother, and then to London for work with the poor in preparation for Holy Orders in the Church of England.

Having withdrawn from society and from its institutions, Griffiths found himself drawn to return to them in order to take the steps that would move him into a new stage of his life. This pattern of withdrawal and return is repeated in Griffiths's life as he works out his ambivalent and prophetic role toward Western cultures. Even while in the solitude of the English countryside, however, Griffiths attended to the dialogue of ideas sparked by both his experience in nature and his philosophical reflection upon it.

2

Reconciling Reason and Imagination

When in his last term at school during an evening walk Griffiths experienced an awakening to the presence of God in nature, his mind and spirit had already been prepared for this kind of spiritual recognition, both through time alone in the countryside and through study.[1] While he was ready for such an awakening, nevertheless Griffiths's intellectual and spiritual search was given new energy, if not direction, by this experience. In the following years, this experience of the divine in nature would stand at the center not only of his spiritual journey but also of his intellectual life.

Reflection upon the Evening Walk

With hindsight Griffiths would conclude that experiences of awakening in nature like his own are, in fact not unusual, especially for the young, and that they can be mediated by a variety of situations, from mountain climbing to war, from illness to falling in love: "Anything which breaks through the routine of daily life may be the bearer of this message to the soul. But however it may be, it is as though a veil has been lifted and we see for the first time behind the facade which the world has built round us." Such experiences, then, transform the mind; encountering "something beyond all words" undercuts one's unconscious attachment to them and to the concepts they express.[2]

It is, therefore, not surprising that while at Oxford Griffiths's continued experience of the divine presence in nature influenced his notion of truth and shaped his method of inquiry for knowing that truth:

Consciously or unconsciously it was this state of ecstasy, which I was seeking all the time, since I had first had a glimmer of it on that evening at school. It was in this state that I felt that wisdom was to be found, not in philosophy, nor in any form of religion, but in an experience which gave one a direct insight into the inner meaning of life.[3]

Direct experience, in contrast to mere thought (whether philosophical or theological), clearly is prominent in his search for "wisdom," "meaning," or what is true. He would later identify the sensory and emotional quality of such experiences in nature as mystical, specifically "a kind of natural mysticism" found in writers like Wordsworth and Mary Webb.[4]

However nourishing such times of awakening in nature remained in contrast to philosophy, Griffiths was habituated through years of education to subject experience, including moments of "direct insight," to reasoned analysis. Thus in attempting to explain to himself the powerful experience of God in nature and its apparent conflict with rationality, Griffiths was drawn into philosophical investigations. He sought specifically to determine the nature of this experience of "seeing" behind the veil of the world, what faculties of the mind such experiences employ, and whether it is indeed an experience of wisdom or truth. However, the goal of Griffiths's quest from the beginning was not merely intellectual understanding but spiritual realization. Perhaps like anyone who has tasted an ecstatic awakening to divine presence, he sought ways to sustain that experience and to grasp its wisdom on a more permanent basis. Thus, the integration of his theoretical understanding of a means for knowing the truth with his actual experience of those means was an ongoing challenge in his reflection on the mind.

Before examining Griffiths's philosophical studies in response to the evening walk, a brief account of his categories for describing mental processes is necessary. Established by early education, his understanding of the mind or soul in terms of its basic capacities or "faculties" provides a common framework throughout most of his writing. This conceptual system for answering cognitional and epistemological questions, known by its critics as "faculty psychology," is based upon Aquinas's classificiation of the soul's capacities into five groups, the vegetative, the locomotive, the sensory, the intellectual, and the appetitive. Griffiths focuses in particular upon the relationship between the sensory (especially the senses and the imagination), the intellectual (especially the active and passive functions of the intellect that he parallels to reason and intuition), and the will (an appetitive faculty).[5] Like any "map" of mental functioning, faculty psychology serves as an explanatory model that has both strengths and weaknesses. Griffiths at times in later writings employs a somewhat different "map" based on a distinction between different types of consciousness.

Reason and Imagination

Griffiths sketches into his portrait of these early years the elements of a tension in his method of inquiry for knowing the truth that would in time become a self-conscious focus of analysis: the tension between two urges or affinities, the desire for direct spiritual knowledge through non-rational means, and a proclivity for rational explanation. As he would later reflect, he spent much of his college years seeking a rational explanation for what his continuing experience of God's presence in nature truly signified.[6] This same tension was exhibited in his movements away from and back into the culture around him. Through his long walks into the countryside (and later through his "experiment in common life" there) and through his return to the culture through college studies and private reading, he alternated periods of retreat from his highly rational modern culture with times of immersion in it. Inquiry into his experience of God in nature thus ignited a conflict (not yet a dialogue) within him between rational and nonrational forces that would later be recognized as an intercultural tension as well.[7] In time, he would explain to himself that the encounter with God in nature had touched a part of himself that had been relatively neglected by Western religion and culture, a part that he would come to associate with the East.

In his desire to understand his continuing experience of God in nature, Griffiths turned first to the Romantic poets, especially Wordsworth, Keats, and Coleridge. With their assistance, he began to articulate a philosophy, that is, a rational framework, to support his spiritual quest as well as his critique of Western culture. In their writings he found ideas and principles to confirm and develop further his own expressions, especially concerning the respective roles of reason and imagination. Retrieving the position he held as a college student on these roles and their current imbalance in Western society, he writes:

> I considered that "thinking" was the disease from which we were all suffering, so that we were incapable of any spontaneous or creative action. The mind moved continually round on itself so that it was incapable of making contact with reality. I was prepared to say with Keats, "O for a life of sensations rather than of thoughts." I felt that it was through sensation rather than through thought that one

made contact with reality, and that it was the imagination and not the reason, which was the one power capable of interpreting sensation and revealing its meaning. . . . I conceived the imagination, much as Wordsworth and Coleridge did, as the faculty of truth; it was the means by which reality was made present to the mind.[8]

Griffiths recognized later that there is a valid place for abstract, rational thought, both in his life and in that of society. Nevertheless, the turn to nonrational means for experiencing "reality" and "truth" led to a lasting conviction that an experience of what is real and true could indeed be "mediated" by what he here calls "the imagination."[9]

Lewis recognized his student's need to think more critically about the type of romanticism and anti-intellectualism that had evolved from a highly ambivalent attitude toward Western culture. To this purpose, Lewis recommended that Griffiths read deeply in Western philosophy after graduation from Oxford. In *The Golden String* (1954), Griffiths recalls step-by-step the effects of this regimen of study, each thinker taking him further toward a more balanced appraisal of the roles of rational thought and the imagination in his own and society's search for what is true: "[A]ll the time I was concerned with the problem in my own life of reconciling reason and imagination."[10]

To understand the respective roles of reason and imagination, it became important to find ways to affirm the value and the role of *both* faculties. In Benedict de Spinoza's philosophy Griffiths found an appealing and sound alternative to his own romanticist spurning of reason. Griffiths later came to believe that it was the Dutch philosopher who first taught him "to think rationally about God."[11] While his experience of God in nature as a student had brought profound depth and feeling into his spiritual life, his understanding of that experience was incomplete, symptomized by his one-sided approach to the divine. With the benefit of hindsight, he writes:

> My experience at school had made me aware of a deeper reality behind the face of nature, but it had been no more than a confused intuition; I had never subjected it to a rational scrutiny. This is what Spinoza did for me. He showed me that the power behind the universe was a rational power, and that to know this reason of the universe was man's highest wisdom.[12]

In Spinoza, Griffiths found a highly reasoned explanation of God's nature and defense of the possibility of knowing God, an account that actually upheld the value of both reason and what Spinoza called "intuition."[13]

Also important in the long list of thinkers cited in *The Golden String* is Samuel Taylor Coleridge, due to his lasting influence upon Griffiths's understanding of means for knowing, especially the imagination. Griffiths had already studied Immanuel Kant's account of the mind and its transcendental principles, an account by which David Hume's skepticism about knowing was refuted for Griffiths. Nevertheless, Griffiths could not accept Kant's conclusion that the mind cannot know what is real in itself, apart from the a priori structure of the mind.[14] In Coleridge's philosophical writings Griffiths found a model for explaining and resolving not only this problem of knowledge but also the many dualisms present in Western thought. Essential to this model was the faculty of the imagination and specifically its role as a mediator between all that is subjective and all that is objective, between the knower and the known, the mind and nature, and the self and the world. Only through this "power" is true knowledge possible.[15]

Coleridge, in his account of the imagination, echoes a traditional distinction in Western philosophy relevant for Griffiths's understanding of his own mental processes, the distinction between "discursive" and "intuitive" approaches to knowledge. "Discursive" means are identified by Coleridge with the philosophies of the past that are comprised of "a crowd of phrases and notions from which human nature has long ago vanished." Such means move via conceptualization from premises to conclusions. The "intuitive" approach, on the other hand, largely associated with German transcendentalism, appears to him both as the philosophy of the future and as a retrieval of the system of Plato and Pythagoras, though now "purified."[16] In contrast to discursive means, intuition apprehends truths without reliance upon reasoned analysis, employing a different mental faculty, the imagination. It is clear both from Griffiths's affection for the Romantic poet-philosopher and from the direction his own thought would subsequently take that he felt greater affinity with the "intuitive" approach, one that affirmed the validity of the imagination as well as reason—in contrast to the hyper-rationality of his culture of origin.

Opening to Faith

Griffiths's study of Western philosophy that he undertook in order to find a rational explanation of his experience of God in nature further heightened in him the tension between direct spiritual knowledge through non-rational means and intellectual understanding through the exercise of reason. What appears to have happened through the regimen of reading, through his retreats in the English countryside during and after Oxford, as well as through his continued relationship with Lewis, is a growing recognition that further experience beyond the emotional awakening to a divine presence in nature was needed. In *The Golden String*, Griffiths reflects upon this need in his life in 1930 as follows:

> I was becoming more and more aware of the limitations of my own experience. I still spent all my spare time in long solitary walks in the country among the woods and commons and on the downs. . . . But it was no longer the face of nature which seemed to contain the meaning of life for me. I felt now that the real mystery lay within.[17]

This change in his spiritual outlook also may have been prompted by the decreasing frequency with which he was experiencing deep emotions in response to nature. It was typical of such experiences that they be ephemeral; and yet, as the awakening in nature occurred less often, a frustration grew that would eventually move him to seek God in a different way.[18] The crisis that initiated the next stage of his life, as he later recalls it, was prompted by the failure of his direct experience to keep up with his intellectual understanding of the spiritual path. Thus, Griffiths's ambitious attempts to seek a rational explanation for his spiritual experience brought not only new insights but new conflicts as well.

One significant contributor to a growing sense of need and conflict was Griffiths's reading of the Bible. His study of both the Old and New Testaments during these years after Oxford evoked deep affinities and inspired new insights in his struggle to reconcile reason and imagination. In the Old Testament he discovered a wealth and depth of poetic expression beyond anything he had read before, including Dante. And in the New Testament, the tight interweaving of realism and the supernatural forced a reassessment of his resistance to, and prejudice about, the latter element—a prejudice that was characteristic of the very scientific mind he had supposedly rejected.[19]

Griffiths further recalls that in John's Gospel and in the writings of Paul he discerned a call to move beyond the way of seeing and knowing characteristic of reason and philosophy. For this new "point of view" Griffiths used the biblical term *faith*. In this concept of faith, he found the fulfillment of what he and his friends "had been blindly seeking with our theory of imagination":

> For us the imagination had been the power to see beyond the phenomenon, to grasp that reality which underlies the appearances of this world. I knew now that this reality was not merely an idea (in the Platonic sense), but a will. Would not faith be the reaching out

of the human will towards that universal will, the discernment of its presence in the person of Christ?[20]

In seeking to know that divine presence he experienced in nature, Griffiths was drawn beyond the faculty of the imagination to open through the will to the divine.

As much as Griffiths acknowledges the change in perspective brought by his reading of the Bible, with hindsight he also perceives the continuity. He characteristically does not cut off the past or deny its value; rather, in the transition from the first period of his life to the second he discerns the steps of a single "path of imaginative experience," symbolized by "the golden string."[21] As is more apparent during the second period of his life, both imagination and faith serve as nonrational means through which Griffiths approaches the mystery he experienced in nature and then in Christianity—means he sought to bring into conscious relation to reason.

Griffiths's new insights regarding faith as a recognition of the truth behind appearances deepened his sense of spiritual need, according to *The Golden String*. As he gradually reevaluated and reencountered Christianity through his study in the countryside and then during his return home and time in London in 1931, he came to recognize the inadequacy of his experience; his insights about faith remained only theoretical. A new depth of experience was needed to resolve the conflict between reason and the nonrational knowledge that he now called "faith." The "face of nature" no longer prompted the depth of awakening he sought, but neither could he find the "real mystery" that he sensed "lay within."[22] Faith was understood as the answer, but it had not yet dawned. Something stood in the way. Was that "something" a limitation within Griffiths himself or within the revelatory potential of nature?

3

God through the Symbol of Nature

Griffiths's efforts to understand his experience of God in nature led him to explore the interrelationship between two faculties of the mind or soul, imagination and reason. It was the imagination, as well as the senses, which served to connect him, like the Romantic poets, to the world of nature and to experience there the presence of the divine mystery. It was reason that sought to conceptualize this experience, drawing it into conscious relation to ideas in the mind and setting it within structures of understanding. By the end of the first period of his life, imagination and reason remain in tension, if not yet in dialogue, within his self-understanding and his theory of the mind. But what is the relation between the mind with its various faculties and the third aspect of the human person, the spirit, the point for Griffiths through which the human opens onto the divine?

Symbols and the Relationship between Mind and Spirit

In one of his earliest articles, Griffiths writes: "It is the glory and the misery of the human soul that it is set between the spiritual and the material world, and can never be happy in either alone." Thus the soul or mind always seeks its conscious integration with body and spirit. But how can this search for integration be fulfilled? While the faculties of the soul normally seem disconnected in their activity, there is an experience described by mystics of "the centre or substance of the soul . . . where all the faculties have their roots"[1]—a depth identical to the "spirit." The spirit, then, is not another part of the person; rather, it is the person's ground, of which mind and body are expressions.

27

Though writing at least a decade after his evening walk, Griffiths conveys in the same early article his continued efforts to understand that experience and the mental faculties in relation to the center of the soul or spirit. Of that center he writes:

> It is here that the imagination receives the capacity to enter into the deepest union with nature and the human soul, and to find the words and images which can represent the inner life of nature and of man. It is here . . . that the intellect learns to embody its ideas in a material form, and to give them symbolic and rhythmical expression.[2]

In other words, it is in the spirit that the faculties of imagination and intellect or reason are integrated, and it is through conscious awareness of the spirit that the faculties' activities are reconciled.

Following this line of analysis, Griffiths examines the role of divine grace in inspiration, found to varying degrees in poetry, philosophy, and revelation. What is common to these various forms of expression is that grace is received through the center of the soul, affecting all of the faculties, including imagination and reason. Drawing upon Christian imagery, he portrays this process of inspiration as the descent of the Word into the symbols employed by poet, philosopher, and prophet.[3] The symbol thus assumes an essential role in Griffiths's understanding of the spiritual journey and specifically of mystical experience. It is through the symbol that the mind opens through its own quiet "center" to the divine; through the symbol, spirit opens to Spirit.

From reflection upon nature and poetry, Griffiths formulated a theory of religious symbol early in his life. Informed by the philosophical writings of Coleridge and Owen Barfield, Griffiths honed his understanding of how central symbols are to human knowledge. Further informed by his own experience, he came to realize how vital religious symbols are to the surrender that alone brings spiritual transformation.

Symbols as Mediators of Knowledge

One may conjecture that Griffiths was first attracted to the power of symbols in his early reading of Romantic poets such as Coleridge, Keats, and Wordsworth. Through Griffiths's imaginative empathy with their poetic imagery, his own experience of nature was deepened; and, after his spiritual awakening during an evening walk at age seventeen, he found it was these poets who captured that experience in words and further enhanced his receptivity to a divine presence in nature.[4] As he would later recognize in analyzing the nature mysticism of others and what he would call the "cosmic revelation," nature itself became for him a symbol of a mystery beyond, yet also within, this world.[5]

Griffiths's earliest theoretical reflection upon symbols in general appears to come in the context of the rational explanation he sought for his early experience of God's presence in nature. He clearly believed that the vision of what lies "behind the veil of the world" that opened for him during the evening walk at school was indeed a kind of knowledge as well. This conviction about the possibility of knowing through nonrational means supported his rejection of Kant's claim that one cannot know anything in itself, apart from the structures of the mind. Griffiths found in Coleridge's philosophical works a convincing and contemporary retrieval of Plato's theory of ideas to ground further his instincts about the mind's ability to know things in themselves or, ultimately, as God knows them.[6]

Griffiths elicited from Coleridge a theory of the imagination and poetic symbolism that explained how knowledge that surpasses the rational activity of the philosopher might happen. Inspired by Coleridge and in disagreement with Plato's claim that the philosopher exceeds the poet in their common pursuit of knowledge, Griffiths writes about the potential power of poetic symbols as follows:

> To me it was clear that the poet was often nearer to the reality than the philosopher, because he sought to embody reality, that is truth itself, in an image which was a living symbol of reality and made it present to our souls in a manner which the abstract concepts of the philosopher could never do.[7]

The "living symbol" used by the poet does more than simply point toward what is real and true. According to Coleridge and Griffiths, the poetic symbol actually makes the reality being symbolized present to the soul so that knowledge in the full sense may occur.[8] Furthermore, Griffiths implies that in making *a* reality present, the reality "that is truth itself," that is, reality *as a whole,* somehow communicates itself through the poetic symbol.[9] Griffiths's general definition of a symbol may thus be identified: A symbol is a sign through which a reality becomes present to human consciousness.[10] But how does the symbol do this?

In further exploring how a poetic symbol might mediate a fuller depth of knowing than is available through reason, Griffiths drew upon an insight received from Owen Barfield's *Poetic Diction* (1928) concerning the potential power of language. Barfield discusses the original multivalent character of certain words that have functioned symbolically in the various religions. The example Griffiths recalls is "spirit," which in various languages has meant *wind, air, breath, life,* or *soul.* Important for Griffiths was Barfield's rejection of the common theory that such terms originally stood for physical phenomena (e.g., *wind, air,* and *breath*) and only later came to be associated with non-physical and even universal realities (i.e., soul, life, and spirit). Instead Barfield claims that such words from primitive cultures originally contained all such meanings at once without distinction.[11] Terms such as *spirit,* then, functioned powerfully in such cultures as symbols, reflecting simultaneously the particular and the universal, the physical and the spiritual, the human and the natural, and the microcosm and the macrocosm.

Griffiths's later analysis of the implications of Barfield's theory indicates the early influence of this text upon his own theory of symbols as well as a connection to his theory of the mental faculties:

> The fact is that in primitive speech a word contains a multiplicity of meanings. The imagination, which is the faculty of primitive thought, expresses itself in symbols (literally, from the Greek, that which is "thrown together"), which reflect this multiplicity of meaning in a single word. In other words, primitive thought is intuitive; it grasps the whole in all its parts. The rational mind comes later to distinguish all the different aspects of the word and to separate their meanings. These are the two basic faculties of the mind, the intuitive which grasps the whole but does not distinguish the parts, and the rational which distinguishes the parts but cannot grasp the whole. Both these powers are necessary for the functioning of the human mind.[12]

In the multivalent character of the symbol resides, in part, its power to mediate a synthetic depth of knowledge quite distinct from the knowledge mediated by analytic concepts. Furthermore, by specifying that the multivalent character of the symbol can only be apprehended fully by the intuitive power of the mind, Griffiths implies that the ability of the symbol to mediate a knowledge of reality depends not only upon the power inherent in the word or poetic image itself, but also upon the quality of mind or awareness of both the poet and the listener/reader. This final point clearly ties into Griffiths's later critique of Western culture for its overemphasis upon the analytic, rational mind and his attraction to the East with its openness to the synthetic, intuitive mind.

The Spirit Opening to the Divine Mystery through Nature

Griffiths's turn to nature in the first period of his life, catalyzed by experiences like the evening walk, served a dual purpose: It fostered "the sense of a Presence, something undefined and mysterious," and it reconditioned his mind by means of a consequent withdrawal from modern Western society with its tendency to secularlize nature.[13] Like Wordsworth he learned that the experience of his spirit opening to the divine in nature was a state of mind *and* body, one that could be cultured. Griffiths records the English Romantic's detailed psychophysiological account of this experience as close to his own:

> that blessed mood,
> In which the burthen of the mystery,
> In which the heavy and the weary weight
> Of all this unintelligible world
> Is lightened: that serene and blessed mood,
> In which the affections gently lead us on,
> Until, the breath of this corporeal frame
> And even the motion of our human blood
> Almost suspended, we are laid asleep
> In body and become a living soul:
> While with an eye made quiet with the power
> Of harmony, and the deep power of joy,
> We see into the life of things.[14]

As noted in the preceding chapter, such an experience was, for Griffiths, not simply a passing psychophysiological state but an awakening to "wisdom" and to "the inner meaning of life."[15]

The slightest detail of the countryside might evoke this "blessed mood" or "ecstasy" for Griffiths, such as the flowers he passed while riding his bicycle.[16] How does he explain this? How could such a state of receptivity be sustained? If nature indeed can serve as a symbol mediating the experience of the divine mystery, then, in the language he would later develop, it would evoke a recollection of the faculties toward integration at the mind's center, the spirit. "Presence" would be felt as spirit opened to Spirit, a recognition registered within the recollected mind. To sustain such a state, one would seek to eliminate anything that might serve to disturb it. For Griffiths at this early stage in his life, the primary obstacle, not only for himself but for his culture as a whole, was thought or reason. Thus in experiencing the spirit's opening to the divine through nature as symbol, much depends on the state of mind. If one is preoccupied with thoughts and not receptive to the "sensations" evoked by nature, if the symbol that is nature does not draw one beyond thought, then "contact with reality," with the divine mystery, is not experienced.[17]

However, given that an experience of God in nature does dawn for Griffiths as for others who inspired him, what does this experience reveal about the relationships between that divine mystery and nature, and between divine Spirit and human spirit?

Intimations of Advaita

Ultimately, Griffiths would come to interpret the goal of the spiritual journey, not only for himself but for all humanity, in terms of nonduality. One comes eventually to realize that one's own spirit is neither identical with, nor separate from Spirit or divine mystery; they are not-one and "not-two," the literal meaning of the Sanskrit term *advaita* that he would later use frequently.[18] Similarly, the created world is neither an illusory appearance of a single Reality nor an existence wholly other from the divine. The cosmos is a revelation, one that is neither simply the same as nor totally distinct from its source. The roots of Griffiths's later expressions of *advaita* may be found within this early experience of the divine in nature.

About his evening walk, he later wrote: "It was an emotional experience in which my whole being seemed to blend with the life of nature."[19] That he says "blend" rather than disappear is significant. The union that he tastes is one in which the self remains a distinguishable participant. He generalizes that in such experiences: "We are no longer isolated individuals in conflict with our surroundings; we are parts of a whole, elements in a universal harmony."[20] Near the end of his life, he would draw a connection between his relationship of "total oneness" with his mother and an intimacy with nature reminiscent of his early experiences as a youth—together symbolized by the Black Madonna.[21]

Nonduality as an interpretive framework appears very early in Griffiths's reflection upon his experience. From an epistemological viewpoint, there was always a link in his understanding between knowing something in itself and a kind of union or "connaturality" with it.[22] From a spiritual perspective, there was an intimate connection between experiencing the self-transcendence inherent in such unitive knowledge and the surrender that is love. Yet ever alive in Griffiths's understanding of the nonduality disclosed in the acts of knowing and loving is the logical necessity, which is at once for him a theological principle, that relationship somehow endures between the knower and the known, the lover and the beloved. In another of his first articles, written early in the second period of his life but nonetheless revealing of long-term directions of thought, Griffiths intimates a nondualistic understanding of knowledge applicable to his experience of the divine mystery through the symbol of nature:

> Now knowledge is a mode of existence: it is the capacity to share the existence of another being, to exist in it in a certain way. This is the innate desire of the mind, to share the existence of other beings, of other people and of other things, so as to multiply one's own existence. And this desire is infinite. The mind has an infinite capacity for being, and will never rest until it has become all things, until the whole universe has come to exist in it. But in getting to know other beings, the mind also comes to know itself. For knowledge is precisely the power to exist in another being *as other*, to become another being without ceasing to be oneself.

Given this exalted sense of the trajectory of the mind in its desire to know, it is not surprising that Griffiths concludes: "Thus the soul's quest for knowledge can only end in the knowledge of God, and it is to this that the whole movement of human thought continually aspires." Knowledge of God reflects the same nondualistic quality discovered in knowledge of persons and things:

> In man . . . through his capacity of knowledge and love, of spiritual communion, nature is transfigured, just as in God man himself is transfigured, not losing his nature and individuality, but transcending it in a communion of knowledge and love of whose depth and intensity we can form no conception but towards which every experience of our life is a summons and a call.[23]

Although Griffiths's spiritual path would take him far beyond what he experienced during his evening walk as a schoolboy, this awakening indeed served as "a summons" toward the loving communion with the divine mystery that he would identify as *advaita*. Thus, even as he began to become aware of the limitations within his experience of God in nature and eventually underwent conversion to Christ, he never disparaged the value of his early awakening.

Limitations within His Experience of Nature as Symbol

When Griffiths read the Bible during his "experiment in common life" in 1930, he brought to the often poetic texts of the Old and New Testaments a sensibility concerning the symbolic power of language.

The specific potency of *religious* symbols now came more fully into view, especially in the Psalms that he began to pray and in the ritual of the Eucharistic celebration, first in the Anglican and then in the Catholic tradition. In time, his abiding sense of God's presence deepened through participation in the symbols of the Christian faith—religious symbols that superseded, though did not totally displace for Griffiths, the symbols of nature and of Romantic poetry.

Griffiths describes how his first reading of the Bible as poetry eased the passage into praying the Scriptures as follows:

> I had gone to the poetry of Wordsworth, Shelley and Keats in my early days at school in order to find my experience of the mystery and beauty of nature renewed and enlarged; for poetry is the means by which the feelings and the imagination are educated and their powers developed. . . . Now my horizon was being enlarged and the mystery of God's dealings with humanity and with the individual soul became apparent to me through my reading of the Bible. But it was the same path of imaginative experience which I had been following all the time; and now I found that the words of the Psalms came to me like pure poetry awaking the sense of God's power over nature and His Providence over the human soul, and I prayed the Psalms almost without realising it.[24]

As the poetry of the Bible enlarges his "horizon" and powers of imagination, the same symbols mediate an awareness not only of the sacredness of nature but also of the divine mystery "over nature." That presence experienced beyond the veil of nature becomes ever more personal; the inchoate intimacy of the evening walk matures into the mutual relationship that is prayer.

It is significant that Griffiths does not clearly distinguish between "poetic" and "religious" symbols nor between religious symbols and symbols in general in his published writing. The general definition of symbol identified above implies that the distinction between different types of symbols resides in the respective "realities" they allow to become present or in the type of experience they evoke in consciousness. While all persons and things symbolize the divine mystery, they do so to varying degrees. In a 1990 letter Griffiths distinguishes religious symbols as those that allow the ultimate Reality to become present within human consciousness most fully:

> [S]ense phenomena and poetic images of all sorts—and I would add scientific theories—are all symbols which reflect reality in some way, but some are very imperfect. Some may be very precise—like

mathematical formulas—but in a limited way. The great religious symbols, above all terms like Brahman, Nirvana, Tao, Al Haqq, En Soph, and the divine darkness, come as near as possible to symbolising the ultimate mystery; but the whole creation "symbolises" God in some way. All this implies, of course, that all symbols and all religious discourse fall short of the divine reality itself.[25]

While all of nature and the creations of the mind as well may serve as symbols, bringing to consciousness the realities to which they point, Griffiths's early experience of the divine in nature with the aid of Romantic poetry convinced him of both the power and the limits of such symbols to bring lasting communion or what he would later call a "nondual awareness of the divine." Although that communion was tasted during his evening walk, it was transient. Did Griffiths understand the cause of his spiritual difficulty to be the inadequacy of nature as a symbol of the divine, or the inability of his mind to remain recollected in its center, in the spirit? Further experience and reflection would be needed to resolve this issue.

The Conditions for Dialogue

During the first stage of Griffiths's life, which he thematized as "God in nature" and which represents his first twenty-four years, he was initiated by the evening walk into experience of a sacred depth, an experience to which he responded with a reverence and devotion usually associated with religious surrender. In attempting to sustain and reflect upon this experience, he found himself without the support of either institutionalized Christianity or the dominant, scientific culture by which he had been conditioned through his education. While he did receive assistance from numerous authors from his culture's past, as well as from C. S. Lewis, Skinner, and Waterman at Oxford, he sensed himself at odds with the prevailing cultural ideal. Like Karl Joachim Weintraub's "culture bearer," Griffiths "lost trust" in that ideal and, in reorienting himself, began to articulate a different standard for his culture.

For the task of reorientation, Griffiths drew upon a variety of sources ranging from Romantic poets to Western philosophers to Eastern sages. This early eclecticism served to establish an openness to dialogue with diverse points of view that would inform his efforts to articulate a new cultural ideal. That openness may be identified at different levels in Griffiths's world.

At an intrapersonal level, the conditions for dialogue were clearly in formation, the key partners being the rational and nonrational styles of mind he not only read about but experienced in conflict within his method of inquiry. Interpersonally, while having a strong tendency to solitude and independence, Griffiths exhibited a willingness to engage his peers and professors in debate on strongly held views from religion to politics.[1] As already discussed, Griffiths's ambivalent relationship with his culture of origin prompted a search for alternative ideals as partners in intercultural dialogue, a search that would in the next period take him to India.

Griffiths's method for reconciling reason and imagination as different means for knowing had implications for his early stance on interreligious matters. Given that his experience of God in this first period occurred totally outside the sacraments and community of the church, it is not surprising that he appears to himself later as having been completely open to recognizing the truth in teachers and religions other than Christ and Christianity. Describing his first reading of the three Eastern spiritual classics noted in chapter 1, he writes:

> It was not that I found anything unchristian in them, but on the contrary that their doctrine seemed to me practically identical with that of Christianity as I understood it. From this time the Buddha and Lao Tzu took their place in my mind with Socrates, Spinoza and Marcus Aurelius, along with the Christ of the Sermon on the Mount, among the great spiritual leaders of mankind.[2]

In his initial theology of religions there is a relatively undifferentiated identity between the authority of different figures as well as their teachings.

On the basis of a theory of the imagination, like Coleridge's, where this faculty serves as the mediator of what is real and therefore true, Griffiths could confidently and consistently affirm the knowledge of truth professed by numerous teachers, irrespective of their religious traditions. Truth is mediated spiritually, not religiously, for Griffiths at this time; that is, as his own awakening to God in nature had shown him, truth could be revealed to and known by the human spirit outside of a particular religious context. This recognition clearly made it easier to conceive of revelation occurring within any and all religious contexts, during both this early period and later ones as well. Thus while these initial conditions for interreligious dialogue would shift dramatically with his Christian conversion in the next period, nonetheless, much of this openness to other religions would remain.

Finally at the cosmotheandric level, essential conditions for Griffiths's participation in dialogue have been set by the end of this first period as well. An intimate relationship between the human spirit, nature, and the divine Spirit has been glimpsed—a realization which, as he would recognize late in life, all of his subsequent experience and reflection would seek to explicate. By this point, Griffiths has also recognized the limitation of nature as a symbol of the divine, sparking awareness of both the transcendence of God and the persistent opacity of the human spirit to the light of divine grace.

Transition from a "Golden Age"

In *The Golden String* (1954), Griffiths would characterize the solitary journey begun in this period as a "rediscovery of religion," beginning with God in nature, which would eventually lead him to Christ and the church. Far from being his challenge alone, this rediscovery, he then believed, was "the great intellectual, moral and spiritual adventure of our time."[3] From this point on, he would discern a close correspondence between his own intellectual and spiritual struggles and those of the culture at large in their mutual search to sustain a sense of the sacred in a modern, Western setting.

Several months before his death, Griffiths offered perhaps the most far-reaching interpretation of the paradigmatic quality of his life. Remembering the powerful awareness of God in nature that both he and Wordsworth experienced, he draws a parallel to Eden, a stage that, while paradisaical, was temporary both for our civilization as a whole and for each individual within it. Inspired by Wordsworth's "Ode: Intimations of Immortality from Recollections of Early Childhood," Griffiths reflects as follows upon the broad implications of this first stage of his life, with both its mystical brightness and the shadows necessarily cast by reasoned analysis:

> I think this is the history of humanity. We all come out of a golden age, the paradise. All ancient people have knowledge of an age when all was bliss and peace reigned. And then we come into this prison house. . . . It's a golden age of childhood, but we have to grow. We have to eat of the Tree of Knowledge of Good and Evil. It brings us down, but it gives us a knowledge that we could not otherwise have. We have to go beyond and return to the source.

What as a youth he had difficulty accepting, the apparent intrusion of reason into "the golden age" glimpsed during the evening walk, as a mature man he now acknowledges as a necessary step on the journey. What he, using Wordsworth's image, experienced as a "prison house" bound by the constraints of his culture's rationality, he now recognizes as a valuable stage toward experiencing a more meaningful return to paradise. As his mention of "ancient people" further suggests, Griffiths also identifies corresponding stages in the evolution of civilization as a whole. Having eaten of the tree of knowledge, we now must make a self-conscious return to a union with our source. He continues:

> That's our calling today. We have fallen away from the golden age, the paradise. We are living in this world of conflict and this prison

house, but we are being called back all the time to the transcendent mystery. To return to paradise. That's the goal of humanity, really.[4]

The return is thus not a simple regression but a mature reappropriation of what has always been present. Griffiths, then, even as he underwent Christian conversion, never needed to let go of the intimacy with nature experienced in this first period: "[A]wareness of the presence of God in nature," he would observe over sixty years after that conversion, "remained with me, and remains with me today, as absolutely fundamental in my life."[5]

Griffiths at age twenty-four, however, finds himself caught in a dilemma, nonetheless precarious because it instantiates a broader cultural crisis in his eyes. Whetted by the evening walk and subsequent experience, his hunger for spiritual nourishment through nonrational means must coexist with an equally powerful tendency toward reasoned analysis, one that cannot simply be dismissed as symptomatic of a degenerate culture. In addition, he has begun to realize that the elusive experience of God in nature that he has tasted will not sustain him. Through study of the Bible, especially the Psalms, he has sensed an even more comprehensive revelation, of God "over nature" and "over the human soul," not simply within them. The pole of divine immanence within his early intimations of *advaita* has outbalanced its complement, transcendence. He seems to sense that correction is needed, but how? By surrendering to the dialogue inherent in relationship at several levels in his life he opened to new possibilities of insight.

PART II

God in Christ and the Church:
1932–1968

—

A correct judgment made through rational investigation belongs to the wisdom which is an intellectual virtue. But to judge aright through a certain fellowship with them belongs to that wisdom which is the gift of the Holy Spirit. Dionysius says that Hierotheus is perfected in divine things for *he not only learns about them but suffers them as well*. Now this sympathy, or connaturality with divine things, results from charity which unites us to God; *he who is joined to the Lord is one spirit with him*.

—Aquinas, *Summa Theologiae* 2–2, q. 45, a.2, resp.

Night of Conversion

How different from the open Cotswolds hills are the dark, close streets of the London slums whose poor he seeks to serve. Only the vegetables in the markets connect him with the distant countryside and with the intentionally simple life he has been living there. Why did he leave such a quiet, natural world for this industrialized one whose noise and suffering weigh oppressively upon him? It had something to do with a sense of calling heard in the silence of prayer, in reading the Bible, in receiving communion; some sense of a spiritual home glimpsed through the words of Paul, Augustine, Newman, and a book of church history by the venerable Bede. But he has followed this prompting to prepare for ordained ministry only by overcoming strong resistance in himself—he who had for years rejected the need for church and clergy. On the other hand, his mother had been overjoyed by his decision.

As he walks along the dirty, shadowed streets in the late afternoon, words from a book he has been reading continually resurface in his consciousness about the need for repentance. Climbing the stairs of the house where he is staying, he is drawn to the small, dimly lit chapel on the top floor. Kneeling there, he hears the thoughts about repentance become a command bearing a force outside his own will. Resolving to remain awake all night in prayer, he returns to his room and kneels at the bedside in response to this call to repent. While his body is relatively still, the mind wrestles, as concepts of what is acceptable, sensible, and rational continually arise.

Years later, he would describe the struggle of that night as follows:

> I had to surrender myself into the hands of a power which was
> above my reason, which would not allow me to argue, but com-
> manded me to obey. Yet this power presented itself as nothing but
> darkness, as an utter blank.[1]

In this darkness, he discovers as his only resource the image of Christ in
the Garden of Gethsemane facing death (Matthew 26.36–39). As he fixes
his mind upon this image, the struggle against a power above reason
subsides. Near the end of his life, he would describe what happened
during his struggle in prayer that night as "a real death experience."[2]
Death of what, death to what?

When the young man rises from his knees in the pale light of morning,
he finds that the night's struggle, this death, has not brought clarity—
only weariness and disorientation. He stands by the window, looking
out onto the still shadowed city. Without resolution he moves toward
the door—when again he hears from within, yet not from his self, another command: "You must go to a retreat."

Not understanding the meaning of this message, he walks to a
nearby Anglo-Catholic Church and inquires. Within hours, he finds
himself participating in a retreat, listening to a priest interpret the teachings of Thomas Aquinas. Later, as he kneels in formal confession for the
first time in his life, tears come, the tall thin frame hunched over and
shaking, his sentences broken by sobs. Later still, in the now holy darkness of the church he lifts his face, eyes closed, to hear the Fathers
singing Ps. 119 in the spare serenity of plainchant:

> With my whole heart have I sought thee: O let me not go wrong out of thy
> commandments. . . .
> Open thou my eyes that I may see the wondrous things of thy law.[3]

When he reemerges into the life of the city, indeed he can see, as though
with eyes washed clean. No longer seeking the refuge of museums and
cathedrals, he moves easily and delightedly through the same streets
whose din and clutter had before oppressed him. Years later he would
write of his struggle and its aftermath:

During that night the mirror had been broken, and I had felt abandoned because I could no longer gaze upon the image of my own reason and the finite world which it knew. God had brought me to my knees and made me acknowledge my own nothingness, and out of that knowledge I had been reborn. I was no longer the centre of my life and therefore I could see God in everything.[4]

At the end of the day, he lies upon his bed in the darkness, his body charged, his mind illumined, his spirit at rest. Beside the bed on a table is a book by St. John of the Cross, left open to a passage that reads: "I will lead thee by a way thou knowest not to the secret chamber of love."[5]

4

The Benedictine in England and India

Griffiths's reevaluation of Christianity in the three years following his graduation from Oxford led him through a painful experience of conflict and self-doubt, especially during the months immediately following his "experiment" in the country. In retrospect, he would explain much of this conflict as a consequence of his attempt to make the spiritual journey on his own "with very little guidance from others and exposed to all the dangers of inexperience."[1] Eventually he came to perceive this independence not as the faithful response to an inner calling born from his early mystical awakening in nature, but as evidence of a deeply rooted spiritual pride. This realization came during a lonely time in London while working in the slums, revealing the "overwhelming need to repent." Through a full night of prayer, fasting, confessing, and his first retreat, he faced and broke through the darkness of his willfulness and despair to receive the light of God's forgiving love in Christ. In Griffiths's own later interpretation of his conversion experience in London, a recurring theme is surrender—a spiritual principle and an experience that would guide and define his life, as he perceived it, from this time forward. It is important to note that what Griffiths felt called to surrender at this time was his reason.[2] His distrust of this faculty in the culture around him was now turned upon himself.

In order to listen more clearly to the all-demanding power that had guided him through his conversion, he again withdrew from society and sought the quiet and simplicity of the countryside, this time as a hermit, following the examples of the mystics he was reading, both Christian and non-Christian. Specifically, he returned to a remote part of the Cotswolds he had remembered from his earlier stay there, and rented a two-room cottage at the top of a valley grazed by sheep. During this two- to three-month period of solitude in 1932, he spent his days reading the Bible and the *Summa Theologiae* of Thomas Aquinas, and in prayer and meditation. As recorded in *The Golden String* (1954), he came to profound realizations concerning the interior life, feeling himself drawn in prayer away from the surface of consciousness toward the center of the soul. He felt himself called by a power within that was both terrifying and loving, called to renounce his own will and to surrender control over his life. This power, he would come to realize, had been directing his life all along, in spite of his prideful sense of being independently in control. He would further characterize this power, to which he opened in prayer, as a nonrational force at odds with his strongly rational mind.[3]

However, Griffiths was not consistently at ease with his contemplative life as a hermit. Seeking guidance from the same Providence that he felt had blessed both his awakening in nature and his conversion experience in London, he turned again to sustained prayer. Shutting himself in the closet of the cottage, he began to pray with unusual fervor, imaging himself again with Jesus, this time at the foot of the cross. Sensitized by frequent fasting, he was soon lost in "a great wave of prayer"; an entire day passed in what he thought was only a couple of hours.[4] When he emerged, the answer to the unsettledness in his style of life was clear. He would take work on the nearby farm. Through sharing the rigors of a shepherd's work and eating his meals with the farmer and his family, Griffiths began to reconnect with nature and with his fellow human beings. In the evening he would return to his cottage to read.

As in the past, the ideas of others sparked continued searching. Prompted by a frustrating need for some kind of rule for his spiritual life and by his reading of John Henry Newman's own reasons for converting to Roman Catholicism, Griffiths found his way to a local Catholic church and soon thereafter to a nearby Benedictine monastery. Convinced by Newman's measured arguments for the efficacy of the Roman Catholic Church, Griffiths was gradually freed of the prejudice instilled by his Anglican upbringing as well as relieved of his reservations concerning the universal claims of the Catholic church. Deeply attracted by his first visits to the monastery, he sensed that here was the proper context and guidance for his ever-deepening surrender.[5]

Within a few months, in December 1932, he was received into the Roman Catholic communion and then, in January 1933 at age twenty-six, into the Benedictine monastery he had visited, Prinknash Priory. When taking the vows of a novice a year later, he was given the name "Bede" after the eighth-century scholar whose history of the Church of England had been influential upon him. Thus began Griffiths's monastic vocation that he would pursue in England for twenty-two years, a calling continuous with the surrender to Christ and to the church initiated in his conversion experience in London.

As a Monk in England: In Dialogue with Modern Secular Culture

In the new setting of the Benedictine monastery, Griffiths felt he had found the proper balance of several key forces and tendencies in his early life: individual and community, independence and submission to authority, and contemplative life and study. Through monastic life, Griffiths would also reevaluate his early experience of God in nature, attesting in the first autobiography to the "still more wonderful way" in which God may be found in the church.[6] The tension between these two types of experience of God, a private experience of God in nature and the corporate experience of God in the church, endures throughout his life.

Griffiths's view of the monastic vocation was expansive, perceiving the monastery in relationship to modern culture rather than estranged from it. Unlike the industrialized society that he had left, every aspect of the monastic life was considered sacred and was supported by the spirit of prayer. Here again, his personal journey of discovery prompted reflection upon the ills of his culture:

> I realised now what it was that I had missed all the time. It was the absence of prayer as a permanent background to life which made modern life so empty and meaningless. Life in the modern world was cut off from its source in God; men's minds were shut up in the confines of the material world and their own personalities, unable to escape their fetters. Here [at the monastery] the mind was kept open to God and everything was brought in relation with Him.[7]

Nevertheless, he writes, "the modern world" is not escaped by living in the monastery but rather is entered more deeply. In the daily sacrifice of the Mass, the monks assist in "the return of mankind to its lost unity"; through their daily observance of prayer, they offer up the needs of all the world. This social dimension and collective impact of the monastic and priestly vocations were essential, then as later, to his sense of what comprises a complete Christian spirituality.[8]

The early years in the monastery appear to have been a time of steady, if less tumultuous growth for Griffiths—at least as he would report them in his first autobiography, *The Golden String*. In the mid-1930s, he began to publish articles in his order's periodical, *Pax*, and eventually in other religious journals. In later years as a monk in England, his articles would focus upon the spiritual power of liturgy and upon the nature of contemplation, offering insights grounded in his own practice of a nondiscursive prayer, the Jesus Prayer, which he had begun in the 1940s.[9] He progressed through both simple and solemn professions to ordination to the priesthood in 1940 and to the office of prior of St. Michael's Abbey at Farnborough in 1947. Five years later he was appointed novice master of Pluscarden Priory in Scotland.

During these years as a monk and priest in England, Griffiths continued to develop his ideas about both Catholicism and the Eastern religions he had begun to study just after Oxford. At this point in his life, he offered a high but qualified estimation of oriental thought. These non-Christian religions could and did serve as preparation for the "final revelation in Christ."[10] Nevertheless, at this time Griffiths also first envisioned "the marriage of East and West" through interreligious and intercultural dialogue that became so thematic in his later thought.[11]

For Griffiths, then, it was providential when he learned in the early 1950s of a proposal by Fr. Benedict Alapatt, an Indian Benedictine living in Europe, to start a monastic community in India. Initially, the abbot denied Griffiths's request to emigrate in order to help with the project, judging that there was too much willfulness involved. Eventually however, in 1955, after Griffiths had let go of all expectations of making the trip, the abbot sent word that he should go. In recalling these events Griffiths later reflected that "The surrender of the ego is the only way in life."[12]

Confronting Hindu Culture and Religion: The Beginnings of Dialogue

Griffiths and Fr. Alapatt traveled by ship to Bombay. In visiting the holy places in this colorful city soon after his arrival, Griffiths had two strong impressions: first, the pervasive "sense of the sacred" in Indian culture, epitomized alike in the great temples and small roadside shrines; and second, the foreign appearance of the Christian churches, modeled upon European styles of the Gothic or baroque.[13] In the symbology of both the Hindu temples and shrines Griffiths found imaged what he came to India to find, the "contemplative dimension of human existence, which the West has almost lost and the East is losing" and a "vision of a cosmic unity, in which man and nature are sustained by an all-pervading spirit, which the West needs to learn from the East."[14] Ever conscious of presenting a balanced assessment, however, Griffiths from the start of his time in India would be equally clear about what the East needed to learn from the West.

After a brief time in Bombay, Griffiths and Alapatt traveled to Bangalore where they purchased some property in the nearby village of Kengeri. In the construction and furnishing of their quarters, as well as in their style of life and worship, they followed the model of simplicity familiar to them from England. They would soon discover, however, that what was considered "simplicity" or "poverty" in England was above the standard of living for almost all of the Indians around them. Furniture as basic as straw beds, tables, and chairs were luxuries in village India.

Proximity to the city of Bangalore afforded interaction with a variety of Hindus, including several university students who frequently visited the newly formed monastery and who, in turn, invited the two Catholic priests into their homes. It was through these latter visits that Griffiths came to experience and appreciate Hindu culture. Years later he would recall that, even in the midst of the poorest villages, he felt from the start a sense of unity with the Indian people that was "almost physical" and a sense of beauty in their family life that had been missing from his own.[15] What had before in England been merely the comparative study of the ideas of different religions now became a fully personal, practical, and even sensory encounter for Griffiths, a deepening of dialogue between the religions of Asia and the Judeo-Christian tradition that continued throughout the rest of his life.

In light of his discoveries in India, Griffiths was prompted to rethink many of the intellectual convictions to which he was most committed and through which he had understood his life thus far. An example is his interpretation of the evening walk and of nature mysticism in general. While in Europe such experience had inspired only a few Romantic poets, in India this awareness of divine immanence was the very foundation of the Hindu religion.[16] Such reassessments, prompted by his pursuit of interreligious and intercultural dialogue, he felt, were not for himself alone. In successfully engaging and learning from the people, culture, and religions of India, Griffiths believed that he had made a discovery needed by Western societies. As in England, his own experience clearly informed his culture critique and articulation of an alternative cultural ideal.

From the start of his time in India, Griffiths began to participate in the regular gatherings of Catholics there who were exploring dialogue with Hinduism and with the other religions of the country—meetings that sometimes included representatives of these religions as well.[17] It was through these dialogues that Griffiths came to know two French pioneers in Hindu-Christian understanding who would have a significant impact upon his own thought and practice: Jules Monchanin (1895–1957) and Henri Le Saux (1910–1973).[18] In 1950, Frs. Monchanin and Le Saux had founded an ashram at Shantivanam, "the Forest of Peace," near the village of Kulithalai in the state of Tamil Nadu. The community was dedicated to the mystery of the Trinitarian nature of

God, symbolized not only in the Christian doctrine but also in the Indian teaching that God is *Saccidānanda* (the Sanskrit term with which the ashram was named, meaning "Being-knowledge-bliss"). The degree of commitment to living out their Christian calling in a way that was fully open to the surrounding culture and religious traditions was further indicated by the French priests' assuming the lifestyle of a *sannyāsi* (or renunciant in the Hindu tradition), including a change of names. Fr. Monchanin took the name Parama Arubi Ānanda, "the Bliss of the Supreme Spirit," and Fr. Le Saux the name Abhishiktānanda or "the Bliss of Christ." Given the contrast to his own continued adherence to Western Benedictine styles of life and dress, Griffiths was no doubt struck by the example as well as by the thought of these two Christian *sannyāsis*. In them he found the contemporary renewal of a type of cultural assimilation for the sake of the Gospel begun by historical figures such as Roberto de Nobili, SJ, and Brahmabandhab Upadhyay.[19] In 1956 and again in 1957 Griffiths stayed at Saccidananda Ashram, also called Shantivanam, not knowing that he would return there little more than ten years later as its spiritual guide.

Griffiths's first years in India, while he and Fr. Alapatt worked on their community in Bangalore, were intellectually productive and spiritually stimulating, as the articles he sent back for publication in the West indicate.[20] However, his efforts to found a monastic community in Kengeri proved unsuccessful. During this brief experiment, Griffiths became increasingly sensitive to the need for a fuller integration of Indian customs and lifestyle into the monastic life he and others were attempting to live in this foreign land.[21] The desire for a fresh start in the project that had brought the two Benedictines to India was provided by an invitation from another monk to help form a community in the most Christian part of the country, the state of Kerala. Fr. Francis Mahieu, OCSO, a Belgian Cistercian who also had arrived in India in 1955, had spent a year at Saccidananda Ashram, seeking the proper Indian form for a Christian contemplative lifestyle. Feeling called to be closer to the center of the Catholic church in India, he obtained land in Kerala and, with Griffiths, founded Kurisumala Ashram in 1958.

During these early years in India, Griffiths had clearly deepened his commitment to dialogue with the surrounding religions and culture as a source of renewal for the church, as a support for his critique of the cultures of East and West, and as a means for his own self-discovery. Kurisumala Ashram would afford increasing opportunities for his inter- and intrapersonal encounter with Hindu religion and culture to mature.

Kurisumala Ashram: Exploring the Relation of Religion and Culture

Under the guidance of Mahieu and Griffiths, the monks of the new community in Kerala patterned the simplicity of their dress and furnishings after that of the Indian *sannyāsi* and the typical villager, allowing for a similar degree of affinity and identification with the surrounding culture as they had found at Saccidananda Ashram. In their monastic discipline and liturgical practice, they followed a strict observance of the Benedictine rule and the Syrian rite respectively. The use of the Syrian rite, widely practiced in southern India, brought them not only into harmony with the Christian culture around them, it also drew them more fully away from their European heritage and into contact with a Semitic worldview, one closer to the Bible and to the early Fathers—in contrast to the worldview shaped in the West by Greek philosophy and medieval scholasticism.[22]

During his ten years at Kurisumala Ashram (1958–1968), Griffiths wrote frequently on the question of how the cultural assumptions inherent within different styles of worship facilitate or impede the liturgical experience of Christians in the East as well as the success of missions.[23] In coming to recognize how thoroughly Western the Christian church in India was, he enhanced his ability to distinguish between truth and the cultural forms in which it is expressed—a crucial distinction for understanding his practice of dialogue.

The social conditions that he witnessed firsthand in the culture surrounding him during his years in Kengeri and then Kerala evoked both appreciation and concern: appreciation for a simplicity of life that engendered familial and spiritual happiness, and concern for the intractable poverty of both village and city. Of particular influence upon Griffiths in his reflection upon the church's and his own roles in response to the needs of Indian society were the life and teachings of Mahatma Gandhi and of Gandhi's disciple, Vinoba Bhave. The Sarvodaya movement (service to all), begun by Gandhi and continued by Vinoba, attracted Griffiths's attention both as a practical and effective response to social realities and as a pure reflection of both Christian and Hindu principles; in this movement he found a potent adaptation of the "social gospel," an example of how Eastern and Western values could come creatively into dialogue for the transformation of culture.[24] Nevertheless, Griffiths's own energies remained primarily focused upon interreligious dialogue in contemplative and theological contexts, seeking to identify the truth who is Christ already present in India. Thus, he continued to participate in conferences and meetings of both an ecumenical and interfaith nature, bringing

Western Christian culture more explicitly into dialogue with the religions and culture of India.[25]

As the community at Kurisumala continued to grow, Griffiths shared in the responsibility of instruction, involving him in much further study of both the Hindu and Christian traditions. Evidence of the development of his thinking in comparing these two ways of life and thought is found in a series of lectures he gave in India near the end of his time at Kurisumala. These lectures were later published in 1973 as *Vedānta and Christian Faith*.[26] It is also clear from some of the articles Griffiths wrote during the later years in Kerala that he was attentive to the social and religious changes happening on the other side of the world, especially the audible questioning of traditional values reported by the media and the response to modernity offered by the Second Vatican Council. Throughout his time in India, Griffiths remained in touch with Western cultures through his lecture tours in Europe, the United States, and Australia, as well as through his reading of current books and periodicals.[27]

Griffiths's discovery of the Christ at work in Hindu culture and religion was fostered not only by his encounter with the Sarvodaya movement, his participation in interreligious discussions, and his study, but in his own spiritual practice as well. While at Kurisumala Ashram, he studied Yoga as a system of philosophy and practiced traditional postures under the guidance of a teacher or yogi who visited the ashram regularly to give instruction to the community. Griffiths became interested especially in *Kuṇḍalinī* Yoga, a holistic approach to personal transformation that involved not only the mind, but the body and emotions as well—a balance of which he was consciously in need.[28] At the same time, his commitment to the value of meditation continued to deepen, still grounded in his own use of the Jesus prayer, though now informed by the principles of Yoga. Thus, the process of dialogue between the cultures, religions, and spiritualities of East and West, heightened by his emigration to India, became even more fully instilled into Griffiths's person—body, mind, and spirit.

As Mahieu focused with increasing depth upon the Syrian liturgy, Griffiths began to discern his own calling in India more clearly and in contrast to his superior's. While the study of the predominant form of Christianity in Kerala was important, he came to believe that the Syrian rite was still essentially foreign to India, reflecting its origins in the cultures of the Middle East, just as the Roman rite and its theology embodied their European sources. Given Mahieu's firm direction of Kurisumala toward exploration of the Syrian tradition, Griffiths began to feel after ten years there that he was in need of a different context to respond to his own intellectual and spiritual callings.[29] As in previous times of transition both in England and in India, this one involved surrender and openness to new opportunities to respond to his vocation as a Christian monk.

The Call beyond His First Self-Orientation

In *The Value of the Individual: Self and Circumstance in Autobiography* (1978), Karl Joachim Weintraub links the efforts of some individuals in orienting themselves over and against the surrounding cultural ideal to the transformation of that culture. These efforts find particularly potent expression in autobiography. It is indicative of the scope of Griffiths's relationship to diverse cultures that two such expressions were needed. In 1954 when *The Golden String* was published, he had participated in the Catholic church and in the Benedictine order in England for over two decades, and felt he was home—physically, mentally, and spiritually. There was a stability in his life situation and a perspective from which a coherent reflection upon his past could occur, interwoven with a maturing interpretation of his culture of origin. Indeed, there is a sense of finality, of completeness at the end of Griffiths's first autobiography—a sense that the opening sentences of his second, *The Marriage of East and West: A Sequel to The Golden String* (1982), confirm:

> When I wrote *The Golden String*, telling the story of my search for God, which led me to the Catholic Church and to a Benedictine monastery, I thought that I had reached the end of my journey, at least as far as this world was concerned. But in fact, even while I was writing *The Golden String*, a new era was about to begin in my life, which was to bring about changes, as profound as any that had gone before.[30]

Indeed, it was one year after the publication of his first autobiography, when he was forty-nine, that a new phase of Griffiths's life did begin as he and Fr. Alapatt set sail for India. His deep spiritual sense, even prescience, about the importance of this taking leave of England and the West was conveyed in a statement he remembers writing to a friend before his departure: "I want to discover the other half of my soul."[31] Clearly, the journey by grace that he conceived in terms of Blake's "golden string" was far from complete.

The Golden String thus constitutes a first "act of self-orientation," an attempt to define himself over and against the reigning cultural ideal, and simultaneously to articulate a new ideal—the task of the "culture bearer," according to Weintraub.[32] The first autobiography portrays one who has both enthusiastically and self-critically immersed himself in his culture of origin, warily identifying with, and distinguishing himself from, aspects of that culture.[33] Through his education—both formal and self-directed, both secular and religious—Griffiths entered with both fascination and suspicion the flowing life of ideas that defined Western societies. Through his experiences in nature and in the monastery, he grounded himself in a spiritual perspective from which to call into question some of those ideas as well as modern secular values. As he transplanted himself into another culture, the simultaneous maturing of his personal, religious, and cultural assumptions continued on new soil. Through his interactions with Indian culture he was called beyond the self-orientation so richly articulated in *The Golden String* and was forced to continue the process of redefining himself, his religion, and his culture—a process that would eventually in the third period of his life necessitate a second autobiographical act.

While the cultures and religions of the East had served an ancillary role in Griffiths's critique of the dominant ideals of the West in the first autobiography, with his move to India that role became more prominent. In his redefinition of the path for his culture of origin, the culture of India came to serve as a vital counterpoint. This development, however, was gradual; continuity with the Western Christian, Benedictine context in which he had lived for over twenty years in England was sustained. Eventually the influence of that context was balanced by assimilation of Indian culture, study of Hinduism, and experimentation with lifestyle, liturgy, and methods of prayer. This change in perspective would demand of him an even deeper degree of surrender, which is reflected in his maturing philosophy of the mind and in his spiritual journey.

5

Faith as a Way of Knowing

How can we explain the role of the individual in the transformation of culture? For Griffiths, it is essential that such an individual undergo a transformation of mind, allowing all of the faculties to develop and to become grounded in their common center, the spirit. He thus portrays the 1932 conversion experience that initiated the second period of his life in terms of an internal struggle, between his reason and a force that opposed his reason from a divine source within. This conflict, present to some degree throughout the prior stage of his life, now became acute, taking on consuming existential significance. In his own interpretation of this struggle, it was the very method of his mind in its pursuit of truth that prompted, and was transformed through, the crisis of conversion:

> [N]ow something irrational seemed to be coming into my life. There had been the desire for fasting which, though I might justify it by reason to some extent, came upon me as an irrational urge, and my reason rose up against it. Which was I to obey, this obscure instinct, this apparently irrational urge, or my reason and common sense? The conflict was the most intense I had ever endured, and it was part of the terms of the conflict, that it could not be answered by reason, because it was precisely the place of reason in my life which was in question.[1]

Clearly there was something about Griffiths's renewed encounter with Christianity, through reading the Bible and returning to church worship after Oxford, which forced a new intensity of self-confrontation and internal conflict to occur. The "path of imaginative experience" that

56

he had been following from his youth, with all of its skepticism concerning the role of reason in himself and in Western society, suddenly appeared to have been overreliant upon this very faculty; the rational mind, in the guise of his theory of the imagination, had limited his availability to the transforming power once found in nature and now encountered through Christianity. What prompted Griffiths's need to "repent" was the experience of a pervasive egoism associated with the domination of reason in his approach to knowing God. What he thought he had recognized as the disease crippling the society around him he now found was infecting his own mind: "I was being called to surrender the very citadel of my self. . . . I do not wish to exaggerate the nature of this ordeal, but it was the turning point of my life."[2]

The surrender of reason experienced through the catharsis of his conversion was both like and unlike that surrender inspired in him by the evening walk and by the Romantic poets who had encouraged his distrust of the rational and scientific mind. In a similar way, Griffiths was forced to realize the limits of reason to grasp what is true and to recognize the existence of nonrational means for experiencing that truth. However, the self-emptying undergone through days and nights of fasting and prayer in London allowed for a more thorough renunciation and letting go of the familiar habits of mind than he had experienced in the past. Of his conversion experience, he would later write: "I was completely in the dark. . . . Is not this the one thing of which we are all afraid? The darkness which is outside the sphere of our consciousness, the abyss where all known landmarks fail?"[3] As fearful as this darkness was, the loss of all rational explanations for what he was undergoing seems to have been a necessary step in the transformation of his mind.

Griffiths recalls that it was during the days of solitude after his conversion experience in London that he came to a deeper understanding of the role of the faculties (i.e., senses, imagination, reason, and will) in relation to the awareness of God's presence. Having transcended even the rich emotional awakening to God's presence in nature and having moved through and beyond the faculty of imagination that had revealed the meaning of such experience, Griffiths followed "the golden string" further. Going beyond thought and feeling, beyond the rational and nonrational faculties, he entered a silence that set all reflection upon the mind and its knowledge of truth in a different perspective. The source and ground of all mental activity was experienced as the locus of contact with God's power and presence. It is this state of utter receptivity to God, reached through and beyond the faculties of imagination and will, that Griffiths called "faith"—a receptivity that brought knowledge in a nonrational way.[4]

Faith Looking toward Contemplative Experience

The struggle to reconcile reason and the nonrational impulses he identified as faith progressed in the more supportive and balanced envi-
ronment of the monastery; here he participated in a diversity of means
for experiencing God's presence, both rational and nonrational.
Living at Prinknash thus fulfilled his desire to find "a life which
would satisfy my whole being, my heart and soul and body as well as
my mind."[5] It was here that his understanding of faith as a way of
knowledge matured.

Rather than arising in the senses, the emotions, or the imagination as
his experience of nature had, faith is a movement of the human will toward the divine will, a reaching out to God that Griffiths recognized in
his early deep experiences of prayer.[6] Implicit in this account of how
God may be known by faith is the principle of relationship—a relationship that is necessarily based upon the experience of a distance, even a
radical distinction, between the soul and God. As the Catholic philosopher Jacques Maritain, one of Griffiths's key philosophical authorities at
this time, affirmed, mediations are necessary and available through the
divine revelation in Christ and in the church to bridge this distance.
Knowledge through faith is "a mediate knowledge."[7]

As Maritain notes, however: "faith will perpetually strive to exceed
its own way of knowing" and inspire in the soul "an unconditional desire for mystical contemplation" that faith by itself is not able to fulfill.[8]
Having gone beyond yet integrated the imagination that was so important in the first period of his life, Griffiths's method of inquiry during
the second period exhibits this very striving of faith toward its perfection in contemplation. This perfection, as he recognized in the first autobiography, was also a knowing through love: "[L]ove can give us a
kind of knowledge which is beyond both faith and reason. The divine
mystery is ultimately a mystery of love, and it reveals itself to love
alone."[9] To the degree possible in this life, love bridges the distance between the soul and God that is presupposed by faith. Echoing Maritain,
he writes in the 1930s:

[I]t is possible to speak of faith itself, at least when informed by
charity, as an obscure intuition of the godhead. . . . Under the influence of the gifts of the Holy Spirit this obscure intuition would
gradually grow in depth and penetration until it developed into
mystical contemplation, and then finally when the veil of faith has
been removed, it would pass into the pure intuition of God in
heaven.[10]

Implicit, then, within Griffiths's understanding of knowledge through faith is its completion in the contemplative vision of an intimate relationship to the divine mystery.

To support his reflection upon the mental processes involved in such nonrational means of knowing, Griffiths turned to both medieval and modern Catholic sources.

Aquinas and the Maritains: Knowledge by Connaturality or Intuition

Inherent within Griffiths's account of faith as a way of knowing is a distinction with which he had been long familiar, at least since his reading of Spinoza and Coleridge: the distinction between discursive or rational thought, and nonrational means of gaining knowledge. To support this distinction in articles of the early 1950s, Griffiths cites Thomas Aquinas, embracing in particular the latter's discussion of "affective knowledge," also translated as "knowledge by sympathy" or "connaturality." This type of knowledge comes through an experience of affinity with what is contemplated *(per quandam connaturalitatem)* rather than through rational examination *(per rationis inquisitionem)* and represents, for both Aquinas and Griffiths, a higher degree of wisdom than the natural exercise of reason can bring.[11] Important for Griffiths is Aquinas's further point that the conditions for, and quality of, such knowledge vary with its object.

Nonrational means, such as the recitation of the Psalms during the liturgy, can mediate two kinds of "knowledge by connaturality" or what Griffiths now tended to call "intuitive" rather than imaginative knowledge. First, recitation of the Psalms may evoke an emotional and imaginative experience that is a kind of poetic knowledge surpassing what a reasoned study of the same Psalms alone might bring. Second, such recitation may mediate the more profound experience of connaturality with the divine reality being communicated through their symbolic language. This kind of mystical experience of wisdom is what Griffiths calls "contemplation," exceeding what discursive theological study can convey; unlike the poetic knowledge of the Psalms felt in the emotions and imagination, contemplation only comes with "the supernatural gifts of the Holy Spirit."[12] Drawing upon the language and authority of Aquinas, Griffiths explains the knowledge of the divine reality that is received through the liturgy as follows:

> We know that the gifts of the Holy Spirit are habits which dispose us to respond to the action of divine grace: they render us "connatural" with God. The knowledge which we have of the

mysteries of faith through the operation of the gifts is therefore knowledge by connaturality. It is supernatural not only in its essence but in its mode of operation: it gives us experience of the reality which we contemplate. It is towards a knowledge of this nature, a supernatural experience of the mystery of faith, that we would suggest that the whole work of the liturgy is directed.[13]

By means of a spiritual gift one may experience contemplation through the liturgy and know the mysteries of faith through one's "connaturality" with them.

According to Aquinas, contemplative knowledge of divine matters by connaturality with them is infused in the mind through love (*per caritatem*). Such knowledge thus not only exceeds an emotional and imaginative knowing of God through the liturgy, it also surpasses, though it presupposes, the knowledge received through the state of spiritual receptivity that Griffiths calls "faith." Contemplative knowledge or knowing through love is, therefore, ordered above knowledge through reason, imagination, and faith because it unites one to the divine mystery being contemplated.[14] This hierarchical ordering of the various ways of knowing endures throughout Griffiths's works.

Griffiths discovered a contemporary elaboration of Aquinas's basic principles concerning "knowledge by connaturality" in the writings of Raissa and Jacques Maritain. In their explanation of "poetic knowledge," the Maritains begin from a very broad definition of poetry, intentionally including various art forms: "that intercommunication between the inner being of things and the inner being of the human Self which is a kind of divination."[15] The interchange between subject and object occurs deep within the individual, close to the very "sources of being," "beneath the sunlit surface thronged with explicit concepts and judgments, words and expressed resolutions or movements of the will. . . ."[16] In poetry, emotion serves as the vehicle through which this communication may occur between subject and object, evoked by a resonance or connaturality between the two. According to the Maritains, the result of this connection between subject and object is a kind of intuitive knowledge that is ineffable and obscure in which emotions rather than concepts serve as the means by which the intellect grasps the reality of the object. Here for Griffiths was a rational explanation of an imaginative or poetic experience of the Psalms as a source of knowledge.[17] Poetic knowledge is defined by the Maritains as "a knowledge *by affective connaturality*," "a knowledge by mode of instinct or inclination, by mode of resonance in the subject, and which proceeds toward creating a work."[18]

The orientation of poetry and poetic knowing toward the creation of a concrete expression of that knowledge is key to the distinction that the

Maritains draw between poetic and mystical experiences.[19] Unlike the knowledge that results from the experience of poetry, the knowledge of the mystic does not tend toward or need artistic expression in order to complete the experience, and it does require a supernatural gift (as Aquinas also said) in order to bring union with its supernatural object.[20] Griffiths's claim is that the liturgy provides opportunities for both kinds of nonrational knowledge, the poetic and the mystical, as well as rational or discursive knowledge.

In Jacques Maritain's *Distinguish to Unite, or the Degrees of Knowledge* (1959), Griffiths also found a clear account of the relationship between knowledge through faith and the knowledge that is received through mystical or contemplative experience. Citing Aquinas as well as more contemporary theologians, Maritain writes:

> When, in the act of infused contemplation, the gift of wisdom, under God's action, frees faith from the human mode of concept and analogy (I do not say from the conceptual formulas that express revealed truth! I say, rather, from the actual use of such distinct conceptual formulas as a formal means of knowing), it suppresses in some way, not by vision, but by the experience of love, that distance from its object, which is the case in faith all alone.[21]

Mystical or infused contemplation is an experience of love that unites one to the divine mystery and provides the very knowledge greater than reason, imagination, and faith that Griffiths sought. The mediations of concepts and analogies, essential to knowledge through faith, have been transcended, and now only the divine effect of love in the soul for God mediates the experience of knowledge.[22]

Suggested by Griffiths's citing of Aquinas and the Maritains is a critique of Western culture, including the Christian church as it has evolved in the West. Griffiths wrote articles on the true way to appreciate the liturgy not only to give voice to his own experience, transformed as it was by the monastic setting at Prinknash, but also because he felt he was not alone in needing greater balance between rational and nonrational means for gaining knowledge. No doubt he agreed with Jacques Maritain's estimation of the importance of the other kind of knowledge that results from "connaturality" or "sympathy":

> Knowledge through connaturality plays an immense part in human life. Modern philosophers have thrown it into oblivion, but the ancient Doctors [of the church] paid careful attention to it and established upon it all their theory of God-given contemplation. I think that we have to restore it, and to recognize its basic role and

importance in such domains as moral practical knowledge and natural or supernatural mystical experience—and in the domain of art and poetry.[23]

Neither Aquinas nor the Maritains disclaim the validity and the need for rational inquiry; their writings bespeak the value of reason, even in portraying and defending the limits of this faculty.[24] Griffiths's experience and theoretical reflection supported this delicate balance between rational and nonrational ways of knowing. Nevertheless, it is apparent from Maritain's and Griffiths's statements that they do not find the proper balance of these two modes in the society around them.

Griffiths also sought to *distinguish* his own position from that of some other philosophers who upheld the importance of nonrational or intuitive means for gaining knowledge.

The Perennial Philosophy and Gregory of Nyssa: Natural versus Supernatural Means

In a 1954 review of some of the writings of Rene Guenon and M. Frithjof Schuon, Griffiths affirms their thesis that a "perennial philosophy" or "metaphysic" underlies the various religions. He also supports their claim, and that of the perennial philosophy itself, for the existence of "a higher mode of thought, which is not rational and discursive but direct and intuitive."[25] However, Griffiths strongly disagrees with Schuon's presentation of Christianity as one among the many historical expressions of this universal tradition of knowledge. The issue at stake in Griffiths's critique arises out of the following question: Is the intuitive or nonrational knowledge of reality espoused by the perennial philosophers necessarily superior not only to the fruits of rational investigation but also to the knowledge of faith spoken of in the Bible and in the church? The essence of Griffiths's response to this question is found in the distinction between natural and supernatural.

Schuon portrays faith as an inferior form of knowledge in comparison to the "direct and active participation in divine Knowledge" experienced through "intellectual intuition"—a mode of knowing grounded in the "Intellect," the uncreated capacity for Truth in the human soul.[26] In response to this claim about the nature of faith, Griffiths first links the position of the perennial philosophy with one of its sources, Plato and the theory of knowledge by innate "ideas." The transition is then made to Aquinas's account of Adam's knowledge of all creation by "infused species," which knowledge was thereby direct, intuitive, and unaided by abstract reasoning. Such intuitive knowledge is now largely absent from human experience, according to Griffiths, but is nevertheless "the mode of knowledge for which man was created."[27] (This knowledge by "infused species" is the basis for the "knowledge by connaturality" of worldly things described by the Maritains in reference to poetic knowledge.) Thus humans naturally yearn for this direct way of knowing, a desire that can indeed be fulfilled through spiritual discipline, as saints of both East and West exemplify.

As valuable as knowledge by "infused species" is, however, it remains a natural human product; the acquisition of such intuitive knowledge may certainly be aided and conditioned by divine grace, but this way of knowing "is not essentially supernatural."[28] Using Aquinas's distinction, such knowledge is a virtue but not a gift. As Griffiths felt he knew from his own conversion, the knowledge received through faith was an unexpected and unimaginable gift of a supernatural order. Even if such a knowledge through faith was inferior in its mode to what Schuon describes as "intellectual intuition," still such a knowledge is greater because of its supernatural quality and its source as a gift from God:

> According to M. Schuon faith is an inferior order of knowledge, which is essentially subordinate to the clear vision of metaphysical knowledge. But if we allow the possibility of such a mode of knowledge, we must still insist that it is essentially inferior to the knowledge of faith. For faith gives us a knowledge of God which infinitely transcends the whole order of nature and can only be received by a supernatural revelation. Though its mode is inferior to that of intuition, its object is infinitely superior to any natural intuition since it gives us God in his absolute transcendence as he can only be known by grace.[29]

In support of placing knowledge through faith above that of "intellectual intuition," Griffiths cites the works of Gregory of Nyssa, a mystical theologian of the fourth century who was very familiar with Platonist theories of knowledge. In his interpretation of Gregory's writings, Griffiths clarifies the important distinction between two types of intuitive knowledge or "knowledge by connaturality." Gregory distinguished between a purely natural intuitive knowledge of the nature of things and a deeper Christian knowledge that approached the mystery of God by supernatural means alone. Thus Griffiths found the same distinction here as in Aquinas and the Maritains: While there is a kind of intuition that produces a knowledge

of things in themselves (e.g., "poetic knowledge" or "knowledge by infused species"), it is a purely natural phenomenon. This is the status of
the "intellectual intuition" of the perennial philosophy. The more profound intuitive knowing through which one experiences "connaturality" with God referred to by Aquinas, the Maritains, and Gregory, is, in
contrast, supernatural in origin; and, knowledge through faith is its essential, supernaturally inspired starting point. God in Christ has provided sacramental, scriptural, doctrinal, and ecclesial means through
which such faith may and must be received. While perhaps not as direct or unmediated as the "intellectual intuition" claimed by the perennial philosophy, this path of faith is still superior because of its source
in divine revelation and its fruition in a knowledge through love of the
divine being.[30]

Griffiths thus positions himself with respect to his past overreliance
upon imaginative and rational means of inquiry as well as with regard
to the tendency of modern humanity in the West to turn away from the
supernatural and toward complete dependence upon what is only natural in origin. Whether distinguishing between different types of intuitive knowledge, or writing of the superiority of Christianity as
embodying the way of faith and love, Griffiths is expressing the same
concern, one based simultaneously upon his own experience and upon
his critique of the surrounding culture: Human beings have been too
self-reliant; they must surrender to the supernatural means of experiencing God's presence, found most fully in the church.

Faith and Reason in Balance

Griffiths's study of Eastern as well as Western thought in the early 1950s
before his departure for India strengthened his view on the value of
nonrational ways of knowing, a view reinforced by the texts he read
from Hinduism, Buddhism, and Taoism. At that time, however, he also
concluded that the supernatural knowledge of faith and its perfection
in loving contemplation exceeded all that Eastern wisdom can offer.
Nevertheless, as early as 1953 he called for a "marriage of East and
West" in the modes of their thought, the intuitive and the rational.[31]

Had the "marriage" of the intuitive and rational means for gaining
knowledge already taken place in Griffiths's overall practice before leaving England, through his research of Western and Eastern philosophies,
and through his efforts over the years to reconcile these two approaches
to truth? While his later writings exhibit further development in his understanding of how one best approaches knowledge of the truth, a sig-

nificant moment of integration is recorded near the end of his time in England. His account of his method of inquiry into the truths of his own tradition (as well as others) at the end of the first autobiography is illuminating in its expression of balance between the receptive and intuitive mode of "faith" and the critical, analytical mode of "reason."

What Griffiths portrays in the first period as a conflict between reason and imagination, he now sees in the second period as a creative interplay or dialogue between reason and faith. Implied here is a structural parallel between imagination (as he understood this faculty in the first period, especially via Coleridge); intuition (as a general alternative mode of knowing, via Aquinas and the Maritains); and faith (as expressed and exemplified primarily in the Bible and in Christian theology). Each mode of knowing has played a role, as Griffiths portrays his self-understanding over time, vis-à-vis the rational mode that he sees as dominant in his contemporary Western culture.

In the first autobiography Griffiths presents his developing ability to integrate the submission of his mind to the teachings of the church and to the monastic rule with his use of critical reason, citing Aquinas as the highest exemplar of this balance. While at times there were "conflicts and difficulties" in his study, he reports, "at each step reason and faith went together." He summarizes the results of this integration as follows:

> As time went on I found that there was immense scope for the exercise of one's critical faculties, and that the use of reason was not impeded but rather stimulated by the constant effort to keep it in vital relation to the truth of faith. Faith and reason could not conflict in reality; where there was an apparent conflict, it gave a certain zest to one's study to try to resolve it without prejudice to the one or to the other.[32]

The balance between reason and faith was sustained by the further realization that both were exceeded and completed by the way of knowing through love in contemplation.

First Years in India: A Reappraisal of Natural and Supernatural Ways of Knowing

When Griffiths arrived in India he did find "the other half" of his soul represented in the symbology of the temples and incarnate in the people who thronged the streets and villages. What he had speculated was a different mode of thinking in the East he found supporting and permeating the very culture of India, just as the rational, scientific mode undergirded and shaped his culture of origin.

In "Fulfillment for the East" (an article sent from India for publication later in the year of his arrival there), Griffiths contrasts the ways in which the West and the East have approached the divine Being. This account is familiar in its comparison of the Western use of "reason acting upon the evidence of the senses as the normal mode of human knowledge" with the Eastern emphasis upon a "higher mode of knowledge than sense or reason—the knowledge of spiritual intuition, a knowledge not dependent on the senses or on any logical process, but on the soul's direct, intuitive awareness of itself."[33] As in the article, "The Transcendent Unity of Religions" (1954), Griffiths supports his discussion of this "higher mode" with references to the contemplatives of East and West, as well as to Aquinas and to the perennial philosophy. Unlike that earlier article, Griffiths makes no attempt to defend knowledge through faith as more perfect, though perhaps less direct in mode, than "the knowledge of spiritual intuition" found outside the Christian revelation. He equates the direct, intuitive knowledge espoused by the perennial philosophy and Eastern spiritualities not with "knowledge by infused species" but with Aquinas's description of contemplation as "a mode of knowledge above both reason and faith, admitting man to a knowledge of God by experience, an infused wisdom in which the soul becomes passive to the divine action, *patiens divina*."[34] Nor is there any mention in his comparison of different ways of knowing God of the distinction applied in his prior article between supernatural and natural. He describes "the knowledge derived from contemplation" or "spiritual intuition" as "a wisdom which descends from above and directly enlightens the soul" and "unites man directly with God."[35] What Christianity adds to "fulfill" the East is not access to a supernatural source of contemplative knowledge but theological precision.

In England in the early 1950s Griffiths portrayed knowledge through faith as the prerequisite to an experience of contemplative knowing that unites one with the mysteries of faith through the mediation of Scripture, liturgy, doctrine, and prayer forms. Such knowledge was contrasted to the direct, immediate intuition spoken of by the perennial philosophers and by the Eastern spiritual teachers. Does Griffiths's different evaluation of the intuitive knowledge claimed by the perennial philosophy and Eastern spiritualities in the 1955 article from India signal a change in his thinking? Has his early experience in India helped him recognize that the direct intuition spoken of by its philosophers and mystics, even if unmediated by the church, is in fact also a grace of supernatural origin and not just a natural virtue? Has he glimpsed the possibility, expressed more fully and explicitly later, that contemplation as a receptive state of consciousness in which knowledge of God may be infused is an experience that unites the mystical philosophies of Aquinas and Gregory with those of the perennialists and the religions of India? The resolution of this discrepancy between two articles written within two years of one another is not clear. Apparently, Griffiths's early experience of India prompted a reappraisal of the natural/supernatural distinction as the basis for differentiating Christian contemplation from all other forms. From such early writings in India it is also clear that Griffiths felt deeply drawn into dialogue with the East on the nature of contemplation.[36]

It is intriguing that there is less philosophical treatment of different styles or modes of knowledge in the writings of the next dozen years, a topic which, as we have seen, had been significant to Griffiths's study and theoretical reflections since his time at Oxford. If any reappraisal of how one knows the truth was happening, it would not be articulated until later during the third period of his life. His discussion of practical matters during these first years in India is clearly more theological and cultural, while less philosophical, in its orientation. It seems that the integrated method of reason and faith continued to operate, although fresh experiences brought some new input into the implementation, if not the understanding, of his multifaceted approach to knowledge.

Kurisumala Ashram: Liturgy and Dialogue

One event is particularly significant for an examination of Griffiths's method of inquiry and theory of mind during the later years of the second period of his life, the move to Kurisumala Ashram in 1958, three years after his arrival in India. While maintaining an observance of the Benedictine rule, this new community brought to Griffiths the regular experience of a different style of liturgy, the Syrian rite. This change in the form of worship that Griffiths as a priest regularly celebrated brought with it "a wholly different tradition," one he describes as an "ancient symbolic mode of thought."[37] Remembering how integral liturgy had become in Griffiths's search as a Benedictine for knowledge of God, one can appreciate how important a shift in liturgical forms would be for him.

The nature of the "mode of thought" expressed in, and evoked by, the Syrian liturgy is reflected in Griffiths's numerous articles during his years at Kurisumala. Recurrent in these writings is the juxtaposition of the character of the Latin liturgy, shaped by scholastic theology, and that of the Syrian rite, embodying the Semitic worldview of the Bible. The value of the Latin tradition, like the faculty of reason to which it primarily appeals, is not devalued by Griffiths, but its limitations are strongly asserted, especially in its applicability to non-Western cultures.[38] In contrast, the Syrian rite is more closely suited to the Eastern mind, with its nonrational or intuitive orientation. Thus this form of liturgy emphasizes the poetry of the Psalms and of hymns, bringing the theology of the Bible to life by utilizing "the biblical mode of thought" that Griffiths would later characterize as based upon a symbolic and poetic rather than conceptual and discursive approach to truth.[39] In particular, like the Bible, the Syrian liturgy reflects and communicates "a wonderful sacramental sense; the sense that through the Incarnation the divine power has penetrated the whole creation."[40] These descriptions echo Griffiths's suggestion expressed a few years before his departure from England that the Psalms must be read in the liturgy with imagination rather than reason in order to experience through them the mysteries of faith. During his ten years at Kurisumala, regular participation in the Syrian liturgy, no doubt, expanded and deepened his appreciation of nonrational means for gaining knowledge of God.

Griffiths eventually grew dissatisfied, however, with the full applicability of the Syrian rite to an Indian context. The Semitic worldview that this liturgy expressed was still foreign to the way in which Indians think and experience, though certainly closer in this respect than the Latin rite and the thought world it reflects.[41] Also, with the cofounder of the ashram, Fr. Mahieu, devoting his energies largely to a deeper scholarly exploration of the Syrian liturgy, the ashram did not afford Griffiths the optimum context for entering thoroughly into the kind of dialogue with Hinduism "on the level of contemplation" that he had envisioned at the beginning of his years in India. Griffiths's sense of purpose and also of method began to diverge from that of the ashram. As will be discussed more fully later, interreligious dialogue, as both a goal and a means for approaching the truth, assumed greater importance for him than continued development of the Syrian liturgy as a form appropriate to India.

Refinement or Reform in Griffiths's Method of Inquiry?

The second period in Griffiths's life, which he has described as a time centered in the experience of God in Christ and in the church, presents a complex picture with regard to his understanding of method. There is a clear line of development from his conversion until his departure for

India resulting in a balanced use of reason and faith. As a monk he had probed deeply into the nature of the liturgy and contemplative prayer as nonrational means for gaining knowledge. Whether through the poetry of the Psalms chanted during the daily divine office, or the sacraments, or the name of Jesus used in contemplative prayer, the knowledge received through the mode of faith is always mediated and thus points beyond itself to its perfection in loving contemplation. As a supernatural gift, such contemplation exceeds the purely natural intuition of the perennial philosophy and of Eastern mystics.

With the move to India, however, from the very first articles written there, it is apparent that an unresolved tension in Griffiths's own sense of method begins to come more powerfully to the surface. Something in his experience of the spirituality present there, and perhaps of the direction of his own spiritual life as well, prompted a reappraisal of the viability of the natural/supernatural distinction as a basis for distinguishing Christian contemplation from all other forms. Reference to this distinction decreases in his writing. Griffiths seems silently open to the profound experiences of truth shared by those of other traditions, received without the explicit mediations of Christ or church, and open to including such experiences as contemplation of the highest order. Simultaneously, as he begins exploring more deeply through dialogue into the general nature of contemplation, any mention of knowledge through faith also decreases as though his own experience was drawing him beyond what he would characterize as "a preliminary stage for knowledge."[42] One may speculate that Griffiths's later characterization of faith as "looking towards experience" captures the very transition he felt himself moving through after his emigration to India. As the experience of contemplation began to grow, it was like the "seed" of faith sprouting and taking on new life; the way of knowing he called "faith" was an important step to make, and yet also to go beyond, in his search for complete knowledge, what the Hindu philosophers call *jñāna*.[43]

Griffiths's reappraisal of means for knowing during the last part of this second stage in his life is supported by the context of Kurisumala, by the experience of the Syrian liturgy, but most importantly by his deepening personal involvement in interreligious and intrareligious dialogue—moving toward what he understood as "the marriage of East and West" both in the world and within himself. The "secret ferment" first created by his reading of Eastern texts was now stirred by his own direct experience of contemplation, enriched by a study of Yoga and Vedānta. Griffiths drew all that he had concluded concerning the various means for knowing fully into dialogue with Indian philosophy and spiritual experience—a dialogue spoken and written about but also one that he lived, incarnated, in all aspects of his life.

The conflict between rational and nonrational tendencies heightened by his conversion experience thus matured into a dialogue through his years in the Benedictine context, a dialogue mirrored in the encounter of "West" and "East" in his mind and in his spiritual journey.

6

God through the Symbols of Bible, Liturgy, and Prayer

A mid the spiritual darkness of his night of conversion when "all known landmarks" failed him, Griffiths held onto an image, Jesus in the Garden of Gethsemane. Later, alone in the Cotswolds, when he shut himself in a closet and prayed fervently for direction, he clung to an image of Jesus on the cross. In both instances, still early in his Christian formation, he broke through darkness into light; guidance from an inner and irrational, yet other and inspired source was received. As in the evening walk, here again was a mystical experience of divine presence; yet the symbols through which that presence was encountered had changed. No longer was he reaching out to God through the sacrament of nature interpreted by the writings of Romantic poets and nature mystics: "The presence of God had been revealed to me on that day at school beneath the forms of nature, the birds' song, the flowers' scent, the sunset over the fields; but now it was another presence which I perceived, the presence of God in the mystery not of nature but of Grace."[1] He had turned inward and simultaneously toward the traditions of the Christian church.[2] The intimations of a path he had discerned during the "experiment" after Oxford had been confirmed and his restlessness had begun to ease.

How does Griffiths understand the spiritual transformation that has happened to him during the conversion and after it? In the second period of his life he realizes more fully the nature of the relationship between mind and spirit and how symbols can mediate the opening of spirit to Spirit—realizations that serve to ground his understanding of both the night of conversion and the subsequent surrender to Christ and church.

Specifically, during his time as a hermit in the Cotswolds after London, he experiences clearly the mind's ability to move beyond the activities of the faculties. After describing how events, study, or the use of imagination in prayer can sometimes lead one to transcend the surface level of consciousness, he generalizes from his experience concerning a deeper level of the mind or soul beyond these activities:

> Beyond this, beyond all thought and feeling and imagination, there is an inner sanctuary into which we scarcely ever enter. It is the ground or substance of the soul, where all the faculties have their roots, and which is the very centre of our being. It is here that the soul is at all times in direct contact with God. . . . It was into this region that I believe I was drawn at this time, and my will in the silent depths of its being reached out to the will of God.[3]

How is it that symbols from Scripture, employed in liturgy and prayer, can facilitate the movement of the mind into this state of receptivity and contact? In answering this question, Griffiths's reflection was informed by several guides from the Western philosophical and Christian tradition, in particular again Thomas Aquinas and the Maritains.

Symbol and Intuition: Raissa and Jacques Maritain

The works of Raissa and Jacques Maritain have already been mentioned in the previous chapter in reference to Griffiths's understanding of intuition. It is clear from his published and unpublished writings that these authors were helpful as well in his formulation of a theory of religious symbols. In the context of their discussions of poetic and mystical (or contemplative) experiences as types of intuitive knowing, they present an understanding of how symbols arise and function in the mind that supports and informs Griffiths's own.

According to Jacques Maritain, in poetic and contemplative knowing, the usual conceptualization process is transcended in analogous ways, resulting in an experience of intuition. In poetic knowing, the subject opens to his or her own creative depths beyond the operations of reason, discovering a connaturality with phenomenal reality that is, as it were, buried there. In contemplative knowing, whether natural or supernatural, the subject goes beyond conceptualization to experience union with a transcendent or divine reality. In both cases, the catalysts for the experience of transcendence are symbols:

> [P]oetic knowledge, like the knowledge of contemplation (when it expresses itself), employs similitudes and symbols—in order to *seduce the reason*, as St. Thomas says; precisely because both of these

kinds of knowledge have to do, in different ways, with the non-conceptualisable.[4]

The symbol, according to Raissa Maritain, functions as an intelligible means for experiencing a mystery that goes beyond all intelligibility, a known word or image for opening to the unknown. Through the symbol one may be drawn into the very depth of experience of which the symbol is an expression. For it is indeed at a deeper or quieter level of experience that both the poet and the mystic intuit the nature of reality in ways that affect the imagination, which is the locus of symbolic activity:

> It is, then, the habit of a certain withdrawal, of a certain sleep of the faculties, of a certain interior silence, which disposes the poet sometimes to divine influences, sometimes to the keen perception of natural causes: "When the soul is abstracted from the sense," say St. Thomas, "it becomes more apt to receive the influence of spiritual substances and also to follow the subtle movements which are born in the imagination from the impression of natural causes, something which is very difficult when it is absorbed by sensible things."[5]

Is this reception of "natural causes" and "the influence of spiritual substances" what prompts the intuition of the fundamental images known as "symbols" both in poetry and in religion respectively? Such an account of the origin of religious symbols would be compatible with Griffiths's own theory.

The subjective depths in which poetic and contemplative knowing through symbols occurs is called by Jacques Maritain the "unconscious." He makes an important distinction here between the "automatic," "deaf," or "Freudian unconscious" and what he calls the "spiritual unconscious." While the former sense of the unconscious denotes a merely animal function cut off from the influence of either the intellect or the will, the latter represents the "preconscious life of the intellect and the will" and is, therefore, the area of the individual psyche where symbols arise prior to their becoming the objects of intellectual, conative, and imaginative activity.[6] As already noted, Griffiths expresses affinity with a different characterization of the "spiritual unconscious" by Jacques Maritain as that area of individual life that lies "[f]ar beneath the sunlit surface thronged with explicit concepts and judgments, words and expressed resolutions or movements of the will. . . ." Within this preconscious life, for Jacques Maritain and for Griffiths, exist "the sources of knowledge and creativity," and clearly the spiritual impulses that take form in the imagination.[7]

In the Maritains' writings Griffiths found a contemporary and psychologically sophisticated interpretation of the origin of symbols within human consciousness and of the manner in which symbols guide the conscious mind back to its own subliminal depths in an experience of intuitive knowing. These writings supported Griffiths's own emerging theory concerning the origin of symbols in an area of human consciousness secluded from rational activity and receptive to the divine; and they informed his own experience of how symbols may mediate an experience of knowledge. With their explicit dependence upon Aquinas, the insights of the Maritains were easily assimilated by Griffiths into his own theorizing in a Western Christian monastic context.

Christian Symbols as Mediators of Contemplative Experience

With his conversion, his joining the Catholic faith, and his entrance into the monastery (all between 1932 and 1933), Griffiths's theorizing about the nature of symbols and their ability to open human spirit to divine Spirit came to be informed by both a full participation in the rich liturgical life of Prinknash Abbey and by a total immersion in the tradition and Scriptures of the church. The results are reflected in his articles as a monk and then as a priest in England.

During the first years after his conversion, Griffiths reassessed his entire view of the spiritual journey, due to his recognition of a fundamental conflict between the Platonist approach that had deeply influenced his early path as well as much of Christian mysticism, and the biblical, incarnational approach at the basis of the liturgy. There was a basic imbalance in the Platonist approach as it had been interpreted in much Western spirituality and as he had implicitly lived it. In particular, he came to reject the negative view of the body characteristic of his own perilous asceticism and of any dualistic philosophy that posed the soul against its "prison house," the body. Similarly, he found in the Platonists' spirituality a tendency to identify the path toward God with an escape from the material world, a world that was fundamentally irreconcilable with the divine realm. Griffiths rejected as well the Platonist tendency to see the spiritual journey as a solitary contemplative ascent and affirmed the value of the church as a context for spiritual growth, based on its claim to be the Body of Christ. His first years in the monastic community tempered what he came to see as his own self-willed independence. As though speaking from his experience of spiritual maturation at Prinknash, Griffiths writes that liturgy offers the most potent corrective for the Platonic tendencies toward a dualistic rejection of the body and the world as well as toward an excessively solitary and ascetic path.[8]

The understanding of liturgy as essential to the Christian spiritual path marks a significant shift in Griffiths's reflections on practical means for knowing the truth. This shift toward a more sacramental, ritualistic, and corporate context for his pursuit of what is true is consonant with the formative spiritual experience of this second period of his life, his surrender of self to God in Christ and in the church. The ascetic and solitary path he had pursued prior to his conversion and just afterward no longer felt appropriate and seemed to reflect some false assumptions about spiritual growth in general. (Nevertheless, as part of his journey, the initial steps had indeed been guided by what he felt to be the same grace that now brought him to new realizations about the liturgy.) Monastic life had fostered a view that the search for divine truth is best lived through the mediations of the body, the community, and rituals of the church, and through the world in general. In other words, Griffiths had accepted the fact that the mediated knowledge through faith that he had experienced in prayer and through the Christian life is a necessary preparation for any higher knowledge of God.

Integrated into Griffiths's understanding of liturgy and knowledge through faith were his convictions about the importance of contemplation, strengthened by his time as a hermit in the English countryside after his conversion. Through the sacramental nature of Christian worship, the reality of God, incarnate in and through the substance of this world, is experienced in both a mystical and a corporate way. Concerning the Eucharistic sacrifice, he concludes:

> There can be no greater or deeper mystical experience than this: it comprehends in itself the purgative, the illuminative and the unitive way. The senses are purified by learning to apprehend the sacred mysteries under sensible forms; the mind is illumined by contemplation and union with the Word made flesh; and the soul is united to God in its inmost depths by the communication of the divine nature. Finally this is no solitary ecstatic experience; it does not take place in the desert or on a mountain. It is the "marriage supper of the Lamb" to which all are invited.[9]

Liturgy may bring one the experience not only of the "mediate knowledge" that is faith, but of contemplative or mystical knowing as well.

Writing after nearly twenty years as a monk, Griffiths sought to broaden the church's understanding of *contemplation*, arguing that this term refers not merely to an aspect of personal piety and one to which few are called, but to "part of the normal perfection of a Christian life" available to all collectively through the Mass. The liturgy offers an opportunity to experience "the profoundly social character of Christian contemplation" toward which the proper spiritual life is ordered and from which all apostolic labors may richly flow.[10] The very purpose of liturgy is "to dispose us to experience the reality . . . of the mysteries of faith," that is, to the contemplative experience.[11] In the early 1950s, Griffiths made similar claims for the role of the divine office and the Scriptures, articulating the effectiveness of these means for the individual and corporate experience of God in the depths of prayer.[12]

Griffiths perceives larger than personal or ecclesial relevance for what he has learned from the monastic liturgy and way of life. He expresses his firm belief that the Christian sacramental life provides an antidote for the social and psychological ills crippling the contemporary Westerner. He laments the fact that the individual in Western society is imprisoned by the world of her or his own making, guarded by the principles of science and reason, and thereby is unable to enter "the vast world of mystery in which the true meaning of man and of God is to be found."[13] Access to this other "world," for Griffiths, is found through worship and adoration, that is, through the mediation of religious symbols.

In other articles of the early 1950s, Griffiths focuses upon the power of the symbols of the liturgy and the Scriptures to mediate a contemplative experience of the "world" of divine mystery. But how is it that things of the created world may give access to this other "world"? While contemplative prayer draws one *beyond* all images, words, and concepts, nevertheless the Christian tradition has affirmed that its symbols may somehow aid the process of becoming present to God, as "means of grace." In his answer to this important question of the relationship between symbols and contemplation, Griffiths delineates the direction that his theory of religious symbol would follow for years to come:

It is quite true that contemplation is generally held to begin when the mind passes beyond words and images and all clear concepts, and comes under the direct influence of divine grace. But this does not mean that the mind must necessarily abandon the use of words and images altogether. When the mind passes into a state of contemplation, it will not use words and images as the proper means of prayer—this will be supplied by the action of grace—but it may nevertheless use them as "supports" to its prayer. The purpose of all prayer is to raise the mind and will to God. All words and actions, all images and concepts, whether of the Mass or the divine office, are so many means—sacramental signs—by which the mind and will are raised to God. We must never stop short at the sign, but use it as a means to ascend to the thing signified—the infinite reality of God.[14]

Griffiths's agreement with these statements never wavered. Key elements of his theory of religious symbols that endured to the end of his
life are expressed here:

> the conviction that the symbols of the faith are intended to mediate an
> experience that transcends all symbols (images, words, or concepts);
>
> the implied Thomistic distinction between the *sacramentum* (sacra-
> ment) and the *res* (or thing symbolized);
>
> the caution that one must never stop at the level of the symbol but go
> beyond into a contemplative experience of the mystery of God;
>
> as well as the insistence that religious symbols are not simply ex-
> pendable means that can be jettisoned by the mature contemplative.

Griffiths applies his insights into the nature and function of symbols
to the liturgical life of the church, including the reading of Scripture, in
great detail. He treats, for instance, the power of particular words in the
psalmody that are often repeated (e.g., *dominus* and *deus*);[15] the place of
art in the liturgy (architecture, painting, sculpture, and music);[16] the
specific symbols of the Mass and the comprehensive range of their sig-
nification;[17] and some of the particular images of the Old and New
Testaments (such as the "cloud" of Exodus and the Gospels' "kingdom
of Heaven").[18]

It is significant that Griffiths applies his theory of religious symbols
beyond the spheres of the liturgy and the Scriptures as well. In redefining the nature of dogmas, for instance, he addresses the apparent
conflict experienced by some contemplatives between the dogmatic expressions of the institutional church and their own more immediate relationship to God. Like many outside the church, these contemplatives
find the dogmas to be hindrances rather than guides to faith.
Diagnosing and resolving the difficulty presented by the fundamental
tenets of the church for one contemporary contemplative, Griffiths
writes:

> Her trouble here arises, we believe, as is commonly the case, from
> a confusion between the dogmas and the mysteries of the faith.
> The object of faith is properly speaking not a dogma but a mys-
> tery. . . . But in order that the mysteries of faith may be made
> known to us, they have to be presented to us in an intelligible
> manner, and the dogmas of our faith are simply the intelligible
> terms in which the mysteries of the faith are presented to us. They
> are not the object of faith, but the means by which the object of

faith is made known. They are like the sacraments, signs of a mystery which infinitely transcends them.[19]

Dogmas, then, like the liturgy and the Scriptures, may serve a symbolic function for the Christian, as means by which the divine mystery is made known.

As Griffiths has noted in the past and would repeat frequently in his writing on this topic, the danger always exists, however, that one "stops short" or gets stuck at the level of the sign, confusing the dogmas with the mysteries of faith to which they point; one then turns the former into the objects of faith rather than the latter. The result of this mistaking the *sacramentum* for the *res* is ultimately one's separation from the truth and from God, for one has turned creations of the mind into idols.[20] What Griffiths implies here and will state more fully later is that only the divine mystery is absolute, not any of the culturally conditioned signs or symbols through which that mystery communicates itself. In fact, certain signs, according to Griffiths, in time may become impotent and die; in contrast, "living symbols" are those that continue to mediate the divine presence and "work a tranformation in our souls."[21]

By extending the range within which symbols might have a sacramental as opposed to merely indicatory function, Griffiths has taken a bold step toward a point of view that will inform all his later writings about the nature and function of symbols in Christianity and, importantly, in other religions as well. In the context of his early articles, Griffiths expanded what may qualify as symbols (in the full sense of sacraments) to include all of creation. In doing so, Griffiths felt he was being faithful not only to his own experience but to the founder of his monastic order as well. Interpreting the "sacramentalism" of St. Benedict, Griffiths writes: "Every created thing is a sacrament, a sign which makes God known."[22] An ongoing tension in Griffiths's theory of religious symbols is thus revealed, one that is prompted by the challenge to integrate his own early nature mysticism with his deepening Christian identity: the experience that all of creation symbolizes (or is a sacrament of) the divine Creator, in tension with the conviction (and the doctrine) that Christian symbols are supreme. Thus Griffiths both affirms that ultimately the universe and all of history are "a great sacrament, in which God is being revealed," and declares that the symbols of the Christian faith are of unsurpassed efficacy.[23]

The special power of the symbols of the church is attributable, according to Griffiths, first to their rootedness in history. In contrast to the timeless context of the symbols of primitive or natural religions, the Bible conveys divine revelation primarily through symbols that are based in historical events. The grounding of revelatory symbols in history and in a linear sense of time is highly significant for Griffiths because this development supports a fuller valuation of this world and of the individual's place in it than the earlier revelations with their cyclic view of time could effect.[24]

A second virtue of the symbols of the church is what Griffiths calls their "supernatural" or "sacramental" quality. It is clear from these statements that, for Griffiths, the Christian symbols in the liturgy, the Scriptures, the divine office, and dogmas may serve as means through which one transcends images and concepts to experience the divine mystery in a contemplative "darkness" of the mind. Such an effect, Griffiths writes, is indeed a "supernatural" one because of the nature of these symbols:

> [T]he symbols of the liturgy are not merely natural symbols; they are supernatural signs, akin to the sacraments themselves, which produce a supernatural effect in us and communicate the divine mystery, which they contain, to our souls. In this sense the divine office may be called *"sacramental."* It is a system of signs or symbols, which manifests the Word of God to us and communicates the grace of the Spirit. If we submit ourselves to its influence and let its special grace act upon us, we ourselves are transformed by the power and enter the mystery of Christ and the Church.[25]

Contemplation as the direct experience of the divine mystery, then, is a "supernatural" effect distinctive of Christian liturgical symbols—a position consistent with his use of the same natural/supernatural distinction with regard to ways of knowing prior to emigrating to India.

This quotation is also noteworthy in its presentation of the power inherent in the symbol itself: The symbol "contains" the divine mystery and thereby "communicates" that mystery to us. To use the Thomistic terminology often employed by Griffiths, the *sacramentum* and the *res* are related more inextricably than by mere convention or by the authority of revelation. The religious symbol and that which it signifies are in the case of the Christian liturgy related at a profound level of intimacy that Griffiths will continue throughout his life to explore, both theoretically and experientially.

From this discussion it is clear that the central conviction underlying Griffiths's reflection upon the value and the limits of religious symbols, especially relevant for his understanding of the unique power of Christian symbols, is that the divine mystery is "infinitely beyond our conception" and so can never be defined by any object of the human mind. Nevertheless, he remains convinced that one may experience the

mystery of God in the state of self-transcendence he calls "contemplation." He is equally certain that such experience is a kind of knowledge;
in fact, it is the goal of the process of knowing.[26]

Consideration of the nature of religious symbols also prompts
Griffiths to suggest, presumably from his experience in the monastery,
the requisite subjective conditions under which the divine mystery
may be known through the kind of symbolic mediations just discussed. Most crucial is the participant's state of mind. Citing Simone
Weil's account of the "attention" with which one should approach the
divine mystery through the symbols of the church, Griffiths writes that
"when we approach the Mass or the divine office, we should not try to
force our attention, but to leave the mind open, so that the thoughts
and images penetrate the mind, while it remains continually quiet and
attentive to God."[27] Only in this state of mind, cultured through the
practice of contemplation, will the "supernatural effect" of the liturgical symbols occur.

Lest it appear that an "attentive" or contemplative state of mind is
somehow a "work" or an achievement by the individual to which God is
subject, Griffiths is careful to emphasize that knowledge of the divine
mystery via the symbols of liturgy, Scripture, and tradition depends upon
a special gift of insight from God, that is, upon grace, "the communication of the Spirit, of God's own wisdom to us."[28] Nevertheless, there is
much that one may do to open oneself to this grace. Griffiths specifically
calls for a recovery of "that ancient tradition of symbolism" which, he
says, "underlies all the Scriptures and the liturgy." Significantly, he re-
minds his reader that this recovery is not just a matter of intellectual understanding; it is a matter of a receptive soul and spirit.[29]

One may still ask how, according to Griffiths, the divine mystery is
experienced by the receptive mind through the religious symbol. While
he does not speculate at length upon this question in any published
works until the second autobiography (1982), Griffiths does give some
preliminary lines of an answer to this question in the 1930s. Griffiths
speculates about how the highly symbolic utterances of the poets and
the authors of religious myths are inspired. Such inspiration, he writes:
"springs from the unconscious depths of the soul."[30] He further identifies such inspiration as a grace received "in the centre of the soul where
the faculties meet." Thus revelation itself, according to Griffiths, is not
merely dropped upon or injected into the intellect as a system of ideas
or pattern of images: "God approaches man through his emotions, his
imagination, his will and his intellect, addressing himself to the whole
man and restoring man to wholeness."[31]

Thus God speaks to humanity from within the very depths of consciousness, communicating revelation through symbols. Such commu-

nication is also found in Jesus' speech, according to Griffiths. Anticipating his later account of how symbols arise within human consciousness as means by which the divine mystery communicates and through which that mystery may be known, Griffiths writes:

> Thus in the order of grace we can see how the Word descends from the height of pure being into the world of the imagination, making use of the images and devices of the poet to manifest Himself. But He does not stop there: He descends even into the world of the senses. "The Word became flesh." He not only expressed Himself in the symbolic forms of the imagination: He made himself to be heard and seen and handled, and He chose to perpetuate His presence among us by making Himself our food and drink.[32]

Here is suggested the potentially provocative claim that Jesus is himself a symbol in the fullest sense, a position to be developed more fully in the next section.

For Griffiths, such a theory of how symbols function again had more than personal and ecclesial implications. Western society in its modern malaise was crying out for the "antidote" offered by a renewal of symbolic experience and intuitive knowing. The legitimacy of Griffiths's diagnosis and claim for the potential healing role of a renewed appreciation of religious symbols is supported by the fact that he was not alone in calling for such a renewal and in envisioning its benefits for Western culture. In formulating this theory of how religious symbols mediate both knowledge and contemplative experience, Griffiths's thought was affirmed and informed by his study of other writers on symbolism, especially the twentieth-century Catholic theologian, Karl Rahner.

Role of Symbols in Divine Self-Expression

According to Rahner, all beings, including the divine being, are intrinsically "multiple" or "plural" as a necessary condition for their own fulfillment in self-knowledge and self-love.[33] In order to possess these two perfections, each and every being must "express" itself as an other so that the relationship essential for knowledge and love may take place. With the being of God in mind, Rahner asserts that the resulting multiplicity is not necessarily a sign of imperfection or limitation. Rather, from the case of the Trinity one knows that plurality of self-expression in unity is itself a higher perfection than simple or undifferentiated being; such differentiation within a unity of being, as in the persons of the Trinity, is, for Rahner, "an ontological ultimate."[34] When this self-differentiation or self-expression is in total "agreement" or harmony with its originating unity, then the expressions take on the full character of symbols: representations that allow the other, that which is symbolized, "to be there." Symbols in this "original," "primordial," or "transcendental" sense—what Rahner calls "real symbols"—may, thus, become first the mediators of self-knowledge for the symbolized being and then potentially the paths to knowledge of that being by others.[35]

For Rahner, the clearest example of this symbolic character of being is what for him is the supreme symbol, the Logos, the image and self-expression of the Father. He writes:

> [T]he Logos is the "symbol" of the Father, in the very sense which we have given the word: the inward symbol which remains distinct from what is symbolized, which is constituted by what is symbolized, where what is symbolized expresses itself and possesses itself.[36]

In turn, this "inward symbol" that is the self-expression of the symbolized is manifested "outwardly" as well in the world as the Word incarnate, Jesus Christ, embodying symbolically in that world the very presence of God. For Rahner, there is only one such "absolute symbol" of God's presence in the world, "the humanity of Christ." This humanity is a "real symbol" because it is not an arbitrary or derivative expression of the Logos; Christ's humanity is "the self-disclosure of the Logos itself, so that when God, expressing himself, exteriorizes himself, that very thing appears which we call the humanity of the Logos."[37]

As the further self-expression of the Logos, the church "continues the symbolic function of the Logos in the world" and is "the primary sacrament."[38] A sacrament, for Rahner, is the effect of God's grace incarnating in the human experience of space and time; it is a symbolic reality which, like those just discussed, re-presents that which it symbolizes. While humans may administer the ritual actions, on the basis of this view of sacrament as symbol, one must say that the sacrament represents God's action upon humanity.[39]

The exteriorization of God's self-expression through the Logos continues further, according to Rahner, in all created things, giving them also a "symbolic reality," one that is infinitely extended by the presence here of the incarnate Word. In light of the incarnation, all things created by God may function as profound symbols of their creator for those who have the eyes of faith.[40] While all things may serve a symbolic function in reference to God, as Griffiths also believes, nevertheless for Rahner, the humanity of Christ remains the supreme symbol of God's presence in the world.

Rahner addresses another issue of interest to Griffiths, the ultimacy of the various symbols and sacraments in relation to the passage of time and in light of the *eschaton* (the divinely appointed end of history). Specifically, Rahner responds to those who claim that at the end of time all symbols will disappear "in favour of a naked immediacy of God with regard to the creature—'face to face.'" Recalling the intrinsic and intimate relationship between the "real symbol" and that which expresses it from within itself, Rahner contends that such symbols do not need to disappear in order for the beatific vision to occur:

> [T]he true and proper symbol, being an intrinsic moment of the thing itself has a function of mediation which is not at all opposed in reality to the immediacy of what is meant by it, but is a mediation to immediacy, if one may so formulate the actual facts of the matter.

Rahner continues in the same passage to affirm that of all Christian symbols, ultimately, only the humanity of Christ will endure, being the supreme symbol of the Logos:

> In the end, of course, many signs and symbols will cease to be; the institutional Church, the sacraments in the usual sense, the whole historical succession of manifestations through which God continually imparts himself to man, while he still travels far from the immediacy of God's face, among images and likenesses. But the humanity of Christ will have eternal significance for the immediacy of the *visio beata* [beatific vision].[41]

The same issue of the endurance of the "real symbol" in the direct experience of the divine mystery became especially important for Griffiths as his relationship to the nondual reality of God grew more intimate.

While it is not clear exactly when Griffiths first encountered Rahner's theology of the symbol, it is apparent that by the time it was written Griffiths had come to similar conclusions himself. For both theologians, the true religious symbol functions as both a means of divine grace, through which God acts upon the human, and a mediator of knowledge, through which the human may approach God. According to Rahner and Griffiths, the symbol does not merely signify but rather re-presents and communicates that which it symbolizes because the symbol itself, to use Griffiths's word, "contains" the divine mystery within it. In Rahner's theory Griffiths undoubtedly recognized a profound working out of this latter point from an ontological point of view, an account that emphasized how the symbol is the self-expression of the symbolized. Furthermore, both theologians claim that, while everything in creation may serve as symbols of the divine mystery, nevertheless the sacraments of the church (differently specified by the two, perhaps) have a unique potency, given their close relationship to the history of the incarnate Logos. Both agree as well that Jesus Christ is the supreme symbol of God as the one who "contains" and "communicates," who is the fullest self-expression of, the divine mystery. Rahner's theory of the relationship of "mediated immediacy" also serves as a valuable counterpoint to Griffiths's emerging understanding of nonduality during this second period.

A possible discrepancy between the two presentations of symbols, and one not necessarily attributable to the particular context of Rahner's article, is Griffiths's apparently greater emphasis upon the need to go beyond the symbol to experience the symbolized. For Griffiths, this experience of transcending the symbol, known as "contemplation," is the very knowing that the symbol intends to mediate. Rahner, by virtue of his ontological account of the intrinsic relationship between the "real symbol" (including, besides the Logos and the humanity of Christ, the church and its sacraments) and what it symbolizes, implies that one never transcends the "real symbol" fully because it is inherent, as an interior moment of self-expression, within the symbolized. Is this apparent discrepancy explainable by the different spiritualities, and thus points of view, engaged by the two authors?[42]

Additional questions are raised by Rahner for Griffiths's emerging theory of religious symbols and how such symbols mediate experience of the divine mystery that are relevant for the change in cultural and religious context he underwent in 1955: Would he find in India a culture more aware of the transformational role of symbols in human mental processes? Furthermore, if the "real symbol" mediates the movement of the soul toward its center, the opening of mind to spirit and of spirit to Spirit, what is the status of the great symbols of other religions? Are they also real symbols, that is, self-expressions of the divine mystery in the fullest sense?

The Impact of India

While the general outlines of his theory of religious symbols were already established by the time Griffiths left England in 1955, it was inevitable that living in India would prompt further reflection upon what symbols are and how they function—not only in Christianity but in the Eastern traditions as well—with clear implications for his view of the spiritual journey and mystical experience.

Griffiths's search for "the other half" of his soul in India was satisfied not only through encountering philosophical ideas and spiritual practices that described and fostered nonrational ways of knowing, but also through his experience of the Indian people and their culture, both of which he found remarkably open to "the unconscious."[43] His early explorations of Hindu shrines and temples revealed to him "graven in stone that profound spirit of contemplation which has given its inner meaning to all Indian life and thought" and "the awareness of the essential holiness of nature." From his exposure to the simple life of the villagers, Griffiths came to conclude that every aspect of Indian life is experienced as symbolic or sacred:

> Perhaps this is the deepest impression left by life in India, the sense of the sacred as something pervading the whole order of nature. Every hill and tree and river is holy, and the simplest human acts of eating and drinking, still more of birth and marriage, have all retained their sacred character. It is this that gives such an indescribable beauty to Indian life, in spite of the poverty and squalor.[44]

What Griffiths had envisioned and actually glimpsed through his reading of the Romantic poets and through his own experience of nature he now found shaping an entire culture.[45] The way of life that he had found so meaningful in the monastery where every activity, however mundane, was viewed as "sacramental," as an opportunity both to serve God and to experience God's presence in contemplation, he now discovered was being lived by the simplest of villagers around him. His early and enduring sense that all of creation and potentially all of human life may be experienced as symbolic or sacramental, he indeed found was the very ethos of India.

With further reflection, experience of the sacred character of life in India would bring Griffiths realizations of the unique philosophical and spiritual insights that his new country had contributed to an understanding of religious symbols. In *Vedānta and Christian Faith* (1973) he writes:

> In India it was understood from the beginning that God cannot properly be imagined or conceived. To my mind this is the supreme achievement of India that at the very beginning of her history she was able to break through the veil, not only of the senses but also of the intellect, and to discover the hidden mystery which lies beyond speech and thought.[46]

In other words, India had long ago recognized the fact that the divine mystery could not be captured within any symbol, whether images or concepts, but could only be experienced through going beyond the symbol and deep into interiority. In living by this recognition of the need to go beyond, Indian teachers, like the ninth-century philosopher Śankara, have upheld a spiritual principle that is neither culture-bound nor applicable only for a few. Rather, they have discerned a key dynamic or direction in the human mind.[47]

While recognizing the need to go beyond all concepts and images in pursuit of the ultimate and the divine, India, according to Griffiths, did not therefore forsake the symbol. Quite the opposite, the symbol and its expression in myth and ritual were accepted, even celebrated, as the necessary means to experiencing ultimate reality—an understanding supported by the "sacramental" way of life just described and by a vision of a "cosmic unity" and by a "sacred universe."[48] Symbolic expressions such as the myths of the Vedas were recognized as arising out of, and potentially leading one back to, a mystical experience of the ultimate reality. It is this firm symbolic or sacramental sense and this grounding in mystical awareness of the one reality, according to Griffiths, that keeps the Indian mind open to experiencing the ultimate in the midst of what to the Westerner may appear as a pantheistic and polytheistic religiosity.[49] To summarize his impressions of India in terms of his own theory of symbols, Griffiths found there a culture that recognized both the necessity and the limitations of symbols in opening one to an experience of the divine mystery, as well as a refined sense of receptivity to such experience.

Griffiths's encounter with India also sharpened his critique of Western cultures. Rarely is his early description of the "sense of the sacred" that pervades Indian life not followed by the claim that this "sense" is, in part, what the West needs to learn from the East. After the passage just quoted on "the deepest impression left by life in India," Griffiths immediately turns westward:

> Perhaps there is nothing which the western world needs more urgently to recover than this sense of the sacred. In the West everything has become "profane"; it has been deliberately emptied of all religious meaning. . . . It is here that the West needs to learn from the East the sense of the "holy," of a transcendent mystery which is immanent in everything and which gives an ultimate meaning to life.[50]

Again, he finds the scientific mind-set to blame for this profanation of life in his culture of origin: "Our science which seeks to explain everything by its causes, has lost the sense of their inner significance. It is so absorbed in the study of the finite, that it cannot see it as a symbol of the infinite."[51]

In response to a recognition of the "sense of the sacred" or of the "sacramentalism" in Indian culture and to the consequent criticism of the cultures of the West, Griffiths frequently calls for a recovery of the church's sense of symbolism, based on an equally important recovery of its sense of mystery. While perhaps inspired by the encounter with Hinduism to seek this recovery in the church, Griffiths suggests that Christians turn not to Eastern religions to guide this retrieval but to their own Christian roots, especially to the Fathers:

> I would say that we have first of all to recover the sense of mystery and sacrament in our own Liturgy. We must try to see our Faith as our forefathers saw it, not as a system of rational and moral concepts, but as a divine mystery, an economy of Grace totally transcending the reach of reason. It is in this way that we can make contact with Hinduism at its deepest level, and perhaps learn from it a deeper sense of our own Christian mystery. In the second place we have to recover our sense of symbolism; to understand how the Liturgy is throughout a symbolic representation of the mystery of Christ. A symbol in this sense is a sign which in some way makes present the thing which is signified. It is in the Liturgy above all that the mystery of the Presence of God, of which the Hindu is so keenly aware, should be made manifest. . . . Finally, this means a return to the sources of our Faith, to that Eastern tradition of Hebrew and Semitic thought, which lies behind all the later development of Greek and Latin theology.[52]

Griffiths's articles from India on the theme of symbolism echo the same call for a renewed sacramentalism found in his articles from England in the early 1950s, but now with an awareness of the implications of such a recovery that extend beyond the church. At first, Griffiths clearly is hoping that a revival of a sense of sacred mystery and of symbolism in the church will make Christianity more attractive to non-Christian Indians. In the sacraments of the church, he believes, Indians could experience the fulfillment of their own quest for the divine pursued for centuries through the symbols of Hinduism.[53] At times, as in the passage just quoted, Griffiths expresses the same need for a recovery of a sense of the divine mystery and of symbolism as a prerequisite to a true dialogue with Hindus.

In summary, what impact did living in India have upon Griffiths's understanding of religious symbols and their role in spiritual transformation? First, the sheer existential challenge of adapting to a culture so thoroughly immersed in a sense of the sacred both affirmed and stretched his own symbolic sensibilities nurtured by the Romantic poets and by the liturgical life of the monastery. Second, in attempting to understand the impact of this culture upon himself and others, Griffiths recognized that this sense of the sacred was grounded in an implicit appreciation of symbols and in the very mystical or contemplative experience that he had already suggested was the goal of the symbolic nature of the Christian life in all of its aspects. Third, his direct encounter with one Eastern culture sharpened his critique of his Western origins, especially his view of the scientific attitudes that seemed responsible for robbing the Western mind of its symbolic openness or sense of the sacred by making idols out of scientific principles. Finally, his appreciation of the symbolic receptivity embodied in Indian culture and his negative assessment of Western cultures, now made from the perspective of the East, both prompted his call for the church's recovery of a sense of the divine mystery and of a sense of symbolism, primarily through a retrieval of biblical and Patristic sources. While not rejecting the better fruits of its scientific and highly rational approach to knowledge, even in Christian theology, Griffiths calls the West beyond its current rational or critical phase into a new level of collective consciousness that is again open to the power of symbols.[54]

Symbols in Comparative Religious Studies and Inculturation

In addition to sparking a call for renewal of the Western church's sense of the sacred and of symbolism, Griffiths's encounter with Indian, especially Hindu, symbols prompts him to address two other tasks: comparing the symbols of Christianity with those of Hinduism to establish their similarities and differences, and discerning the relativity of cultural symbolic forms to help legitimate a liturgical style that would speak more effectively to Indians than the Latin rite. In technical language, these two tasks are known as "comparative religious studies" and "inculturation."

In his early articles for the West from his new home, Griffiths, no doubt, felt it necessary to support his recognition of the powerfully "sacramental" character of Indian culture and religion by both comparing and contrasting the symbols of Hinduism with those of Christianity. In the writings of his first decade in India one finds many attempts both to account for the potency of Hindu symbols in terms accessible to Christians and to distinguish Christian symbols as, nevertheless, fulfilling the aspirations and conceptions embodied in those of Hinduism. The Christian symbols of the Eucharist and of Christ serve as clear examples of how Griffiths applied his understanding of religious symbols to comparative religious studies.[55]

In a paper delivered at the "All India Study Week" at the end of 1956, Griffiths speaks of the common element of sacrifice found in all religions and of the "special character" of the Eucharistic sacrifice. Through their religious rituals, according to Griffiths, human beings of all cultures have sought to invoke and come into the presence of God. In developing symbolic forms for this purpose, no one has surpassed the Hindus, by Griffiths's estimation, especially in religious music and architecture. Hinduism thus represents one of the highest expressions of what Griffiths calls the "primeval revelation" through which God spoke to humanity before the revelations made to Israel in the Law and then in Jesus Christ. Though many gods and goddesses may be worshiped by the Hindu through sacrifice, these remain clearly understood as symbols of the one God known as Brahman.[56]

Griffiths thus argues that Hinduism has much to contribute to the Christian's understanding of the Eucharistic sacrifice. Nevertheless, the Mass, when properly presented, has even more to offer to the Hindu. The sacrifice celebrated by Christians is unique, according to Griffiths, in at least two ways. First, the Mass represents, that is, makes present, a sacrifice that took place in history, once for all time in time. Second, this sacrifice was instituted by Christ himself in the Last Supper; it is not merely of human design but is itself of the order of Revelation and is grounded in "the authority of Christ."[57] While the Mass is analogous to the sacrificial rites found in Hinduism, it fulfills in time the timeless aspirations of humans seeking God through the "primeval revelation."

Griffiths characterizes the respective contributions that Hinduism and Christianity might make to one another with respect to their sacrificial rites as follows:

> If the Hindu sense of the divine mystery, of the sacramental nature of the universe with all the depth of symbolism which springs from this view of life, and the Hindu conception of sacrifice as the essential means by which man enters into union with God, could all be brought to centre on their proper object, that is on Jesus Christ, God and Man, the Redeemer of the world; then surely not only would Hinduism receive its supreme fulfillment, but the Church also would be enriched by the genius of India and we should see an Indian Catholicism, which would be the authentic expression of the soul of India.[58]

Here is an assertion of the need for and value of Hindu-Christian dialogue, but one set clearly in relation to the finality and universality of Christ.

Griffiths's characterization of the Christ symbol illustrates a similar attempt to express affinity and distinction. The Incarnation, Griffiths asserts, is "the supreme 'sign'" of God's work in history—again, in contrast to the semihistorical, mythical figures of the Hindu gods and even the *avatāras* (lit., "descents"). While there are similarities between the Hindu teaching of the *avatāras* as manifestations of God in human form in times of great need and the Christian doctrine of the Incarnation, Griffiths contends that Rāma, Krishna, and Śiva do not effect the same power as symbols of God because of their fully divine (i.e., suprahuman) and semihistorical character. Again upholding the value of Hindu symbols and yet claiming that their supreme fulfillment is found only in Jesus Christ, Griffiths writes:

[W]hen we confront Rama, and Krishna and Siva with the person of Christ, we have no need to reject or despise them. We have only to show that they are shadows of the reality. They are symbols which have been realised in Christ—He alone is the historic fulfillment of all man's dreams of a saviour: He alone answers the deepest need of the human heart and reveals the ultimate truth of the divine love.[59]

In other articles from Griffiths's first years in India, one finds very similar accounts of the symbolic character of the Eucharist and of Christ in comparison to the symbols of Hinduism. From the dual nature of Christ as symbolic (or mythical) and historical, Griffiths is, thus, able to conclude that "Christ alone is capable of reconciling the ancient tradition of religion in India with the demands of the modern mind."[60]

Griffiths has identified, then, what he considers to be a weakness in Hindu sacramentalism, its tendency to see the symbol outside of any historical relationship to what it symbolizes. This inadequacy in the Hindu theory of symbolism, according to Griffiths, is symptomatic of a basic flaw in Hindu philosophy—a flaw seen in the Hindus' inabilities to recognize the importance of religious differences and to account adequately for the relationship between God, the human soul, and the world.[61] These criticisms will be discussed at greater length in the next section.

Turning to the second primary topic in Griffiths's writing on religious symbols during his first decade in India, the project of inculturation, one finds an important principle that qualifies his presentation of the supremacy of Christian symbols: the relativity of cultural symbolic forms. Prompted specifically by the challenge of composing a liturgy that would speak more effectively to Indians than the Latin rite, Griffiths joined others in seeking "to distinguish what is permanent and essential in the liturgy of the Mass, and what is variable and subject to the vicissitudes of human culture, of language, custom, habits of mind and body." Not all Christian symbols are of the same timeless value; many are clearly culture-bound and not universally applicable. For this reason, according to Griffiths, the church has developed rites within a few different cultures and must be open to developing more, including an Indian rite.[62]

Behind Griffiths's concern about the recognition of the relativity of many cultural forms found in Christian practice is not only the project of inculturation but also the danger expressed in his earlier articles on symbolism that many in the church "stop short" or become stuck at the level of the symbol. As evidenced in the resistance to replacing some of the cultural forms associated with the Latin rite (including the Latin language), many Catholics had become attached to the symbols in a way that limited their openness to experiencing the divine mystery that is communicated by, yet always transcends, the symbols. According to Griffiths, only by dropping this resistance to recognizing the relativity of many cultural forms associated with the Christian faith can the church renew itself and assume a universal status.[63]

In the context of Griffiths's efforts toward inculturation, the distinction between the divine mystery and the symbolic means whereby this mystery is encountered is again operative in his understanding from the beginning of his time in India. Nevertheless, in the interest of making the liturgy intelligible and meaningful for those of a non-Western-European culture, one cannot, Griffiths writes in 1956, merely incorporate cultural forms and concepts into Christian worship without substantial prior consideration of just what those cultural forms and concepts entail. The reason for caution on Griffiths's part at this time is his appreciation of the potential power of symbols as not only expressions of the divine mystery but also as communicators of cultural assumptions that may or may not be in harmony with Christian teachings.[64] Griffiths acknowledged in 1956 as well that the time might soon come when more thorough assimilation would be possible. Given the style of worship and even architecture later adopted at Shantivanam, it is clear that the times did indeed change and Griffiths with them.

Encountering Advaita

As already suggested, the fundamental intuitions underlying Griffiths's attraction to, and convictions about, the principle of nonduality may be identified very early in his writings and in his experience, especially of nature. From an epistemological viewpoint, there has always been a link in his understanding between knowing something in itself and a kind of union or "connaturality" with it. From a spiritual perspective, there has been an intimate connection between experiencing the self-transcendence inherent in such unitive knowledge and the surrender that is love. Yet ever alive in Griffiths's understanding of the nonduality disclosed in the acts of knowing and loving is the logical necessity, which is at once for him a theological principle, that relationship some-how endures between the knower and the known, the lover and the beloved. These intuitions about nonduality and relationship inform all that Griffiths experienced and wrote concerning *advaita* and were as consistent over time as the elements of his theory of religious symbols.

Once Griffiths had emigrated to India in 1955 and directly encountered exponents and interpreters of Vedānta philosophy, he frequently wrote on the experience and doctrine of *advaita*. A deep affinity for the nondual experience itself and a nagging skepticism about the various interpretations of the experience found in Indian philosophy character-ize these early writings. Emerging out of this ambivalent response to Indian *advaita* come Griffiths's attempts to articulate a Christian under-standing of nonduality.

As evidence of his positive appraisal of the Indian sense of mystery and sacramentalism, Griffiths in works of the 1960s frequently lifts up the Hindu witness to *advaita* as vitally significant for all, including Christians, to acknowledge. This experience of nonduality is a mystical intuition of, not just a metaphysical conclusion about, the human soul at its "center" in relationship to the divine mystery, spirit in relation to Spirit. In agreement with Western interpreters of the nondual experi-ence like Jacques Maritain, Griffiths describes it as

> ultimately an experience of the soul in its inmost depths; through it we get beyond the world of the senses, beyond our imagina-tions, beyond all the world of thought which always occupies us, until we reach the inner centre where the soul is resting in itself. Maritain calls it an "experience of the substantial being of the soul", the soul in its ground of reality.

While for Griffiths this intuition of *advaita* is "a very great thing," for other Western interpreters, such an experience of "the soul resting in it-self" is suspect.[65]

R. C. Zaehner, for example, interprets Hindu *advaita* as an experience of the soul in "isolation," and "closed" in on itself, separated from rela-tionship with God and others, and thus "the deadest of dead-ends." Significantly, Griffiths disagrees with this potentially devastating critique:

I agree with Professor Zaehner that the Hindu experience is an experience of the soul in itself, beyond image and concept in the "ground" of its being, but so far from its being "closed" I would maintain that it is precisely in this "ground" that the soul is "open" to all being. So far from a "dead-end", it is a living point, which opens on the infinite. In other words, it is at this point above all that man is open to God.

In support of his evaluation of the nondual experience, Griffiths cites both "the extraordinary fertility" that such experiences have shown in human history, specifically through Hinduism and Buddhism, and the lives of those shaped by this experience who clearly exhibit compassion and devotion rather than egocentrism and spiritual pride.[66]

For Griffiths, the experience of the soul in its "center" beyond all images and concepts is an encounter with the divine mystery. Hindus and Buddhists may describe this experience quite differently, the latter speaking in negative terminology and avoiding God language, but, Griffiths claims, the realization is phenomenologically the same. It is this experience of the "center" and the general orientation toward the interior life that Christians may learn about from the Eastern traditions. But equally important is what Christianity has to offer the East in the interpretation of this essential type of experience that is also found in Christianity.[67]

The distinction between experience and interpretation is fundamental to the numerous critiques of Hindu *advaita* found in Griffiths's writings throughout his time in India. Distorting the Hindu understanding of their intuition of *advaita* is the same "weakness" or "defect" in Indian philosophy just noted: its inability to account adequately for the relationship between the divine mystery or ultimate reality and the world of time and space.[68] It is as though the Hindu's experience of nonduality comes to overshadow the reality of differences, and thus removes the ground for relationship, whether between the divine mystery and the world, or that mystery and the individual soul. The obvious danger of such an experience is that it undercuts the reality, and thus the value, of the individual self, of the community of persons, and of the world in which one must act.

The primary exponent of Hindu *advaita* with whom Griffiths disagrees in his early critiques is Śankara and the school of Advaita Vedānta. According to the interpreters of Śankara's teachings whom Griffiths first encountered in India, all differences do disappear in the experience of nonduality, confirming the unreality of all distinctions in relation to the divine mystery or Brahman. In fact, the entire world of differences, including souls, is, as the human experiences it, a misperception or "superimposition" upon the nondual reality and is thus "illusion" or *māyā*. When one awakens through mystical discipline to recognize this fact, then the dream of this world of appearances disappears and one realizes that only the one, Brahman, is truly real. Griffiths concludes that on this point of the reality of the soul and the world there is a fundamental difference between Hindu and Christian experience and not just a difference of interpretation.[69]

Within Vedānta itself, as Griffiths notes, there were strong objections to Śankara's interpretation of *advaita*, particularly from what Griffiths calls the other "stream" or "tendency" within Hinduism, the *bhakti* or "devotional tradition." These objections arose because of a further implication of Śankara's Advaita philosophy, as it was often interpreted, the relativizing of the personal God. Due to the fact that a personal God with name and form also necessarily belongs to the world of differentiations, such a God is ultimately illusory as well—a tenet that the various devotional sects within Hinduism clearly could not accept. At least two other schools arose within Vedānta in specific opposition to this interpretation of the personal God and in strident defense of the legitimacy of the devotional path as a means for liberation: the qualified nondualism (*viśiṣṭādvaita*) of Rāmānuja (eleventh century) and the dualism (*dvaita*) of Madhva (thirteenth century). While more attractive to Christians as interpretations of spiritual experience because of their defense of the absolute nature and reality of the personal God, neither school, for Griffiths, provides a satisfactory answer to the fundamental quandary posed by the experience of nonduality, that is, the relationship between the divine mystery, the soul, and the world.[70]

The Hindu philosopher with whom Griffiths exhibits the most affinity is the early-twentieth-century sage, Aurobindo Ghose, though relatively little appears in Griffiths's writings about this teacher. Rather than the world dissolving like a dream or illusion with the onset of spiritual awakening, Aurobindo teaches that it is taken up, transformed, and experienced as within the divine mind itself. Nevertheless, Griffiths remains skeptical of whether even Aurobindo's system adequately resolves the fundamental issue of the relationship of the world to the divine mystery.[71]

In response to the various Hindu interpretations of the nondual experience, Griffiths articulates the lines of a Christian understanding of this same fundamental intuition that reality is nondual. These insights are later systematized as a "Christian *advaita*" and confirmed by his own contemplative experience. Underlying Griffiths's suggestions of what Christianity has to offer Hinduism in understanding the experience of *advaita* is the basic principle just discussed concerning the relationship of knowledge and love that must exist between the soul and God, and a further equally strong conviction to maintain the reality of this world. Both principles are grounded not only in his own experience but in Christian doctrine. Thus, out of Griffiths's early critiques of Hindu philosophy three key, closely related issues emerge that continue to shape his reflection upon nonduality and his articulation of a Christian *advaita:* the nature of the divine mystery itself (including the question of the personal God), and the relationships of that mystery to the soul and to the world.

First, regarding the soul and the divine mystery, in order for a relationship to endure, some difference or at least distinction must remain between them as the knower and the known, and the lover and the beloved. According to the Christian revelation, even with the highest realization of union with God, the individual does not merely dissolve and cease to exist. Griffiths distinguishes the Christian viewpoint from others on the relationship between God and the soul in this way:

> For the Hindu and the Buddhist, as for certain currents in islamic thought, in the ultimate state there is an absolute identity. Man realizes his identity with the absolute and realizes that this identity is eternal and unchangeable. In the christian view man remains distinct from God. He is a creature of God, and his being raised to a participation in the divine life is an act of God's grace, a gratuitous act of infinite love, by which God descends to man in order to raise him to share in his own life and knowledge and love. In this union man truly shares in the divine mode of knowledge, he knows himself in an identity with God, but he remains distinct in his being. It is an identity, or rather a communion, by knowledge and love, not an identity of being.[72]

This distinction between identity and communion as descriptions of the final states of God-realization in the Oriental and Christian religions respectively persists throughout Griffiths's writings.[73] Also significant here are the metaphors from human experience of knowledge and love used by Griffiths to distinguish the Christian understanding of nonduality from the Advaitic that tends to use images like the drop-ocean analogy (e.g., *Muṇḍaka Upaniṣad* 3.2.8; *Praśna Upaniṣad* 6.5).

Second, equally fundamental to Griffiths's critique of Advaita philosophy is the conviction that the world must be understood as real and not just as illusory. Griffiths defends this position in order to avoid what he identifies as two tendencies in Hindu thought about the relationship of the world to the divine mystery: monism, the belief that all apparent diversity is in reality only one indistinguishable being; and pantheism, the belief that the diverse world is God in manifest form. In the first extreme, sometimes interpreted as Śankara's position, the reality of the world is completely lost in God. In the second, the transcendence of God is lost in the world, and God becomes subject to the vicissitudes of time and space. Through its particular affirmation of the reality of the world, Christianity, according to Griffiths, stands between these two extremes.[74] The Christian position also lends support to cultural development and moral values. The desperate poverty in India serves as evidence of the dangers inherent in taking the doctrine of *māyā* too strictly.[75]

Specifically, Griffiths claims that the Christian doctrines of creation and incarnation serve to resolve the difficulties inherent in Advaita Vedānta. First, regarding the relationship of the soul to God, the doctrine of creation supports a clear delineation between God as Creator and the human soul as created. Whatever degree of "participation" may occur on the basis of the soul being created in the image of God, nevertheless the distinction always remains. The example of Jesus' incarnation further clarifies that even one who experiences profound union in love with God speaks in terms of a relationship, never of an identity, with God.[76]

Second, with reference to the reality of the world, a doctrine of creation, as another twentieth-century Western Christian theologian in India, Fr. Pierre Johanns earlier discerned, establishes the proper relationship between God and the created world such that the reality of the two are distinguished and yet said to be analogous. Furthermore, Jesus' incarnation, in contrast to the mythical and only semihistorical *avatāras* of Hinduism, affirms the reality and purpose of this created world, especially human history. By choosing to reveal divinity so fully in the world of space and time, God consecrated that world and the human events that became symbolic of that revelation. Such a world, then, does not disappear in God when one comes to know its Creator, but nor does it retain its present character. This world, Griffiths paraphrases Christian teachings, is destined to be transformed into a "new creation" in which God is realized as fully present.[77]

Given the distinctions established by Christian doctrines between God and the soul, and between God and the world, one may ask whether Griffiths can legitimately identify his account as presenting a nondual vision of reality. Can one affirm so strongly the importance of distinctions and yet also assert that all may be experienced as nondual? Can the Christian experience of relationship to God, to the world, and to all humanity, truthfully be interpreted as an experience of *advaita*? The key to resolving this apparent contradiction, for Griffiths, lies in the third central issue, the nature of the divine mystery itself, as expressed in the doctrine of the Trinity, or, more fundamentally, in Jesus' understanding and experience of his relationship to God the Father.[78]

An early and enduring model for Griffiths in articulating a Christian *advaita* is the thirteenth-century mystical theologian, Meister Eckhart. In Eckhart, Griffiths and others have found a clear example of nondual realization, one that may be fruitfully compared to Śankara due to their similar claims concerning an experience of identity between the soul and God. While some of Eckhart's expressions about this experience in relation to the doctrine of the Trinity lack caution, Griffiths affirms that the core of the controversial theologian's insights is orthodox, precisely in maintaining the distinctions that are necessary for a relationship to persist both within the Godhead and between God, the soul, and the world. Griffiths interprets Eckhart's Christian *advaita* as follows:

> [W]e must remember that Eckhart was building on the christian doctrine of grace. This ascent to God takes place for him "in Christ," that is in the Word, and what he seems to be seeking is the participation of the intellect in God's own knowledge of himself. Now it is strictly true to say that in God's own knowledge of himself in his Word there are no real distinctions. God knows himself and all created things in one simple pure act of knowledge, which is identical with his being. In this sense it is true to say that the knowledge of God is "advaita," without duality. As Aquinas teaches, "ideas" in God, that is God's knowledge of created things, are identical with the divine essence. If therefore the soul by grace should participate in God's own mode of knowledge it would know all things, itself included, in this simple mode of knowledge "without duality."[79]

Griffiths identifies in Eckhart the insight that, for a Christian, the nondual experience is entered through God's own self-expression in the Word, opening the experiencer by grace to the intimacy with the divine mystery that Jesus knew through his sinless nature. By sharing in Jesus' experience of God the Father, one participates in the very life of the divine persons who represent the mystery of love who is God. Again, Christian nonduality is imaged in terms of knowledge and love. The knower and the known, the lover and the beloved, the soul and God, the Son and the Father, are united yet remain distinct.

It is in the doctrine of the Trinity that the Christian Revelation has symbolized both the oneness and the interrelationship characteristic of the God whom Jesus experienced. Identity may indeed be experienced between the soul and God, but it is a participation in God's self-knowledge and not a realization of a preexisting simplicity, as Śankara's Advaita Vedānta implies. It is not proper to say that either the soul or the world is lost in the kind of Christian *advaita* articulated by Eckhart:

[I]t remains true that, though "identified" with God by knowledge, the soul yet remains distinct by nature. Though the mode of knowledge is different and distinctions, as we conceive them, cease to exist, yet the distinctions remain in reality. Man and the world are not lost in God, nor are the persons absorbed in the unity of the Godhead. It is these distinctions which christian orthodoxy is concerned to maintain, since they allow for relationship both between man and man in the mystical body of Christ, and between man and God. They leave a "space" for the relation of love between persons, between the person of God and his creatures and between the persons within the Godhead. It is probable that Eckhart intended to retain these distinctions but his language often obscures them.[80]

The reality of the distinctions within the created world, as well as between that world and its creator are based not upon human conception but upon their reality in the mind of God, that is, Aquinas's "ideas." Furthermore, these important distinctions are grounded in the fundamental differentiation between God and God's self-expression, symbolized as God the Father and God the Son, who exemplify the paradox of relationship within unity characteristic of all knowing and loving. It is this interpretation of *advaita* that Griffiths felt Christianity could offer to Hinduism.[81]

It will become apparent that in Griffiths's early attempts to articulate a Christian *advaita* are the key elements in his understanding of how a Christian might appropriate but reinterpret the Hindu's experience of nonduality. The same three basic issues remain central to Griffiths's efforts: What is the nature of the divine mystery and is that nature somehow personal? Is the relationship between that mystery and the human soul such that the latter disappears when mystical union is experienced? And, can the relationship between the world and the divine mystery be understood in a way that maintains both the reality of that world and the transcendence of the divine?

Religious Symbols as Mediators of Surrender

Reflecting near the end of his life upon the night of conversion and its aftermath more than sixty years earlier, Griffiths refers to the love he then felt overwhelmed by as "total . . . like a marriage."[82] The presence he had awakened to in nature had become a deeply personal one, yet an "other" whose role in his life seemed irrational, uncontrollable. If divine immanence had predominated in Griffiths's conception and experience of God after the evening walk, conversion brought the radical humility of faith characteristic of encountering divine transcendence. Nevertheless, Griffiths consistently describes his relationship to this transcendent other as one of love, suggested most powerfully by the metaphor of marriage.

As Griffiths will later explicate in his theory of *advaita*, marriage entails both oneness and twoness, unity and distinction; what characterizes the relationship between wife and husband is a reflection of the relationship between human and divine, between spirit and Spirit. In order for unity in distinction between human and divine to be experienced, according to Griffiths, the mind with its various faculties must be converted (*convertere*, "to turn round") toward its center, its ground in the spirit. It is the role of the religious symbol, as an expression and communication of the divine mystery (Rahner), to facilitate this turn. Specifically, it is by means of the religious symbol that the reason is seduced (Aquinas) and the individual will turned toward the divine will.

For Griffiths in the second period of his life, the primary religious symbol is Jesus Christ—a "real symbol" experienced during his night of conversion through imaginatively placing himself in the Garden and later at the foot of the cross. Within the Benedictine context, this symbol was also regularly operative through the Scripture, the divine office, the Eucharist, and beginning in 1940 his lifelong practice of the Jesus Prayer. Jesus Christ, and the church that is his body, thus become the focus of the nonrational means of knowing that Griffiths identifies with Paul as faith; Jesus Christ is the "real symbol" of the reality beyond the veil of appearances that he encountered in the evening walk, and more fully during the night of conversion. Jesus Christ is thus also the primary symbol of the reality that he comes increasingly in the second period to know through contemplation.

Griffiths's move to India enhanced his familiarity with the experience of contemplation in Jesus Christ but also relativized his sense of religious symbols. The Hindus, he found, have not only a profuse range of divine images but also a sense of symbols and of the mystery beyond them from which Christianity needs to learn. Nevertheless, Griffiths remains committed to the belief that Jesus Christ is the supreme symbol, one that excels and perfects the divine images of Hinduism and other religions.

New conditions and insights continued to arise for Griffiths that needed to be reconciled with his evolving theoretical understanding, thus generating questions to be addressed in his frequent publications. For example, if Jesus Christ is the real symbol of the divine mystery does the mature experience of contemplation entail going beyond that symbol, transcending the duality between human and divine essential to faith? What of the symbols of other religions such as Hinduism that appear to have mediated such a profound sense of the divine mystery? Are they also *real symbols,* in Rahner's strong sense of the term? If they are "real symbols," then what are the implications for a Christian theology of religions and for the missionary task?

A discussion of Griffiths's spiritual journey, his theory of religious symbol, and his exploration of *advaita* must return to the principle and experience of surrender traced throughout his interpretation of his own life as a transcending of self, a giving of oneself in love to the greater love who is God. Just as surrender pervaded Griffiths's understanding of how the mind is transformed, allowing him to move to new levels of awareness in which previously opposed values in tension could be resolved by a deeper vision of their underlying unity, so the same principle and experience inform Griffiths's theory and experience of mystical transformation via symbols. Only if one is willing to renounce and transcend the world of signs, including those of the church, will one be fully naked and open before the divine mystery "in the darkness." Yet one must always remember as well, as Griffiths often repeats, that "we need these signs if we are to approach the mystery."[83]

Ultimately, what motivates a high degree of surrender, according to Griffiths, is love for the mystery beyond the signs, the mystery that one only knows at first through its expression in those particular signs that function as religious symbols. For the Christian the supreme symbol of this degree of surrender in love is Jesus' sacrifice upon the cross—a sacrifice that is symbolically reenacted in the Eucharist and that images the death required for awakening to one's nondual relationship to the divine. In the third period of his life, through the difficulties in establishing a contemplative community at Shantivanam, through the controversies he faced as an internationally recognized figure, and through torments of illness unto death, Griffiths entered ever more deeply into the mystery of the surrender imaged by the cross.

Into Dialogue

———

The conditions for dialogue established in Griffiths by the end of the first period of his life fostered creative interaction and mutual discovery between self and other during the second. Intrapersonally, the conflict between rational and nonrational means matured into a dynamic interplay of different ways of knowing, while interpersonally his intellectual and spiritual journey advanced through immersion in community, that of the Roman Catholic Church and the Benedictine order. With his move to India, the early fascination with Eastern religions was transformed into a daily, living dialogue with Hindu scholars, yogis, and villagers, while interculturally his discovery of "the other half" of his soul grounded his critique of Western cultures. Dialogue at each of these levels, in turn, informed his experience and interpretation of the creative interrelationship between the cosmic, divine, and human realms, fostering insights about nonduality that would set the stage for the third period of his life.

Griffiths's openness to dialogue as a process potentially transformative of body, mind, and spirit is especially apparent in his evolving view of the relationship between Christianity and other religions.

Evaluation of Other Religions: The Fulfillment Theory

During the first period of his life, as reported in *The Golden String* (1954), Griffiths assumed an attitude of relatively distant acceptance toward other religions, a perspective from which all great teachers seemed to speak almost the same truth as Jesus Christ. The differences between religions were not of much importance. As he himself notes, with the

101

serious reading of the Gospel that took place during the transition to the second stage of his life in 1931, this attitude would change.[1]

In a 1937 article, Griffiths applauds the guidance that Justin Martyr offered to the church in its relationship with non-Christian religions.[2] Like Justin, Griffiths acknowledges that seeds of truth *(logoi spermatikoi)* are to be found in the various forms of religion and philosophy, and that Christians should affirm these "seeds" rather than attack the errors and superstitions among which they are found.

The principle behind Justin's relating of the various "seeds of truth" found in other religions to Christ is the Greek concept of the Logos or "Word," identified with Jesus Christ in John's Gospel. This seat of reason and truth is found in all humanity, as reflected in their search for knowledge of God, but is fully revealed and incarnated only in Jesus Christ. While thus establishing the common basis for the truths of other religions and for the truth of Christianity, Justin, according to Griffiths, overemphasizes the similarities between Christian and non-Christian teachings—a flaw of which Griffiths himself would always be mindful. Nevertheless, Justin's overall approach to non-Christian religions and philosophies, with its principle of the *Logoi spermatikoi* and the belief that Christianity "fulfills" the aspirations of all other religions, would guide Griffiths's own reflection and help to define a position he calls the "fulfillment theory"—a stance that would endure throughout the second period of his life.[3]

It is intriguing to note that in this same article Griffiths cites his reading of one of the pioneers of a Christian understanding of Hinduism, Rev. Pierre Johanns, SJ, and affirms the latter's claim that "almost all the elements of Christian religion . . . are to be found among them [the Hindus] in a higher form than they were ever known among the Greeks."[4] This claim prompts Griffiths's own further insight concerning the potential role of an encounter between Christianity and Indian thought:

> Thus it may well be that just as the contact of Christianity with Greek philosophy, of which we have the first example in St. Justin, led to the gradual development of Catholic philosophy and theology along the lines of Greek thought, so the contact of the Church in the coming centuries with the philosophical and religious mind of India may lead to a corresponding development of Christian thought.[5]

This insight would guide Griffiths's theological efforts years later when he, too, ventured to India. Clearly, the transformation in point of view brought by his conversion and by his discovery of knowledge through faith did not restrict his openness to other traditions.

Little more on non-Christian religions is found in Griffiths's writing until the 1950s, when he begins to write frequently on this topic. Drawing from a text by Henri de Lubac, *Catholicisme,* Griffiths describes in a 1950 article an inclusive view of the church, incorporating all those who do not deliberately choose to place themselves outside of it and who live by the "Natural Law" of reason and conscience found in the hearts of all. This law is a means of divine grace whereby humans are drawn toward the truth who is Christ, and thus all religions are "different expressions of the Natural Law." Through an openness to this guiding power within, all religious people are alike and all are related to and saved by Christ whose grace alone it is that brings one to salvation. But the differences between these religions are also significant, according to Griffiths. While Christians must search for the elements of truth in all other religions, they must also lead the other traditions "to recognize the fulfillment of what they believe in the doctrine of the Church," and "to see in Catholicism the fulfillment and completion of every form of religion. . . ."[6]

In other writings prior to his traveling to India, Griffiths articulates two additional ideas concerning the relationship between Christianity and the other religions. The first concept is one integral to most versions of the fulfillment theory, the idea that the truths found in other traditions served a propaedeutic function in relation to the teachings of Jesus Christ and the church. The religions that emerged prior to the Incarnation do function as a kind of revelation of truth but as what Griffiths calls "the Primitive Revelation," based in a timeless metaphysical tradition well articulated by the perennial philosophy. This prior revelation, however, was neither final nor complete; it served as "the divine preparation by which the people of the ancient world were prepared for the coming of Christ." As a uniquely historical, rather than a timeless and metaphysical, Revelation, Christ fulfills the other religions through and in time. All that the ancient myths and rituals had intimated was completed in history through the life, death, and Resurrection of Jesus Christ.[7]

The second point that Griffiths brings into creative interaction with the fulfillment theory and its view of other religions as preparatory is the claim that interreligious dialogue will help Christianity to express more fully the Truth who is Christ. Even before his departure for India, he writes:

This is not merely a question of introducing some new concepts into western theology, but of introducing a new way of thought and a new outlook on life. For centuries now Christianity has developed in a westerly direction, taking on an ever more western character of thought and expression. If it is ever to penetrate deeply into the East it will have to find a correspondingly eastern form, in which the genius of the peoples of the East will be able to find expression. For Christianity will never realise its full stature as a genuine Catholicism, that is, as the universal religion of mankind, until it has incorporated into itself all that is valid and true in all the different religious traditions. If we believe that in Christ is to be found the revelation of Truth itself, then we must recognise that all truth wherever it is to be found is contained implicitly in Christianity. As St Justin Martyr again said, "All truth wherever it is found belongs to us as Christians."[8]

Thus, for Griffiths, the Christianity that fulfills the other religions is not one that eventually should replace these other traditions as much as it potentially includes them, in all the richness of their particular cultural forms and expressions of truth. Similarly, the Christian tradition and its knowledge through faith do not deny the value and place of other ways of knowing, including the type of intuition spoken of by the philosophers that Griffiths studied in his youth and in the monastery. Nevertheless, at the end of the first autobiography, Griffiths is unequivocal in his assertion of the superiority of the Christian religion. Grace is universal, but one way to salvation and one way of knowledge alone lead to the final Truth who is Christ:

> All religious traditions contain some elements of the truth, but there is only one absolutely true religion; all religions have taught something of the way of salvation, but there is only one absolute Way. Christ is the Way, the Truth and the Life, and without him no man comes to the Father.[9]

Clearly, Griffiths's evaluation of other religions, succinctly identified as the fulfillment theory, did not close him to the possibility of learning from other religions through dialogue with them. Not forgetting totally the disillusionment of his youth with Western culture and religiosity perhaps, he remained vigilantly open to what could be learned from other cultures and religions, particularly those of the East. The interior dialogue between rational and nonrational forces sought its resolution in part in an exterior dialogue between the religions and cultures of East and West, even before his departure from England.

By the time of Griffiths's emigration to India, dialogue emerged from his exploration of other religions as the best method for learning from them and for seeking their fulfillment. One should approach dialogue not by attacking the imperfections of non-Christian religions but by affirming the "seeds of truth" in them, seeing how they relate to the Gospel, and then showing how these "seeds" may be fully developed in Christianity. The goal of dialogue is a more explicit expression of the truth already contained inherently within Christianity. Griffiths sensed that just as there was a lingering restlessness or incompleteness in his own soul, so there was in the church and in the West as a whole, signal-ing the need for what he called in 1953 "the marriage of East and West":

> What is required is a meeting of the two traditions at a deep level of understanding, so that their full potentialities can be realized. This will require on our part a real effort to assimilate the mode of Eastern thought, for Eastern thought differs from our own most of all in its mode. Whereas Western thought tends to be rational and discursive, Eastern thought is intuitive and contemplative. The one is the product of the *animus* the other of the *anima*. The differ-ence is therefore primarily psychological.
>
> The meeting of the Eastern and the Western minds will thus be a true marriage of East and West, the masculine mind of the West meeting with the feminine mind of the East in a fertile union.[10]

Both East and West will benefit from such a "marriage," according to Griffiths. The West will receive guidance in renewing "intuitive thought and interior life," while the West may remind the East of the importance of its own spiritual roots, at a time when the East is coming under in-creasing cultural influences from outside.[11]

It is through dialogue that Catholicism can give "precision" to, and "strengthen," the spiritual and metaphysical tradition ("the Primitive revelation") founded upon contemplative knowledge and integral to all religions by bringing this tradition into relation with the grace and per-son of the incarnate Christ in history. He is specific, for example, in call-ing for meetings between representatives of the various traditions "on the level of contemplation," a challenge that will necessitate for Christians the recovery of their own contemplative sources.[12] Griffiths remains clear, however, that the goal of such dialogue between contemplatives as well as through the study of comparative religions developing at this time is

> to show how Christ is, as it were, "hidden" at the heart of Hin-duism, of Buddhism, of Islam, and show how it is the one Word of God which has enlightened mankind from the beginning of his-tory and manifested Him to all different nations according to their different psychologies, permitting many errors to remain but never withdrawing the guidance of His Spirit.

While Christ did not come to destroy the preparations made by other religions for his teachings, he did come "to correct, complete and fulfill them."[13]

Griffiths's openness to learning from the religions of India fostered his endorsement of a nontraditional approach to missions, one lived by the group of Christian *sannyāsis* or renunciants who preceded him. Rather than seek to convert the "heathen," which as an approach to the missionary task had borne little fruit, Griffiths from this time forward would support the view that "mutual assimilation" and dialogue comprise a far more effective approach, one more in tune with the spirit of the Gospel that Jesus compared to a leaven.[14] Rejecting the ethos of conquest that had characterized the missions in centuries past, Griffiths argues that Christians should "approach the peoples of these different religious traditions not as our enemies but as our friends, who share in part the Truth which we claim to possess."[15]

As Griffiths in India entered more deeply into dialogue, especially with Hindus, he remained sensitive to the danger of syncretism, a facile blending of teachings from various religions with little attention to the importance of differences. Essential to avoiding this error while still entering fully into dialogue with another tradition, according to Griffiths, is the ability to discriminate between what is common and even universal in the various traditions and what is unique and particular.[16] Thus, he differed with Vinoba Bhave's call to "bury" the different religions with their many differences and retain only their common spiritual principles. During his conversation with Vinoba, Griffiths argued "that there are real and essential differences in each religious tradition which affect their whole view of life and that we ought to respect these differences."[17] Only through an honest attempt to understand the differences can a reconciliation, and perhaps someday a unification, take place. The result of such a discriminating but tolerant attitude toward other religions would be what Griffiths calls in several articles an "ecumenical approach" similar to that found in the movement among Christian denominations.[18] To chart a course between syncretism and the thoroughly exclusivistic attitudes of the past, one must balance both elements of the internal dialogue: the discriminating faculty of reason and the intuitive ability to appreciate what unifies diversity.

In the midst of the changes forcibly expressed in Western culture during the 1960s, especially by Vatican II, Griffiths came to recognize that such dialogue was also essential to the continued development, even the survival, of the world as a whole. What he needed was a context within which such a dialogue could be facilitated more deeply both within him and in community. Griffiths already seemed to sense what such a context would be in his earlier estimation of the purpose of communities like Kurisumala:

> What is required is a meeting of the different religious traditions at the deepest level of their experience of God. Hinduism is based on a deep mystical experience and everywhere seeks not simply to know "about" God, but to "know God," that is to experience the reality of God in the depths of the soul. It is at this level that Christian and Hindu have to meet, to discover in their experience of God, what is really common and where the real difference arises. It is here that we believe that a monastery can play a decisive part. It should be the work of the monk by the practice of prayer and contemplation to enter ever more deeply into the experience of God, to seek for an ever closer union with God in the depths of the soul. Such an experience will lead him to understand the Hindu mystical experience, as it were from within.[19]

Because of Mahieu's direction of the ashram toward a deeper commitment to the Syrian rite and worldview, one may legitimately ask whether Griffiths's eventual discomfort at Kurisumala was due to the ashram's inability to facilitate such a dialogue with Hinduism for him, especially as contemplation became ever more prominent in his own experience and reflection.

Consistent with Griffiths's point of view after his conversion and entrance into the monastery, he still identified the truth in its wholeness as Christ at the end of this second period of his life. An "ecumenical approach" to other religions, reinforced by his early experience in India, operated in tension with his version of the fulfillment theory. Thus in 1966 he would still speak of Christ both as present in Hinduism *and* as "the Saviour who alone can bring to fulfillment the inner meaning of Yoga and Vedānta."[20] Yet, near the end of this second period of his life, Griffiths began to speak in terms of the "complementarity" of the different world religions, including Christianity, a principle that would become thematic in his writings of the third period.[21] The direction that a resolution of the tension inherent in his position on dialogue would eventually take was thus already apparent in the mid–1960s.

Transition via Dialogue

It is clear, then, that Griffiths's evaluation of other religions in relation to Christianity underwent a significant change as a result of his conversion to the Catholic church, his study of Eastern and Western thought, and his experience of a Benedictine context in England and India during this second period, leading him to espouse the fulfillment theory of religions. It is also apparent that in his attempts to articulate a coherent evaluation he strove to balance nonrational and rational means of inquiry to express an inclusive but nonsyncretistic view of the Church in relation to other religions. But the equilibrium in his understanding of means for gaining knowledge and in his evaluation of other religions was slowly stirred by his experience in India. Just as direct experience of India thrust him into some lack of clarity about the relationship between different ways of knowing God, so firsthand experience of Hinduism began to prompt a reevaluation of all other religions in relation to Christianity. Simultaneous with these developments in his interreligious and intercultural perspectives was an evolution of his intimations of nonduality in the relation of cosmic, divine, and human realms. It is the ongoing dialogue of self and other at various levels—the "other" now forcibly present via India and Hinduism—that fostered fresh insights and pushed him toward what he necessarily had to identify as a third, distinct period of his life.

Further connecting the second and third phases of Griffiths's life are three key issues raised by his praxis of dialogue that focus the exemplary character of that life: To what degree is it possible to bridge two different cultures in order to benefit one's own? Can the intellectual frameworks characteristic of those cultures be productively integrated to exemplify a common search for truth? Is it possible and fruitful to draw upon the spiritual riches of the "other" in order to foster mystical awakening and still maintain the integrity of one's faith commitments? Griffiths's attempts to live out the answers to these questions, not only for himself but for his culture and tradition, underwent significant development in the third period of his life.

PART III

${\mathcal{N}}$onduality (${\mathcal{A}}$dvaita): 1968–1993

I do not pray for these only, but also for those who believe in me through their word, that they may all be one; even as thou, Father, art in me, and I in thee, that they also may be in us, so that the world may believe that thou hast sent me. The glory which thou hast given me I have given to them, that they may be one even as we are one, I in them and thou in me, that they may become perfectly one. . . .

—John 17.20–23

OM. In the center of the castle of Brahman, our own body, there is a small shrine in the form of a lotus-flower, and within can be found a small space. We should find who dwells there, and we should want to know him. . . . The little space within the heart is as great as this vast universe. The heavens and earth are there, and the sun, and the moon, and the stars; fire and lightning and winds are there; and all that now is and all that is not: for the whole universe is in Him and He dwells within our heart.

—Chāṇḍogya Upaniṣad 8.1

The View from His Window

Illumined by the light from the window are the gaunt features of the aging monk. The blue of his eyes is clear, though crested now by thick, graying eyebrows. Gray there is as well in his hair and beard. With all of his senses he takes in the view that is deceptively still in the afternoon heat.

What meets his eyes are but a few simple huts, a small brick chapel, a guest house, and a tiny library where the books are protected from the animals by wire mesh. Above the buildings stand palmyra palms, and not far is the sacred river Kavery. Before his eyes briefly dance the fleeting images of how the "Forest of Peace" had first appeared to him when he arrived from Kurisumala, strangely reminiscent yet eerily absent of its two French founders. Then appear the faces of the first two monks who had come with him and soon left, of the young family who had managed the ashram for him during several years when he was for most of the time a community of one, and finally of the two young monks from Kerala who sought him out to be their guru and stayed. Now down the dirt path from the main road walked villagers and foreigners, coming and going, somehow drawn to this place—as though the seed planted two decades before by the ashram's founders had finally begun to germinate.

A question familiar from the years of hardship and loneliness arises but now with ever lessening urgency. Years later, putting words to the answer lived out at this ashram, he would say:

> One trusted in Divine Providence the whole time, really. You weren't expecting things to happen regularly at all. If somebody came, we welcomed them; if they left, we had to accept that. I

think that is the only way to be, really. . . . That to me is the Great Principle: to allow things to grow.[1]

As the past moves through the mind, so may the future. While he gazes through the window, thoughts come about rebuilding the library, enlarging the guest house, expanding the chapel; thoughts about guiding the brothers, adapting the liturgy, preaching a sermon; thoughts about submitting an article or traveling to speak in England, Europe, or America. As the mind moves, he watches it, as through a window, and recognizes that in this movement there is a rhythm not his own:

> You have to learn to fit into the rhythm and allow it to carry you, then it carries you forward in the end. . . . Then you get confidence that something is guiding. I have that strong feeling: that the ashram has been guided from the beginning, from the time of Monchanin onward. There has always been a Providence at work, and people feel it today. Many attribute it to me, but I don't think it's so. I think there is something far beyond that. . . .[2]

As he watches the mind moving between past and future, suddenly it stops in the present and opens in realization: "But I am much more than this." Meditation happens.[3] There with unexpected clarity is simply the view from the window: marigolds and roses lifting silently from the dark earth into the brilliant light—the light that at once enlivens them and enables him to see them; a light that surrounds the flowers and their viewer, penetrates them all, unites them, is their source. It is a light he has come to know as a person, yet beyond what we normally conceive as personal; one to whom he has surrendered, yet also one with whom he is united:

> I look at the flowers which are growing in the garden outside my window. . . . I see them in the light of the Word. And the same Spirit which stirs in them stirs in me, awakening feelings of joy and delight in their beauty. They are in me and I am in them, and both of us are in the Word and in the Spirit. This is a theophany. . . . The same Spirit moves the flowers to spring and me to contemplate them: both in them and in me it is the one Lord who rejoices in his works.[4]

A warm breeze ripples through the uplifted petals and across his sunlit brow.

Gazing through the window, he has returned to the center, in light of which all of the dualities characteristic of time and space tremble within a vast, embracing presence: "[T]here is a window in my consciousness where I can look out on eternity, or rather where this eternal Reality looks out on the world of space and time through me."[5]

7

The Guide of Shantivanam and Prophet of Dialogue

It was fortunate, if not providential, that as Griffiths's discomfort at Kurisumala was becoming acute an opportunity to move to the ashram founded in 1950 by the two French priests, Jules Monchanin and Henri Le Saux, was given. Monchanin had died years before (1957), and by the late 1960s Le Saux, by then more commonly known as Abhishiktānanda, felt physically and spiritually in need of remaining at his hermitage in the Himalayas. When Saccidānanda Ashram was turned over to Mahieu, it was decided that Griffiths would go to try to revive a community there in 1968. Griffiths would later relate to one bi-ographer that the first years at Shantivanam, as the ashram is usually called, were a test of faith, a time when he was often left alone with an unreliable manager as monks from Kurisumala came and went. Referring to such difficult times at Shantivanam over the years he said: "More than once I have surrendered the whole thing. That's the secret. If you really renounce somehow it comes itself."[1]

In the move from Kerala to Shantivanam Griffiths would later rec-ognize the opportunity to begin again and "in a more radical way" his experiment in monastic life in India.[2] Eventually, he was joined by two Indian monks from Kurisumala, Amaldas and Christudas, who felt both a strong personal bond to Griffiths as their spiritual guide and an affinity with the direction he was giving to the life of the ashram. From this stable nucleus, the ashram began to flourish, both practically speaking, in the cultivation of land and the relationship to the nearby village, and spiritually, in the formation of a community based upon the pursuit of "a genuine religious ecumenism."[3] Griffiths thus took advantage of this new beginning to reshape the ashram life in a way that was indeed radically different from that found at Kurisumala and more in line with the traditional Indian sense of what an ashram should be. Unlike a Benedictine monastery that centers around the common life and liturgy of the monks, an ashram is a community of disciples gathered around the guru or master in whose experience of God they seek to share. The time of personal meditation and prayer is primary in the ashram, out of which the expression of common prayer and liturgy breathes forth, rather than vice versa. However, like Kurisumala Ashram, Shantivanam's relationship to the local villages was also important. Griffiths directed the ashram to serve as a spiritual center, as an employer and source of food, and as a provider of nursery school and dispensary services. He thus continued to pursue the proper balance for himself and for his community between the familiar complements of individual and community, of private and corporate contexts for spiritual growth.[4]

The new arrangement bore fruit in the health of the ashram, as reflected in the number of visitors and vocations it attracted, as well as in the spiritual lives of its members. For Griffiths in particular, the shift in emphasis from the liturgy to contemplation in the new community prompted a deepening of the mystical dimension of his life. While he was not one to speak in depth about his spiritual experience, one may discern in the articles and books written after 1968 Griffiths's greater attention upon the contemplative life and, with this maturing of experience, a simultaneous shift in his appreciation of other religions.[5] In charting the spiritual course for both himself and the ashram, he seems to have acted consciously in relation to the examples of his predecessors, the founders of Shantivanam, taking a more ambitious approach to a life of dialogue than was possible for Monchanin yet pursuing a more integrated and cautious path than Abhishiktānanda. Griffiths's greater success in building a monastic community at Shantivanam than was ever achieved by the two French priests reflects Griffiths's ability to integrate the divergent gifts of the ashram's founders and the greater openness of the church after Vatican II.[6]

With the move to Shantivanam, his engagement in the dialogue between "East" and "West" deepened as he opened more profoundly to his contemplative depths, even as that same dialogue came to shape the spiritual and social life of his ashram.

Recognition and the Broadening Scope of Dialogue

With time, more foreign visitors were attracted to the ashram, necessitating an expansion of the facilities. Through conversations with them, as well as through his own reading, correspondence, and travel, Griffiths pursued dialogue not only with India and its Hindu religion and culture, but also with other religions and cultures. As he entered his seventies, the scope and volume of his published writings increased; he produced four books between 1977 and 1987, as well as numerous journal articles. In these writings, he often speaks quite boldly and generally about the nature of religion, its role in the midst of a quickly changing world, and the need for deeper dialogue not only between religions but between cultures. During these years of his eighth decade, Griffiths also began to receive greater recognition, accepting opportunities to speak in various countries. In order to provide an ecclesiastical foundation for his community, Griffiths sought affiliation for the ashram with an existing monastic order in the West, joining the Camaldolese in 1982.[7]

In the same year, Griffiths published a sequel to his 1954 autobiography. In *The Marriage of East and West: A Sequel to the Golden String* (1982), he not only briefly recounts his years in India but also introduces themes characteristic of his then current thinking on intercultural dialogue, especially the role of the "new science" in helping to bring about the dawning of a "new age."[8] Reminiscent of, and yet moving beyond, the type of cultural critiques found in the first autobiography, the work reveals greater optimism concerning the transformation of Western cultures and of world consciousness as a whole:

> There are signs already that this new consciousness is beginning to dawn as the West comes into contact with the East. The age of scientific materialism, which dominated the nineteenth century is passing and a new age of spiritual wisdom is coming to birth. Western science itself has prepared the way for this.[9]

The theme of a cross-cultural change in consciousness taking place as a result, in part, of the dialogue between Western science and Eastern spirituality is prominent as well in Griffiths's 1990 work, *A New Vision of Reality*. Here he suggests that Christianity, as a primarily Western religion that is opening to its own mystical depths and to its interreligious responsibilities, has an important role to play in these cross-cultural developments. Particularly in the final chapter where he speculates concerning the "new age" he feels is coming to birth, it appears that his perspective has changed yet again. It is as though he speaks from a vantage point that *assumes* the marriage of cultures he himself has explored and thus offers a more unified, global perspective.

As one reads *The Marriage of East and West,* and the works that followed it, one senses that the scope of Griffiths's life's work continued to broaden. Far from resting in the fruits of his study and experience of Hindu-Christian dialogue, he appears to have been propelled toward

new horizons—a movement forward that became less of a struggle as
the world began to join in the project of interreligious and intercultural
exploration.[10] Drawing strength from encounters with other pioneers
like the Dalai Lama with whom he met in 1985 and then again in 1992,
as well as from the support voiced by the Pope in 1986 for the challenges of inculturation and dialogue, Griffiths continued to speak and
write into his ninth decade. Such projects were as diverse as "a
Christian commentary on the Bhagavad Gītā," an attempt to articulate
the integration of "Western science, Eastern mysticism and Christian
faith," a treatment of Christian meditation as it continues to evolve in
dialogue with the Eastern traditions, and an anthology of Scriptures
from various religions that speak symbolically of the nondual nature of
reality.[11]

Critical Responses from Christians and Hindus

Although Griffiths attempted to balance his vision for Shantivanam with
practicality and respect for existing church structures, controversy with
the local bishop was frequent in the early days, sometimes prompting
Griffiths's despair about whether the experiment represented by the
ashram would survive. Some of the ecclesiastical issues seem petty to an
outsider, such as whether monks from a different diocese and state were
welcome in Tamil Nadu. But others, involving liturgy and especially the
ashram's attempts to assimilate local Hindu customs into their worship,
are more significant. Objections were raised, for instance, concerning the
use of readings from Indian Scriptures, such as the Vedas, the
Upaniṣads, and the Bhagavad Gītā, in the context of the ashram's worship services. The appropriateness of incorporating elements from
Hindu ritual into the celebration of the Mass, such as circling a flame before the Blessed Sacrament, was also questioned. Even the ashram's attempts to harmonize the architecture and symbology of its temple with
local customs provoked controversy. In particular, when the dome of the
ashram's temple was erected incorporating Christian images in a traditional Indian design, some saw the result as more Hindu than
Christian—for instance, Christ portrayed cross-legged in a meditative
pose. Such local objections were quieted by Griffiths's appeal to the liturgical commission in India that often gave him its support.[12] Nonetheless,
his interpretation of the church's project of inculturation was clearly controversial for some, both in India and outside, both Christians and
Hindus.

In the midst of such times of change in the church, it was perhaps
inevitable that groups attempting to respond to the call of Vatican II

and new interreligious realities would be criticized by those who resisted such a call or who interpreted it differently. Objections were
raised to Griffiths and Shantivanam by both conservative Christians
and by those involved in social movements in India who saw such
communities as encouraging an escapist or individualistic spirituality.[13] In addition, the comparative theological methods behind such
ashram experiments came under attack. The Fordham University professor Jose Pereira specifically criticizes Griffiths's efforts at inculturation and some of his interreligious conclusions as more theosophical
than Christian.[14]

In a later version of the same article, Pereira, joined by Robert
Fastiggi, describe Griffiths's efforts at integrating Hindu customs into
Christian liturgy and spirituality as follows:

> The purpose of true Catholic inculturation is to express the rich-
> ness of the Gospel and the Catholic faith through concepts and
> symbols which reflect the native culture. Anything that is "good
> or honorable and beautiful" within the culture can be adapted and
> absorbed by the Catholic faith—be it a gesture, mode of dress, or
> spiritual concept. Bede Griffiths, however, appears to offer a form
> of Neo-Hindu Christianity which obscures rather than enriches
> the Catholic faith. A close examination of his theology reveals a
> superficial attempt to give Hindu concepts Christian meaning or
> Christian concepts Hindu meaning. The result is a system which
> is neither truly Hindu nor Christian.[15]

The authors specifically object to what they interpret as Griffiths's attempts to "identify" concepts such as *saccidānanda* (being-knowledge-
bliss) and the Trinity. Given his efforts to maintain the integrity of
different religious symbols as unique self-expressions of the divine
mystery, it is clear that Griffiths does not "identify" or equate the symbols of Hinduism and Christianity but rather seeks to discern and articulate their analogical character as symbols of the one divine mystery.
He claims thereby that part of the task of inculturation is the respect for
religious differences while also seeking common ground.

Griffiths's prophetic role in relation to the church represents not a
continuation of his youthful resistance to such institutions but a commitment to integrating the fruits of his interreligious experience into the
self-understanding of the church, based on the conviction that it is in
such dialogue that the future of the church lies. Nevertheless, in some of
his later writings, Griffiths critiqued the slowness of the church's response to the creative initiatives expressed in the Second Vatican
Council. He proposed, for instance, several structural and theological

changes within the Roman Catholic Church that would facilitate re-union with other Christian churches and help the projects of incultura-tion and dialogue. In the general prophetic role being addressed here, Griffiths often responded to controversial issues in the church, particu-larly through the vehicle of the English journal, *The Tablet.* Such articles again evoked critical responses, such as that from Fastiggi and Pereira who question Griffiths's respect for the Vatican.[16]

Conservative Hindus have also responded critically to ashram proj-ects like Shantivanam and to Griffiths in particular. *Catholic Ashrams: Sannyasins or Swindlers?* (1994), edited by Sita Ram Goel and published by the Voice of India, levels a scathing attack upon what it perceives as Griffiths's deceitful missionary strategies in the name of dialogue. Griffiths illustrates for the editor just "[h]ow negative, hostile, and ag-gressive the missionary mind remains toward Hindu society and cul-ture."[17] He is "a Hindu on the outside, a Catholic on the inside," and, according to another contributor to the volume, "the worst kind of spir-itual colonialist."[18] Griffiths attempted to engage in dialogue with such Hindu critics with little or no constructive results beyond further alien-ating them. It was perhaps experiences such as this that led him to draw away from dialogue with Hindus during his later years and to turn to-ward what he came to recognize as his most receptive audience, con-templative Catholics in the West.

Completing the Odyssey

In January 1990, Griffiths suffered a stroke at his ashram that might eas-ily have crippled him and prevented further study, writing, or travel. Instead this crisis sparked a profound spiritual awakening and a more urgent sense of mission. Having recovered his physical strength, he trav-eled to North America in the fall of the same year, a trip that initiated what he characterized as yet another stage of his life. After 1990, Griffiths regularly visited the United States with the intention of contributing to the renewal of the spiritual life there, especially among Christians, and to the formation of lay contemplative communities. Having borne his Western culture of origin to India and lived there for over thirty years of intensive dialogue, he returned to the West on a more regular basis to share the fruits of that dialogue with a culture he found simultaneously in collapse and in the throes of rebirth. It was as though he returned with a boon of insight nurtured through his journey to the East, insight that he felt Western countries were more ready to receive.[19]

The 1990 stroke not only sparked a stronger sense of mission to the West but also transformed his personality in a way that reflected, more than ever before in his life, an opening to what he had called "the other half of my soul." Apparent especially to his close friends and disciples was Griffiths's greater willingness to express his emotions, quite in contrast to the reserve of prior years. His "surrender to the Mother" shortly after the stroke corresponded with his assuming a more mutual relationship to his community, exhibiting strength and charisma through weakness and vulnerability. His reflection upon this change in himself, especially in reference to his closest spiritual companions, drew a connection between this newfound intimacy and the theological principle that he also suggested was the keynote of the final period of his life, nonduality. He wrote to Russill Paul D'Silva:

> The Holy Spirit, Christ in us, pierces through every level of our being & makes us one in this ultimate ground. I feel it with you as something quite definite, there is a hidden bond beyond our conscious selves to which we have always to return, & this is true in measure of all of us. This is what it means to love with the totality of one's being.[20]

The profound connection between the nondual quality of the communion of love that is God represented by the Trinity and the same quality of the communion of love that is interpersonal relationship was thus realized, deeply enriching Griffiths's final years.

In the evening of his life, at an age when many rest from their journeying, Griffiths continued to be drawn willingly, if sometimes painfully, forward. In a present unsettled by startling global changes, he and his ashram endured in their impact as examples of the openness, the creativity, and the movement toward integration that he believed were born of the surrender called "love."[21] The drama of his final months of illness, including additional strokes in late 1992 and 1993, exemplified "the final stripping" that Abhishiktānanda, his predecessor at Shantivanam, had said characterizes *sannyāsa*. Griffiths died at his ashram on May 13, 1993.

Tensions within His Self-Understanding

As is apparent from the expositions of Griffiths's life in chapters 1, 4, and 7 of this study, there are discernible themes within the picture he draws of that life. Admittedly, any attempt to summarize these elements from his writing simply creates an interpretation of his own self-interpretation. Yet, even with this distance from "what actually happened," such an exercise can illumine some of the principles behind Griffiths's sense of himself. Analysis of the themes implicit in his self-interpretation also prepares the way later in this study for a discussion of the role that such a life may play in the ongoing development of a culture and a civilization.

The following threads within Griffiths's self-understanding may be drawn together as pairs of themes in creative tension with one another:

1. his position as a prophetic critic of his religion in tension with his sense of calling to integrate his experience and ideas into the church's viewpoint;

2. his experience of a personal revelation of God in nature and within himself in tension with the traditional revelation of God in Christ and the church;

3. an attraction and critical response to Eastern cultures, especially their spiritual wisdom, in tension with an ambivalence toward Western societies, especially in their reliance upon science;

4. his identification with "an immemorial past" in tension with his vision of the evolution of society toward a "new age";

5. the nonrational or intuitive mind in tension with the rational mind.

Each of these tensions is resolved in Griffiths's experience through a dynamic that is, for him, foundational: surrender.

1. Griffiths found himself at times in the role of a rebel or prophet, especially in relation to organized religion. In his initial denunciation of Christianity, in his unusual road to conversion, as well as in his interreligious activities once formally affiliated with the Christian church, Griffiths often did not follow the conventional course. Yet one also senses that at every step of his journey since his conversion he was conscious of a vocation to integrate what he was experiencing and thinking into the church's self-understanding. Some discomfort and conflict seems to have been created by the fact that he at times felt he was out of step with, or perhaps ahead of, official positions in the church. But it is significant that he never broke ecclesiastical ties at the local or international level, even when conflict did arise, as described earlier in this chapter. To the end of his life, aligning his ever-advancing insights with the orthodox teachings of the Roman Catholic Church remained a challenging priority. Thus, this tension between his affiliation with an inevitably slower-moving institution and his attentiveness to his own quickly unfolding experience and thought endured.

2. A related tension exists in Griffiths's writing between the poles of community and individual, particularly in regard to what experiences

of God are deemed authoritative—those endorsed by the official community or church, or those received by individuals apart from their affiliation with any organization or indoctrination. The clearest instance of this tension arises from the experience of God in nature with which Griffiths begins *The Golden String: An Autobiography* (1954), a personal awakening that remained a significant and enduring point of reference in his self-understanding. As he believed is common among youths, he first clearly experienced the presence of God not in the context of organized religion but mediated personally by God's creation. Griffiths never rejected the value of this experience of God in nature, even after his conversion to Christianity. He appreciated that first opening to the divine presence as "one of the decisive events" of his life, as the beginning of his search for God, as an instance of "the grace which is given to every soul, hidden under the circumstances of our daily life," and as "the end of a golden string," the following and winding of which would lead him "out of the labyrinth of life" to "heaven's gate."[22] The status given by him to such experiences clearly informed his confident assertion later that some other traditions, such as the Vedic, represent *revelations* in the same sense of the term used by Christians for the Gospel.[23] Thus, his own broad and personal experience of God's self-revealing presence helped to establish on a more than intellectual level his openness to the truth of other traditions.

The kind of personal experience of God in nature Griffiths describes came into creative tension with his experience of God in Christ and in the church at various times in his life, affecting his estimation of other religions. At the time of writing *The Golden String,* for example, he spoke of the "still more wonderful way" in which God may be found present in the church.[24] When he came to India, however, much that he had written before had to be rethought. In particular, he found that the experience of God in nature, which in Europe had inspired a few Romantic poets and his own first sense of what religion should be, had been the foundation for the centuries-old religious tradition of the Hindus. His gradual appreciation of the religious culture surrounding him in India was thus informed by his own early experience, *and* vice versa. In short, Griffiths himself experienced God's presence through various revelations, while belonging to a religion that claimed the primacy of one. The resulting tension seems to have been more the source of creative exploration concerning both the Christian and Hindu revelations than the cause of anguishing conflict.

In the tension between Griffiths's different ways of experiencing God a related pair of principles in the account of God's relationship to the creation appears: immanence and transcendence. In his self-understanding,

Griffiths was forced by the power of his own experiences to reconcile the intimacy of God discovered through nature and felt in the faculties with the terrible God who stood over and against his own willfulness and pride during his conversion experience. Into his eventual reconciliation of God's immanence and transcendence, Griffiths would also incorporate an understanding of the distinction between the Oriental and Semitic religions—the former emphasizing divine immanence, the latter, divine transcendence.[25] Ultimately, the two elements in this tension would be subsumed in the theory and experience of nonduality.

3. One may discern a tension within Griffiths's relationship to Western cultures that is similar to the ambivalence in his relation to the church as doctrinal and spiritual authority. In the 1920s in England, the voices of social critics such as Leo Tolstoy, George Bernard Shaw, Oswald Spengler, and T. S. Eliot influenced Griffiths through his avid reading. Specifically, he joined in pacifist and socialist rejections of many of the values of Western societies. As he matured and read more, his objections to religious dogma and moralism as well as to Western materialism and industrialization became more focused upon the character of the Western mind—a mind shaped primarily by rational and scientific inquiry divorced from nature, imagination, and feeling.[26] While having immersed himself in Western thought through study and participation in the church, Griffiths remained detached to varying degrees from the activity of Western cultures, whether through his early experiments in communal and solitary living in England, his years as a Benedictine monk there, or in his emigration to India. This distance also allowed him to recognize the thoroughly Western character of Catholic Christianity as it has been brought to the East, a fact that has undermined the success of missions. Implicitly thematic in his self-understanding is the role of the outsider who may see and critique Western cultures more clearly because of this self-imposed distance, while recognizing at the same time that his persona has been shaped by those cultures.

Informing Griffiths's critique of Western cultures is an attraction for what he calls "the East," in both its cultural and spiritual aspects. His early and enduring exposure to the philosophies and cultures of Asia in particular helped to nurture "the new vision of reality" that he claimed is necessary for the survival of the West and the East. In *The Golden String* he characterized his early reading of some of the Asian spiritual classics as having colored his thought and affected his soul in unconscious ways. The "secret ferment" brought by Asian wisdom prompted his further studies of other religions while a monk and eventually his desire, and its fulfillment, to experience the culture of India for himself.

One must imagine that, with his emigration and the discovery of "the other half" of his soul, the unseen turbulence felt in England came powerfully to the surface. What began as a somewhat personal "meeting of East and West" gradually matured into a "marriage," whose public and even prophetic character began to attract growing recognition in his later life. After the institutional and cultural changes signaled and further provoked by the Second Vatican Council, the encounter with the East that had come to dominate his self-understanding began to appear as thematic in Western cultures in general—as though the "secret ferment" he had identified in himself was no longer so secret but was creatively at work in his culture of origin as well.

From early on, then, "West" and "East" became comprehensive symbols for Griffiths, serving as a further pair of principles in tension with one another, with a corresponding list of correlates, such as rational and intuitive. Neither Griffiths's critique of the West nor his attraction to the East were one-sided. As critical as he was of his culture of origin, Griffiths nevertheless was consistent in his assertion that this culture (including the rational theologies of Christianity) has much to offer to the East to remedy the latter's own weaknesses, faults that Griffiths was equally willing to point out. As the title of Griffiths's second autobiography implies, this pair of principles in tension, East and West, are not presented as opposites or as irreconcilable, but as complementary. Nevertheless, as claimed by his Hindu critics, and as discussed in this book's Conclusion, Griffiths's exploration of the relationship of "West" and "East" inevitably retains a Western Christian character, limiting its effectiveness for some readers.

4. Inherent within Griffiths's conscious positioning of himself at the edges of modern Western cultures and his immersion in one culture of the East is an identification with "an immemorial past."[27] While he did not call for a simple return to the past, Griffiths did at times praise a balance between the material, mental, and spiritual dimensions of life found in prior centuries, a balance in life to which, he thought, Western cultures should return. For Griffiths, the perspective given by the Judeo-Christian myth and the evolutionary viewpoint of theorists like Ken Wilber are not aligned but can be reconciled. While supporting Wilber's evolutionary perspective (somewhat similar to Pierre Teilhard de Chardin's) according to which humanity since the Fall is moving toward a new degree of integration with the divine, Griffiths also interprets the myth of the Garden of Eden as portraying a state of life, a paradise, to which humanity is being called to return.[28] In both his theological and social reflections, the resolution of this tension comes in accepting a paradox: what appears as an evolution from one stage in

the development of consciousness to another is, in fact, a return to the state of freedom and union with God from which humanity began, though now with fuller awareness—a return that occurs not in spite of cultural wanderings, however lamentable in the West, but through them.[29]

In the earlier stages of his self-understanding and critique of modernity, a strong ambivalence toward Western cultures, especially science and its fruits, was evident. Through his reading of Wilber, Fritjof Capra, David Bohm, Rupert Sheldrake, and others in the 1980s, however, Griffiths came to recognize that Western science would have a role to play in its own transformation. The result of this reappraisal was a more optimistic attitude about the future place of Western science in a "new age." Working the same paradox just discussed in relation to his attitude toward modernity, Griffiths affirms that the progress of science will be found in renewing a view of life antithetical to its modern model and harmonious with traditional wisdom, thus reviving an ancient vision and at the same time extending it further.[30]

5. As just mentioned in relation to his critique of Western cultures, from his school days on, Griffiths was distrustful of the rational scientific mind, even while relying upon it so heavily in his own life's work. Concomitant with this distrust was an attraction to alternative ways of knowing, generally labeled "intuitive," whose place in Western cultures has become problematic. To be discussed further in the next chapter, the tension between these two styles of thought or ways of knowing is present in both the content and the method of all his writing. One might justifiably claim that this tension is not only fundamental to his own personal journey of mind and spirit but also essential to his understanding of the cultural changes surrounding him in England and India, and further to his view of global transformation.

The theme of the relationship between the rational and intuitive minds is closely linked to a final, central, and enduring principle in Griffiths's evaluation of Western cultures and attraction to Eastern ones, a principle equally essential to his understanding of the key changes in his life: surrender. In resolving the personal crises caused by the tension within his self-understanding, Griffiths returned again and again to what he believed was the only effective response, to let go of his own will and intellectual insistences in order to allow something beyond the opposing values to emerge and integrate them into a more comprehensive unity.

It was through surrendering to God's will, as he experienced it, that Griffiths struck for himself the difficult balance between challenging the church and nurturing its development. Only through letting go of his own will could he insure himself against a prideful independence in his role as prophet. Similarly, to resolve the tension between his various experiences of God, as well as between the various revelations of truth, Griffiths renounced his own concepts of who God is and how God works in order to remain open to the unpredictable power of God's Spirit, as evidenced in his conversion, his providential journey to India, the move to Shantivanam, and later his stroke. In relation to Griffiths's appraisal of East and West, his life and thought prompted him first to see the differences between these two worlds very clearly and then to transcend to a level beyond differences from which the complementarity of East and West could be appreciated. Only through such a surrendering of one level of understanding to receive another was he able to discern what each worldview has to offer the other—to the degree of even being able to accept a positive role for science in the transformation of both worlds into a "new age." Finally, in his own spiritual psychology, it is through surrender that the rational mind submits itself "to a higher law of its own being" and relinquishes its domination, allowing a more receptive, intuitive mind to dawn.[31] In Griffiths's later years, this constantly unfolding mystery of surrender would become embodied in the ideal and life-style of *sannyāsa* or renunciation, taken to a spiritual extreme reminiscent of Abhishiktānanda.[32] Their mutual conclusion is that only in receiving this state of life as a grace can the paradoxical nature of God, of God's Revelations, and of the spiritual path, as well as the inevitable tensions between individual and collective authorities be resolved.

A final quality of Griffiths's self-understanding also is brought to light through the interpretation of these themes. Throughout his writings, the language and the principles by which he explains his own experiences become thematic in his interpretation of the malaise and the cure of cultural and global ills. Here is his apparent conscious appropriation of the role of culture bearer: By seeking to replace the ideals inherited from his culture of origin, he articulated an alternative paradigm for that culture to consider—one he found echoed with increasing frequency by other Western thinkers in his later years. In response to the first of three questions posed at the end of part two above, he also simultaneously suggested to other intercultural explorers of his time the limits in any person's abilities to translate herself into another culture. As serious as his engagement with Indian culture was for his final thirty-eight years, and as profound as its influence proved to be upon him, Griffiths nevertheless recognized the fact that he remained fundamentally Western in his outlook and thus that the most appropriate audience for his insights was in the West as well.

While aware of his limits as a culture bearer, Griffiths still speculated boldly concerning the transformation that both West and East must undergo, especially the surrender of the rational mind and the opening of the intuitive that he claimed that the West needed and that the East was losing. It is to this particular identification of the transformation needed by his culture with the changes he himself had undergone that the discussion now turns.

8

The Way of Intuitive Wisdom

Underlying and informing Griffiths's relationships to the cultures of West and East is the ongoing internal dialogue between rational and nonrational ways of knowing. Definitive for the direction of this dialogue in the third period of his life is the move from Kurisumala Ashram in Kerala, with its emphasis upon Syrian liturgy, to Shantivanam, where Griffiths in 1968 began to structure an ashram community more thoroughly centered upon contemplative practice. The implications of this shift in his ashram's priorities for his understanding and experience of the mind were significant, consonant with the theme of nonduality.

Meditation and the Experience of Advaita

During the year of his move to Shantivanam, Griffiths gave a series of lectures at Madras University, later collected and published under the title *Vedānta and Christian Faith* (1973). These talks reveal ideas about the mind that were shaped by the deepening contemplative experience characteristic of his final twenty-five years. Signaling a significant change of attitude, Griffiths offers a more positive appraisal and nuanced interpretation of the ninth-century Indian sage Śankara's Advaita Vedānta philosophy than he had in the past.[1] According to Griffiths, Śankara's teachings are based upon the direct experience of ultimate reality beyond the world created by perceptions and thoughts. In order to appreciate the perspective from which Śankara writes, one must undergo this same experience of going beyond the world as it is presented through the senses and the conceptual mind. It is revealing that Griffiths's descriptions of this entry into Śankara's philosophy are

128

similar to his own accounts of what happens to the individual through a contemplative means of knowing:

> Sankara has seen with extraordinary penetration that the human mind cannot rest on any image presented to the senses or on any thought presented to consciousness. It has to go beyond both image and thought, if it wants to reach the ultimate reality, the ultimate truth, which cannot be thought or imagined.[2]

As becomes clear in Griffiths's discussion, the realization underlying Śankara's perspective upon appearance and reality is the experience of *advaita*, "an awareness of being which is nothing but a reflection of being on itself."[3] This experience is described further as a state of self-transcendence where one goes beyond the distinction between subject and object and experiences a knowledge that is complete, a knowledge of truth itself.

Reinforcing the importance of the Indian sage's insights through comparison, Griffiths sets Śankara's teachings on the nondual nature of God, and the human experience of that divine nature, alongside those of Aquinas. Both authorities conclude that ultimate Reality or God is without any duality and that divine mind or consciousness knows all things through identity with them—the same kind of knowing that dawns through the human experience of nonduality.[4] Griffiths summarizes his comparison of Śankara and Aquinas as follows:

> Thus we find that Christian doctrine holds with Sankara that the ultimate end of man is to "participate in the divine nature," to share in God's own mode of consciousness, and hence to know himself and all things in their identity in the divine essence. We are justified therefore in saying that there is a Christian tradition of the ultimate state of man and the universe, which is identical with that of Sankara. God himself is "without duality," his knowledge or consciousness is "without duality," and the end of man is to participate in this "non-dual" mode of being and consciousness in God.[5]

While it is impossible to deduce the nature of Griffiths's own experience from such theoretical comparisons, it is safe to infer that his understanding of the mind had begun to articulate itself in a different way as he moved to Shantivanam, a shift signaled by his intensified focus upon *advaita*.

In *Return to the Center*, written around 1972 and published in 1976, Griffiths offers a more intimate glimpse into the meditative experience that by then clearly supported his theoretical comparisons.[6] Put simply, meditation is the means by which one may transcend the normal functioning of mental faculties to know oneself, one's world, and God in their true relationship as a nondual, yet differentiated wholeness— what Griffiths identifies as an experience of *advaita* or "the One 'without a second'":

> Meditation goes beyond the conscious mind into the unconscious. In meditation I can become aware of the ground of my being in matter, in life, in human consciousness. I can experience my solidarity with the universe. . . . I can get beyond all these outer forms of things in time and space and discover the Ground from which they all spring. I can know the Father, the Origin, the Source, beyond being and not-being, the One "without a second." I can know the birth of all things from this Ground, their coming into being in the Word.[7]

In the language of his earliest writings in England on the mind and contemplation, meditation provides an intuitive or nonrational means of knowing.

In a passage especially revealing of his understanding of the mediatory role of the mind, Griffiths speaks of the relationship between the world as it is perceived through the senses and understood by reason, and "the world as it really is," experienced through meditation:

> I look out on this world of things around me, each one separated in space, each one moving in time, and beyond this comparatively stable world I know that there is an almost infinite dispersion of matter in space, a perpetual flux of movement in time. . . . In my consciousness this diffusion of matter, this flux of becoming, begins to be ordered in space and time. . . . When I turn back beyond my senses and beyond my reason and pass through this door into eternal life, then I discover my true Self, then I begin to see the world as it really is.

Through meditation, then, one may indeed transcend the mediatory role of the mind to some degree, with the result that one does see the world more clearly. As he continues his description of this experience, the scope of its nondual quality becomes strikingly apparent:

> This is the archetypal world, not known in its diffusion in space and time, not reflected through a human consciousness dependent on a material body, but the world in its eternal reality, gathered into

the one consciousness of the Word. Here all is one, united in a simple vision of being. All the long evolution of matter and life and man, all my own history from the first moment that I became a living cell, all the stages of my consciousness and that of all human beings, is here recapitulated, brought to a point, and I know myself as the Self of all, the one Word eternally spoken in time.[8]

Through transcending the usual functioning of the mental faculties, one transcends the self. Through going beyond the self, one becomes aware of the true Self—the Self of all, the Word through whom all things were created and in whom all things are united. It is this "world in its eternal reality" that comes into view from the window of his hut at Shantivanam.

Almost twenty years later, Griffiths would offer further detail regarding the practice of meditation developed at Shantivanam that would endure as the key means for his opening to the experience of nonduality. In his lectures at the 1991 John Main Seminar on "the evolving tradition" of Christian meditation, Griffiths defines contemplation (used interchangeably with "meditation") as "the practice of the presence of God," aligning himself with the tradition of "pure" or nondiscursive prayer. Such prayer was taught by the Desert Fathers and communicated through John Cassian, Benedict of Nursia, and more recently through the contemplative renewal in the Roman Catholic Church beginning in the 1970s, as well as with the medieval Orthodox tradition of the Jesus Prayer.

Drawing explicitly from his experience with Yoga in India, Griffiths emphasizes the importance of an integrated practice, involving all three aspects of the Pauline anthropology, body, soul or mind, and spirit. Beginning with the body, he endorses the common instruction on keeping a firm, still, but relaxed posture during meditation so that it is of minimal distraction. Furthermore, he consciously brings his breath into the practice as a means of integrating the body and mind, so that one prays as a whole person, envisioning the Spirit (recalling *spiritus*, "breath") descending throughout his body and then ascending again.[9] Silence is thus brought to the body and to the senses, in preparation for an experience in which the physical aspect of one's existence is transcended and yet also integrated.

In order to instill silence in the mind or soul, Griffiths endorses the Eastern tradition of mantra and specifically John Main's adaptation of that practice for Christian meditation. In the course of his discussion, it is clear that Griffiths also considers the Jesus Prayer that he himself practiced since the 1940s as a form of mantra meditation, bringing to light for him important common ground between Christian, Hindu, Buddhist,

Sikh, and Sufi spiritualities.[10] In general, the purpose of the mantra, according to Griffiths, is to center the person by unifying the faculties and focusing them on the indwelling presence of the divine mystery. The mantra's specific effect of silencing the dualistic or discursive mind brings transcendence of the ego and openness to the unconscious, within which dwell both positive and negative psychic forces. The opportunity is thus created for both profound psychological healing of past wounds and dangerous encounters with destructive internal and even cosmic forces. The Christian engaged in meditation is protected by the mantra, which often is, or includes the name of, Jesus Christ or his words, and by the faith and love nurtured through the rest of the Christian life that form the foundation of contemplative practice.[11]

Finally, in addition to bringing stillness to the body and recollecting the faculties of the soul, Christian mantra meditation opens one to the divine Spirit through one's own spirit. By the human spirit Griffiths means "the point of self-transcendence" where "body and soul go beyond their human limitations and open to the infinite, the eternal, the divine."[12] Here one's separation from God, from other persons, from the entire creation, in fact all duality created by the conscious mind is transcended, following the path made by Jesus Christ. Nevertheless, one must also acknowledge, according to Griffiths, that Christian meditation is not unique in bringing one to the experience of the spirit open to the divine mystery. In the terms of Griffiths's theory the mantra is a *real* or religious symbol found in many traditions through which one may transcend all dualizing habits of mind to experience *advaita,* the nondual nature of the divine mystery. Furthermore, by going through and beyond the mantric symbol, one may realize that humanity is an organic whole, part of the even greater cosmic whole, all of which stands in a nondual relationship to its creator.

With meditation as a tool, Griffiths refined his lifelong analysis of the mind more confidently in relation to the experience of nonduality.

The Limitations of Reason Revisited

In the context of Shantivanam, Griffiths's maturing experience of nonduality informed and was informed by his continuing reflection upon the dialogue between rational and nonrational forces. From his exploration of various nonrational or what he calls "intuitive" means of gaining knowledge in the prior period (sensory and emotional experience, imagination, faith, and contemplation) a tension had emerged. What is the respective status of knowledge that is mediated through and remains on the level of the symbols of Christ and church (knowledge through faith), and the more complete knowledge that dawns when the symbols are transcended and the nondual reality is experienced (contemplative or mystical knowledge)? With the contemplative orientation of Shantivanam, Griffiths was able to experience the latter way of knowing more frequently and fully and to recognize its importance in both the Christian and Hindu traditions. As he became increasingly familiar with this highest degree of intuitive knowing, all the other levels were seen more clearly in relation to it. Simultaneously, the dialogue between rational and nonrational forces appeared less as a struggle in himself and in the cultures around him and more as the interplay of the faculties within an awareness of the nondual reality that is their center or source, the spirit.

Griffiths's conclusion that the experience of *advaita* leads one toward a state of complete knowledge has clear implications for his understanding of the various ways through which truth may be known. As before, he affirms the role of intuition relative to, while still upholding the value of, the faculty of reason and another important source of knowledge, the experience of the senses. In his discussion of Śankara, for example, he confirms the integrity of experience from within different "modes of knowledge," implicitly distinguishing between the mode of the senses, the mode of reason, and "the highest mode of knowledge above sense and reason," which he identifies with intuition and contemplation.[13] Given the comprehensiveness of what he calls "intuition" or "knowledge by identity," Griffiths claims that such a mode of knowing, long revered in the East, deserves more attention in the West. Even though such knowledge "cannot be strictly verified, because this knowledge transcends all ordinary forms of consciousness and cannot therefore be properly expressed," yet its value is universally recognized; the experience of *advaita* is the knowledge of God and all things in God through an "unknowing" attested to by Śankara and Dionysius and sought by all religious traditions.[14]

Griffiths's comparison of Hindu and Christian theories of contemplation as ways of knowing prompted further reflection upon what is unique and what is common in each. Both the Christian and Hindu contemplative traditions claimed to be attaining a high level of intuitive knowledge. How could they be distinguished?

Griffiths's early articles from Shantivanam illustrate his enthusiasm about what the Christian could learn from Hindu spirituality but are also clear about how the Christian experience of contemplation is unique. Referring to the goal of Yoga to achieve a state of inner silence so that the mind or soul can experience its own "center," he writes:

This idea of the centre or substance of the soul is well known in Catholic mysticism, but our scholastic philosophy and theology have tended to obscure it. Even in our prayer and worship we tend to remain on the level of the rational consciousness, and "meditation" becomes little more than an exercise in discursive reason. But the aim of all meditation should be to pass beyond the limits of the rational consciousness and awake to the inner life of the Spirit, that is to the indwelling presence of God. It is to this discovery of the indwelling Spirit, the source both of being and consciousness, that the Church in India is being called.

Transcending the rational mind in meditation, then, constitutes a common goal for the two traditions. What is experienced when the mind or soul reaches its center, however, is different:

> [F]or a Christian this Ground of being and consciousness is not only the source of life and truth, it is also the ground of the presence in us of the Holy Spirit. What we discover when we enter into the depth of the soul is the love of God "which is poured into our hearts by the Holy Spirit who is given to us." In other words, we encounter God not only in his immanence in nature and the soul but in the free gift of himself in the Holy Spirit.[15]

What Hindu spirituality offers Griffiths, then, is a systematic method for, and understanding of, the contemplative experience of transcending "rational consciousness" to reach the center of the soul. What Christianity offers to him, and he believes to others, is an added richness to the experience and understanding of this center. As he acknowledges, the Hindu also knows the "mystery of God's love," as exemplifed in the Bhagavad Gītā. But a "Christian Vedānta" would reveal how the contemplative experience unites one with the Christ within and with all of humanity, and empowers one to serve the world rather than to withdraw from it, as Advaita Vedāntins known by Griffiths proposed. The Christian contemplative also experiences not just an "ontological identity" with transcendent Reality, but "a participation in the personal life of God," in the Trinity, through the relationships of knowledge and love—or, in St. Paul's words, to "know the love of Christ which passes knowledge."[16]

Nevertheless, Griffiths draws substantially upon Hindu sources in his account of what happens when the mind goes beyond the limits of rational consciousness to experience nonduality. Relying upon traditional Indian philosophical distinctions, he characterizes *advaita* as an experience of the union of the knower, the object of knowing, and the process of knowing, the familiar separation between subject and object being transcended.[17] More than just a theory, this knowledge is a direct experience, one that is unavailable to the rational faculty because reason always presupposes the existence of an objective world distinct from the subject or knower. In order to transcend the limitations posed upon reality by the rational faculty, the mind must turn back upon itself and away from the senses to know itself intuitively, in its undivided wholeness, in its nonduality.

What the two different types of knowing, the rational and the non-rational or intuitive, represent for Vedānta are two different means for experiencing the same reality. When experienced through the senses and reason, reality appears multiple, everchanging, and finite; when experienced through the height of intuition (meditation), reality is found to be unified, unchanging, and infinite. The truth from the Upaniṣads embraced by Griffiths is that these are two different experiences of *one* reality or Reality. The ground of consciousness (the Ātman) is identical with the ground of creation (Brahman)—precisely because the creation itself, including the human mind, is an expression of the one universal consciousness. Through the human mind this universal consciousness comes to know itself, in its parts through what is called "reason," and in its wholeness through what is named "intuition." Thus both types of knowledge, the rational and the intuitive, have their value; and, therefore, both experiences of reality, as multiple and in its nondual ground, have their integrity.[18]

After his move to Shantivanam, the import of reason is obviously not forgotten or rejected; Griffiths's scholarly inquiry depends upon it. But one may say that the limitations of the role of reason, in both personal and cultural contexts, are now experienced and understood more clearly. He writes, for example, that the social and spiritual ills of humanity are caused primarily not because the activity of reason in itself is flawed but because this faculty remains turned toward the world of the senses and disconnected from its source that is the Word of God within, the ground of consciousness.[19] Similarly, the knowledge of science and technology is not evil in itself but becomes so when not used in relation to the higher wisdom that dawns through the transcending of reason. The limited role of reason is apparent in the following ranking by Griffiths of the different "modes of knowledge":

Science is the lowest form of human knowledge—the knowledge of the material world through discursive reason. Philosophy is above science, because it goes beyond the material world and explores the world of thought, but it is still confined to discursive reason. Theology is above philosophy, because it is open to the world of transcendent reality, but its methods are still those of science and philosophy. It is only wisdom which can transcend reason and know the Truth, not discursively but intuitively, not by its reflection in the world of the senses but in its Ground, where knowing is also being.[20]

In Griffiths's mind, nothing less than the survival of humanity is at stake in establishing the correct priority between these different ways of knowing, especially between discursive reason and wisdom born of mystical intuition or contemplation.[21]

Griffiths's critiques of both Western and Indian cultures are closely tied to the question of the proper balance between the rational and intuitive ways of knowing. He continues to connect his criticism of both cultures to their respective overreliance upon one way of knowing at the expense of the other: the West upon the rational, the East upon the intuitive means. What is needed is the balance between these two elements symbolized by a "marriage." Griffiths is clear, however, that just as Western culture has sought and in many instances succeeded to dominate other cultures, so the rational way has threatened to supersede the important role of the intuitive, even in countries such as India where the intuitive way has virtually defined the culture.[22]

The Way of Intuitive Wisdom

Griffiths's most sustained analysis of the mind and, specifically, of its nonrational capacities is found in *The Marriage of East and West: A Sequel to the Golden String* (1982). After describing the current imbalance between the partners in intercultural dialogue (West and East, male and female, rational and intuitive), Griffiths probes deeply into the question of what is the intuition, a question that he says has occupied his attention from early on in his education.

"Intuition is a knowledge which derives not from observation and experiment or from concepts and reason but from the mind's reflection on itself."[23] Such a knowledge relies neither upon sense experience nor a conceptual or linguistic exercise, but upon a subtler and less active capacity of the mind—its ability to be present to itself. For Griffiths, intuition as a way of knowing is grounded in the self-awareness that accompanies every physical and psychological event, a self-awareness to which one rarely adverts but that is nonetheless everpresent. Such knowledge does not appear on the familiar surface level of the mind upon which one normally operates. The knowledge born of what Griffiths calls the "intuition" arises, as it were, from "beneath the sunlit surface" of the mind, from "the moonlit world of dreams and images, before they emerge into rational consciousness."[24] This "world" is the "I am"-ness or pure existence presupposed, and also to varying degrees present, in every moment of human experience. In an earlier work Griffiths referred to this same level of awareness as an experience of "the mystery of being"—a mystery constantly present and always available through the power of self-reflection.[25]

Griffiths's description of intuition and its ground in self-awareness relies upon metaphors, images that have their limits as well as their usefulness. The image of the surface and depths of consciousness, corresponding to the sources of rational and intuitive knowledge, provides one picture that illustrates the relationship between these two ways of knowing. Another tool for presenting the relationship between these two types of knowledge is the distinction between an active and a passive intellect, corresponding for Griffiths to the distinction between reason and intuition. While the former "abstracts rational concepts from our sense experience," the latter faculty "receives the impressions of the experience of the body, the senses, the feelings, the imagination."[26] The active intellect through its power of analysis supports the rational means for gaining knowledge, while the passive intellect through its receptive capacity provides the raw material for the intuitive means. While the active intellect conceptualizes the data received by the passive intellect for the purpose of rational knowing, intuition as a kind of knowing that arises from self-reflection attends more immediately and passively to the impressions left in one's awareness through the various channels of experience.

Unlike the fruits of the active intellect, Griffiths writes: "[I]ntuition cannot be produced. It has to be allowed to happen."[27] Through self-reflection or attending to one's everpresent self-awareness, one may receive the knowledge inherent within sense experience, the emotions, the imagination, and mystical experience—knowledge that is potential by virtue of the fact that, while the passive intellect receives every minutia of experience, not all that is received will be actualized in consciousness because of limited self-awareness. Thus, while the "world" available to the active intellect or reason is potentially vast, in actual experience it is severely restricted. By opening to the layers of consciousness beneath the surface of the mind, one may extend the range of one's knowing to include more of what reason may comprehend and more of what transcends reason. How does one transcend the surface level of the mind to access one's innate capacities for intuition?

Griffiths begins his account of the various sources of intuitive wisdom by stating that "intuition exists at every level of our being." In his ordering of the corresponding levels of intuition, each one subsumes that which has gone before it. Using images drawn from Wordsworth, Griffiths portrays the process of intuitive knowing as comprised of successive refinements of feeling, eventually opening "into the purer mind."[28] Thus he first describes the physical level of intuition, how the mind's reflection upon bodily sensations can lead to a kind of knowledge, one that results not in rational concepts but expresses itself in gestures, images, ritual, and prayer.[29] As examples of this physical level of intuition he cites the primitive's knowledge of the earth, the farmer's instinctive knowledge of the seasons, and the lover's "knowing" of the beloved through physical union—in each case a knowledge independent of, though potentially enhanced by, rational or scientific knowledge. One is reminded of Griffiths's own early and enduring experience of intimacy with nature, both in the English countryside and then later with the land around Shantivanam.

Closely related to the first level is what Griffiths calls "emotional, affective intuition."[30] Using the example of human relationships (mother and child, wife and husband), he cites the knowledge of another person and of oneself that may arise through psychological as well as physical intimacy—again a knowledge that may be supported by conceptual knowledge but is distinct from it. Living in monastic communities since the age of twenty-five, Griffiths had the opportunity to experience this type of affective knowledge in yet another context.

Related to, but "beyond" the levels of physical and emotional intuition is the knowing that may arise from the mind's reflection upon the images of one's internal and external worlds, what Griffiths calls "imaginative intuition."[31] Penetrating more deeply, the light of one's awareness illumines not only the physical and emotional impressions but the primordial images or archetypes that spontaneously structure experience. As these images are brought into reflective consciousness one simultaneously receives a different kind of knowledge of the world and of the self whose nature these images reveal. Griffiths thus implies that the imaginative intuition begins to synthesize the diverse experiences of the complex world into the terms of these fundamental images, bringing forth a depth of meaning unavailable through rational exercise of the mind. This way of knowing, found obscurely in all, is perfected in the great poets and artists who thereby succeed in communicating deep understandings of human nature. Whether in the common experiencer or the poet, the activity of the imaginative intuition remains equally passive, as though guided by its own law. According to Griffiths, Western education has stunted the natural development of this intuitive capacity in human beings by focusing so fully upon the exercise of abstract thought. This is the very education within which Griffiths was raised and whose limitations he confronted and critiqued throughout his adult life, often citing theorists of the imaginative intuition, like Coleridge and Jacques and Raissa Maritain.

It is in the context of a critique of the West's overidentification with the rational mode of consciousness that Griffiths chooses to remind his reader of the necessary balance between the two primary ways of knowing: "Both reason and intuition by themselves are defective. . . ."[32] Having already described the perilous consequences of a mind dominated by reason, Griffiths cites the equally dangerous results of a mind in which intuition is unchecked by rational investigation. The ideal balance is again portrayed using the image of a marriage between reason and intuition, and between the active and passive intellect. In a great poet such as Dante, Griffiths states: "Reason itself, the active intellect, is taken up into the intuitive mind, that is, into the reflective knowledge of the self, and reason becomes intuitive."[33] In other words, in the great artist (and also, one might suggest, in the great scientist) the mind's rational activity in abstracting concepts from sense experience itself becomes an object of intuitive inquiry. Rather than being mistaken as the only true mediation of knowledge of the world, reason assumes a place alongside the other modes of inquiry as a valid but relative means for gaining knowledge—each of which supports the other and, when taken together, result in what Griffiths calls "an integral knowledge" embracing the whole person. The active mode of the intellect is then in balance with the passive mode, the one faculty turning in proper order toward both the abstract and the concrete, the world of appearances and the reality within, all embraced by an effortless gaze of self-awareness.[34] In this way, "reason becomes intuitive," that is, a source of knowledge through self-reflection. Griffiths appears to have recognized here what was only implicit in his thinking before, that even the dualism of reason and intuition can and must be transcended.

The intuitive knowledge expressed in great art and poetry, however, does not represent the deepest penetration of human self-reflection, according to Griffiths: "The poet synthesizes all these elements of human experience into a unitive vision, but he remains dependent on images and concepts."[35] Through imaginative intuition one has come to know the Self or "the mystery of being" that accompanies every event of consciousness (i.e., consciousness itself) through the archetypes, through poetic images, through artistic forms in the imagination. But, as Griffiths so often says, one can and must "go beyond," transcend the sense of self represented by the archetypes to experience complete knowledge of one's identity.

Reflecting on his earlier experience of faith as a preparatory stage of knowledge in comparison to contemplation, Griffiths describes faith as "a function not of the rational but of the intuitive mind" and as an "openness to the mystery of God."[36] This opening of the spirit to God is completed by the union in love he calls "contemplation" or the highest level of intuitive knowledge. In describing this final stage of the intuition's journey, he writes: "It carries with it all the deep experience of the body and the blood, and all that the emotions and the imagination have impressed upon it, and now passing beyond images and thoughts, it 'returns upon itself' in a pure act of self-reflection, of self-knowledge." This is the same contemplative or mystical experience he has described before of the spirit beyond body and soul or mind. He continues:

This is the experience of the mystic, who, set free from all the limitations both of body and of soul, enters into the pure joy of the spirit. The spirit is the culminating point of body and of soul, where the individual person transcends himself and awakens to the eternal ground of his being. The obscure intuition of physical being, the broadening intuition of emotional and imaginative experience, the light of reason discovering the laws and principles of nature and of man, all these are reflections of the pure light of intuition, in which the soul knows itself, not merely in its living relation with the world around or with other human beings, but in its eternal ground, the source of its being.[37]

Through attending to the various levels of experience comprising "the way of intuitive wisdom" (physical, emotional, imaginative, rational, fiducial, and contemplative) via self-reflection one has come to know intuitively and fully that "mystery of being" that underlies all of existence, "That" which is at once one's unchanging identity, the ground that connects one to all in creation, and the very basis of all being, all reality. The fundamental truth or intuition to which Griffiths's inquiry leads him, then, is identical to that which he has recognized in Vedānta: When one journeys through the various levels or modes of consciousness to experience that which is consciousness itself and one's deepest (because unchanging) self, one simultaneously realizes that which is the ground of all beings and all being; Ātman is Brahman. At the end of that journey, as the multiple worlds of experience have gradually become unified through the various layers of intuitive knowledge, the soul opens to that experience of oneness in which all the divisions created by the mind drop away, the experience of the nondual reality (*advaita*) in which all the diversity is contained. Again, Griffiths emphasizes, this entire "way of intuitive wisdom" unfolds through grace, not through the design or effort of the human mind. So also the rational mind will always fall short in attempting to describe this "way"; the most that words can do is point toward the experience.[38]

Griffiths summarizes the "way of intuitive wisdom" by setting its goal of complete knowledge not only in the context of the individual life but in the life of the universe as a whole. In a passage reminiscent of Pierre Teilhard de Chardin and Aurobindo Ghose, he writes concerning the development of matter as follows:

> [I]t has to go through various stages of evolution before it can be capable of life; and again life has to go through many phases of development before it can become conscious; so finally consciousness has to develop through sense, through feeling, through the imagination, through reason before it can become fully conscious of that being which is the source of matter, of life and of consciousness. But the hidden germ of intuition, of receptivity was present from the beginning, and the ultimate mystical experience is only the flower of that intuition which was hidden in the root of matter.[39]

Here in brief form is Griffiths's vision of the path that life follows in becoming conscious, a path replicated in the life of each individual. Writing from the perspective of his midseventies, Griffiths conceives that all means of gaining knowledge have their role to play in human evolution, culminating in the mystical intuition in which the source of all being becomes conscious and knowing of itself, unmediated by the thought structures of the human mind—an experience of nonduality, *advaita*.

In Dialogue with the "New Science"

When in the early 1980s Griffiths first encountered the "new science," he discovered in Fritjof Capra, Ken Wilber, Rupert Sheldrake, and David Bohm persons with a similar vision of how Western science must change, and how Eastern wisdom must be assimilated, in order for civilization to endure. These scientists affirmed Griffiths's analysis of rational and intuitive means for gaining knowledge and challenged him to integrate their insights into his intercultural and interreligious understanding. In short, they illustrated the fact that the "marriage of East and West" for which he had called since at least 1953 had begun to take place.

In *The Tao of Physics: An Exploration of the Parallels Between Modern Physics and Eastern Mysticism* (1975), Capra introduces his comparison of the insights of modern physics with Eastern wisdom by describing "two kinds of knowledge, or two modes of consciousness" that have predominated in the West and East respectively: "the rational and the intuitive."[40] In a similar fashion, Wilber discusses "two modes of know-ing" in *The Spectrum of Consciousness* (1977), a text cited by Griffiths in lectures and writings. Wilber distinguishes between the "dualistic" mode employed by science ("dualistic" because it always presupposes the separation of the knower and the known) and a "non-dual knowl-edge" long known in the East and now being envisioned by some mod-ern physicists—a knowledge that is independent of observation and conceptual theorizing ("wherein knower and known are one pro-cess").[41] Influenced by the late Indian sage Jiddu Krishnamurti, Bohm speaks of a distinction between thought, as the everchanging factor in the "process of knowledge," and awareness, as the abiding factor. Like Griffiths, Bohm envisions a method of inquiry in which rational thought processes are taken up and integrated into a holistic awareness, similar to what Griffiths calls "intuition."[42]

The impression that the "new science" made upon Griffiths is evi-dent in the lectures he gave during the 1980s, including those edited and collected for both his commentary on the Bhagavad Gītā and *A New Vision of Reality: Western Science, Eastern Mysticism and Christian Faith* (1990). Specifically with regard to his understanding of the mind, a few points can be added from these two texts. In his Gītā commentary, Griffiths discusses the familiar two types of knowledge of which the text speaks and again associates them with the West and the East: *vi-jñāna,* or the "discriminative knowledge" exalted by science; and *jñāna,* or the "unitive" or "intuitive wisdom" praised by the Upaniṣads and Lord Krishna. As in his earlier account of "the way of intuitive wis-dom," he again calls for the full integration of these two essential means of gaining knowledge, means that correspond to what scientists have proposed as the distinct functions of the two sides of the brain. While the left side is "rational, discursive, discriminative, analytical and di-viding," the right side is "intuitive and unitive." The effects from al-lowing either part of the brain to dominate, according to Griffiths, are dangerous. The faculties must work in balance with one another, a har-mony that can take place through combining the exercise of reason and the practice of meditation.[43]

In *A New Vision of Reality,* Griffiths elaborates upon further episte-mological and intercultural implications of the relationship between reason and intuition suggested by the "new science." Following Ken Wilber's *Up From Eden: A Transpersonal View of Human Evolution* (1981), Griffiths describes how individual human development replicates the evolution of consciousness in the species as a whole. Like the human race at the beginning (symbolized by Eden), the child begins life in the womb fully one with all of nature and experiences an undifferentiated awareness of identity with the cosmic whole. In time, consciousness of the body, then the mind, and the self gradually develop, leading to an increasing degree of separation and fragmentation in the young person's awareness of the world and her or his relation to it. According to Wilber, with the advent of language, that is, the representation of objects by signs, an inner world begins to develop within human consciousness in relation to the concrete outer world, reinforcing the awareness of a self separated from what before was experienced as an undifferentiated unity.

Griffiths, in agreement with Wilber, notes that first through the imagination and later through logical thought, the capacity of the human brain evolves further, enlivening the right and left sides of the brain respectively—thus setting Griffiths's discussion of these two complementary ways of knowing in an evolutionary framework. At the stage when only the imaginative mode is active, the child, like the human race millennia ago, is open to the sacred via symbols and myths but also to "all sorts of confusions and superstitions."[44] When this level of consciousness is transcended, both individually and as a species, then reason develops to test and purify the workings of the imaginative mind. Soon after this breakthrough occurred historically during the "axial period" (800–200 B.C.E.), a temporary balance of the imaginative and logical modes produced the powerful and at times mystical philosophies of India, Greece, and China.[45] But this balance would not last long as civilization developed further; the integration of reason and imagination is not easily sustained.

The balance evident in the great philosophies of the seers of the Upaniṣads, the Greeks, and the Chinese was overcome as the power of reason developed further, especially in the West. Griffiths cites a similar imbalance that occurs in the development of the child.[46] The consequences of the ascendance of reason to a dominant position over the imagination are dire, by Griffiths's estimation. As reason develops, so does the ego and the aspiration to control oneself, others, and the surrounding world. In the West, science and technology progress as a result of this development of the rational faculty, but so does a culture oriented toward serving the individual ego. What these consequences represent is a case of "arrested development," a stopping at one level of consciousness and a failure to move on to the next, that is, a failure to achieve the level envisioned and experienced by the great philosophers of the "axial period" where imagination and reason are fully integrated.[47]

Griffiths uses the concept of nonduality to describe further the present, "arrested" state of consciousness of most individuals, particularly in the West. Most people are dominated by a dualistic awareness, an inclination toward separation and division that may be traced back to the mythology of Eden and that may be found fully developed in the West's current overdependence upon rational consciousness:

> The fall of humanity is the fall from the unified state of being, when humanity was in harmony with nature and with God, into the state of division and duality. It is a fall from the unified or non-dualistic mind into dualistic mind, that is, into our present mode of consciousness. The human mind as we experience it thinks always in terms of duality, of subject and object, of mind and matter, of truth and error, and everything is perceived in terms of time and space. All our science, philosophy and theology are products of this dualistic mind, and our normal way of perceiving the universe around us is in terms of an inner and an outer world.[48]

This "normal way" of perception and thus knowing is therefore limited. Modern science has come to this recognition that all the senses and language systems can provide is a description of the appearance of reality, not "the truth of reality."[49] In other words, the dualistic mind can only perceive and conceive a dualistic reality. The products of such a mind do not constitute full knowledge or truth because ultimately reality is nondual (*advaita*); or, to use Capra's phrase that Griffiths often quotes, reality is "a complicated web of interdependent relationships."[50]

In order to move beyond the "arrested development" in the evolution of consciousness Griffiths has described, individuals and the species must experience the transcending of reason and of the dualistic mind. One may gain access to such an experience through the variety of means generally described as "meditation."[51] When one goes beyond the rational, dualistic mind, one knows in a different and more complete fashion. Griffiths also turns to the mystics of the various great religions to support this claim that knowledge arises through transcending reason and experiencing union with reality as a nondual wholeness. He cites the *jñāna* of the Upaniṣads and Bhagavad Gītā, the *prajñā* of the Buddhists; the experience of the oneness of being (*wahdat al-wujud*) that is a "perfect knowledge" for the Sufis; and the "knowing by unknowing" described by Dionysius, the Christian mystical philosopher, and taken up by Ruusbroec, among others.[52] Implicit in Griffiths's account, then, are the claims that the distinction between subject and object (knower and known) fundamental to most people's experience may indeed be transcended, and that the result is a more complete way of knowing that will empower continued evolution.

In Wilber's account of the evolution of consciousness through various stages, Griffiths found a principle that he had likewise intuited, especially regarding the relationship between the two primary ways of knowing, the rational and the intuitive. From the experience of his own maturing as well as of his culture, he knew that either mode by itself leads to the dangerous consequences of partial knowledge. The challenge for the developing individual, as it is for the evolving species, is not only to transcend an earlier stage of consciousness, but also then to integrate the positive aspects of the earlier stage into the succeeding one.[53] This principle of transcendence and integration, essential to Wilber's account of the stages of consciousness, is applied by Griffiths to the emergence of rational thought, into which the prior imaginative level must be integrated, and to the current challenge to go beyond and integrate rational consciousness into what he calls "the perfect marriage of imagination and reason in intuitive thought."[54]

In the evolution of human consciousness, at both the individual and cultural levels, beyond an overidentification with its rational mode, reason is transcended but not left behind; it is "taken up" or integrated into the higher levels of consciousness that Griffiths, again following Wilber, labels the "psychic" and the "advaitic." Reason should be used, for example, in interpreting the great Scriptures of the various world religions—revelations that are, in fact, "messages from that transcendent world" to which one opens fully at the highest level of consciousness.[55] He also affirms the necessity of using reason to process experiences of levels of consciousness beyond the rational. Speaking of the subtle or psychic realm of experience to which one opens through meditation, Griffiths writes:

> The ordinary, rational, mental level of mind has no access to this realm and ordinary scientific methods are useless to map it. It is important to remember, however, that in these investigations we do not discard our reason. The method is to open ourselves through intuition to these deeper insights and then to try to understand them, to relate them and appropriately to systematize them through the reason. Reason and intuition always have to be used together. . . . It is a matter of the right and left brain, the right being the intuitive and the left the rational. . . .[56]

More than simply the balanced use of separate faculties, what Griffiths envisions here is the fluid dialogue of varied means of gaining knowledge within an encompassing awareness.

Regarding the larger questions of social and cultural transformation, Griffiths is clearly intrigued by the image of a "paradigm shift" suggested by Capra, Wilber, and others, marking an abrupt change in the worldview of civilization as a whole and the onset of "a new vision of reality." The increasing predominance of the rational mode of consciousness during the common era has supported what Griffiths and Capra identify as a materialistic and mechanistic model for life in the West—a model that has in this century begun to influence the East strongly, a matter of great concern to Griffiths. But he becomes convinced after his exposure to the "new science" that a change of models, a "new age," is at hand. As more individuals and even science itself begin to experience levels of consciousness beyond the rational level, a shift in paradigms will indeed occur.

The confirmation of his own ideas from the "new scientists" supported Griffiths's growing sense that the dialogue between rational and nonrational forces that he had experienced in his own life and envisioned between East and West was now being lived by many around him as well. As he traveled in the 1980s and 1990s, he discovered a growing number of persons experiencing and thinking along the same lines as himself. The paradigm shift that he and others had envisioned indeed seemed to have begun.

A Psychological Breakthrough to the Feminine

While meditating outside his hut early one morning in January 1990, Griffiths felt a sudden force like a sledgehammer hit him on the left side of the head, pushing him out of his chair and blurring his vision. He eventually found his way to his bed where he was soon discovered and where in the subsequent weeks he would be cared for by the ashram community. Gradually he returned to health. However, profound changes in his awareness endured, changes that he would interpret using language clearly reminiscent of the theory of mind just described.

Griffiths describes "the greatest grace I've ever had in my life" as follows: "I had died to the ego, I think. The ego-mind and also maybe the discriminative mind that separates and divides, all seemed to have gone. Everything was flowing into everything else, and I had a sense of unity behind it all."[57] Completing what Griffiths characterizes as "a death experience" was the new life brought by a further profound opening to the Holy Spirit. Several days after the stroke, while he was still convalescing, he felt an urge from within to "surrender to the Mother." As he responded to this call, he underwent what he describes as "a psychological breakthrough to the feminine." "An overwhelming experience of love came over me. It was like waves of love." Drawing upon the psychological distinctions underlying his understanding of the mind, Griffiths suggests that the feminine within him, identified with the intuitive mode that had so long been repressed as in many men, was finally released, catalyzing within consciousness a new sense of wholeness.[58]

The silencing of the discriminative or dualistic mind by mantra meditation occurred in a complete and conclusive way as a result of the stroke, allowing a more intuitive and thus unifying style of mental activity to arise—an event Griffiths explains as the release of the feminine within his unconscious. With the dominance of the rational mind thus broken, a different quality of mental experience was allowed to come into being. It is interesting that he has no memory of the following several days during which he was unable to speak. Gradually, his "normal" conscious awareness returned but without overshadowing the simultaneous awareness of nonduality. Rational activity resumed but now accompanied by the intuitive in a profoundly integrated fashion.

Here is the experience of what Griffiths had described as reason and the other faculties being "taken up" into an intuitive mode, into a nondual awareness. In response to the second thematic question posed at the end of part two above, here as well is a taste of the "marriage" of the intellectual frameworks associated with his culture of origin and with India that he labeled "West" and "East." Here also is an experience of the soul outside of meditation with its faculties active and yet centered on "the point of the spirit," where all dualities are transcended and yet integrated. Finally, here is an experience of the "love of God" "poured into our hearts by the Holy Spirit."[59] Not surprisingly, this experience sparked further reflection upon the nature of *advaita* and the role of symbols in facilitating the experience of it.

9

God beyond the Symbols of the Religions

A s we trace the evolution of Griffiths's critique of cultures, his theory of mind, and his spirituality, the question arises of what moves
him from one stage to the next, from one point of view to its successor.
Griffiths's answer, as already suggested, is surrender or, more techni-
cally, self-transcendence. It is also significant to his self-understanding
that this movement is mediated by symbols, in the first period those of
nature and then in the second those of Christ and the church. The trajectory of this movement becomes ever clearer in the third period, as
disclosed in his account of what he sees through the window that opens
onto both the world outside and the world within. The ultimate goal of
the process of self-transcendence or surrender is, for Griffiths, portrayed most powerfully by the image of *advaita*, nonduality. The realization that reality is a nondual yet fully differentiated wholeness
echoes throughout his later writings on his intercultural journey, on
various means for gaining knowledge, on the nature of God, and on the
relationship between the religions. In each of these areas, Griffiths resolves tensions between diverse elements through a process of transcending the level of differences and then integrating the diversity into
a greater unity or wholeness. The secret to this ongoing process of realization is not an intentional act or expertise; nor can the principle of
transcendence and integration be effective if it remains merely an element of theory or an intellectual rule. The realization of *advaita* must
dawn within every sphere of one's life through an ever-deepening receptivity to the work of the Spirit, in other words, through surrender.

As in discussion of the previous two periods, implicit throughout the
following account is Griffiths's claim that his life is exemplary; that is,
out of his experience arise principles that are suggestive for the path of
all.

Symbolic Life of Shantivanam

It is not surprising that the transformation in Griffiths's point of view that accompanied the deepening of his contemplative life at Shantivanam affected not only his theory of the mind but also the way in which he applied his theory of religious symbol in the life of the ashram. Again, what seems to have happened to Griffiths at the time of, and especially after, the move to Shantivanam is a radical opening in his experience of contemplation and thus of his awareness of that which transcends all concepts and images, that is, all symbols. His subsequent discussion of the nature of religious symbols does not reflect a significant change in the theory already articulated while a monk in England. But a change is evident in the way in which he applied this theory to the practice of interreligious dialogue and to the liturgical life of the ashram.

The impact of Griffiths's deepening understanding and experience of *advaita* is evident in the bold statements that he makes in his writings from Shantivanam concerning the experience of the divine or transcendent mystery and the various symbols used to evoke and express that experience. Something in Griffiths's contemplative life has transformed his perspective: He speaks now with great assurance about the absolute and universal nature of the experience of the divine mystery beyond all concepts and images. Consequently, his sense of the relativity of all symbols as expressions of that mystery is heightened. In the clarity of this new perspective the common ground and the common symbolic character of all religions become strikingly apparent. In *Return to the Center* (1976), he writes: "All religion derives from a mystical experience, transcending thought, and seeks to express this experience, to give it form, in language, ritual, and social organization."[1]

The effort to express the mystical experience of the divine mystery is both necessary and inherently flawed for all religions, according to Griffiths. Words, like all thoughts, fail to capture the fullness of the experience that only the silence beyond all thoughts and words can represent. Nevertheless, words can help turn the mind toward this mystical experience; and the great religious symbols, if entered into with what Griffiths calls "faith," can mediate an opening to the divine mystery itself.[2] Where human effort fails in achieving and expressing the experience of this transcendent mystery, the divine is found reaching out through its own self-expression to provide access to the human. Writing in a fashion reminiscent of Karl Rahner's "Theology of the Symbol" (1966), yet with a far more synthetic perspective upon the various religions, Griffiths describes the power of the religious symbol in terms of a divine, as well as human, initiative:

This one Truth, which cannot be expressed, is present in all religion, making itself known, communicating itself by signs. The myths and rituals of primitive religion, the doctrines and sacraments of the more advanced, are all signs of this eternal Truth, reflected in the consciousness of man. Each religion manifests some aspect of this one Reality, creates a system of symbols by which this Truth may be known, this Reality experienced.[3]

Griffiths's appreciation of the role of symbols in relationship to the divine mystery is thus very similar to that expressed in the 1950s in England. But his application of this theory of religious symbols has broadened dramatically as a result of an intensified identification with that mystery itself more than with any particular symbol system—although Christianity remains his preferred context of experience and discourse. Thus, he expresses the familiar lines of his theory of religious symbols within a more accepting view of the truth in other religions characteristic of the third period of his life:

In each tradition the one divine Reality, the one eternal Truth, is present, but it is hidden under symbols, symbols of word and gesture, of ritual and dance and song, of poetry and music, art and architecture, of custom and convention, of law and morality, of philosophy and theology. Always the divine Mystery is hidden under a veil, but each revelation (or "unveiling") unveils some aspect of the one Truth. . . .[4]

Through their respective and diverse symbols members of all religions are drawn to experience the very same "Mystery," "Reality," and "Truth" because it is this "Mystery" that has expressed itself, and thus "hidden" itself, in the finite forms of the symbols of these various traditions. Griffiths may thus conclude that "The goal of each religion is the same."[5]

It was, then, with an accepting attitude toward the power of the symbols of other traditions that Griffiths reshaped the liturgical life of Shantivanam, participating thereby in the important project of the church in non-European cultures known as "inculturation." The worship life of Shantivanam prompted continuous reflection and decision regarding the role and effect of Christian symbols in an Indian context and Indian symbols in a Christian one, such as the use of non-Christian Scriptures in daily prayer services and the introduction of symbolic gestures usually found in the Hindu puja into the celebration of the Mass—efforts that some Christians found objectionable.[6]

Griffiths's openness to the potency of non-Christian symbols, however, raises an important question for him as a Christian: What is the status of Jesus Christ as a symbol in the fullest sense in comparison to the central symbols of other traditions?

The Christ Symbol in a Comparative Context

In the contexts of applying his theory of religious symbols to both comparative religious studies and inculturation after the move to Shantivanam in 1968, the synthetic direction of Griffiths's statements about the nature and role of religious symbols raises with greater urgency a question that was briefly treated in chapter 6. Are all religious symbols of equal spiritual value? Or, do "real symbols" exist outside the Christian Revelation? In particular, one may ask whether the transformation in Griffiths's point of view during the third period of his life affected his understanding of Christ as "the supreme symbol" of God in the context of dialogue.

In *Return to the Center*, Griffiths avoids the adjective "supreme" used in the 1950s and instead describes Christ as a unique revelation of God, complementary with others.[7] In his account of Christ as "the symbol of God," Griffiths again presents both the timeless and the historical dimensions of this self-expression of God as Logos, emphasizing the uniqueness of the latter in comparison to other "symbols," such as Buddha or Krishna. Unlike Rahner, Griffiths, however, does not uphold the humanity of the historical Jesus as being of equal revelatory status as his divine nature.[8] Jesus' humanity, like the form in time and space of any symbol, is conditioned by his context and, therefore, is somewhat limited. In his interior life, however, Jesus knew his unlimited and unconditioned relationship of love with the Father.[9]

Griffiths actually undertakes a comparison of a few of the key religious symbols found in different religions, specifically Krishna, Buddha, and Christ. After discussing their similarities and differences as symbols of the divine mystery, Griffiths concludes:

> The Buddha, Krishna, Christ—each is a unique revelation of God, of the divine Mystery, and each has to be understood in its historical context, in its own peculiar mode of thought. . . . Each revelation is therefore complementary to the other, and indeed in each religion we find a tendency to stress first one aspect of the Godhead and then another, always seeking that equilibrium in which the ultimate truth will be found.[10]

From Griffiths's perspective, then, these various religious symbols both reveal and hide the divine mystery through their historical forms, a quality that may be most fully affirmed through the concept of complementarity.[11]

The question concerning the status of the Christ symbol may be sharpened in response to the synthetic statements concerning the "one Truth" and its many symbols evoked by his experience of *advaita* at Shantivanam. If Jesus Christ is truly a "real symbol" in the Rahnerian sense, a self-expression of the divine mystery that is intrinsic to that mystery itself, then how can it be complementary to others unless they, too, are in some way "real symbols"? Griffiths's answer to this question is grounded in a Logos theology informed by both Justin Martyr and Rahner.

The Logos, whose "seeds" are to be found among non-Christian peoples according to Justin, is the full self-expression, the "real symbol," of the Father according to Rahner. To varying degrees the divine mystery has thereby expressed itself within the other cultures and religions of the world, revealing and hiding itself under symbols. For Griffiths, in contrast to both Justin and Rahner, the great symbols of the different traditions should indeed be considered "real symbols."[12] These diverse symbolic self-expressions represent different aspects of the divine mystery and thus should all be accepted in order to gain the fullest possible understanding of that mystery.

In identifying Christ as the Logos or "real symbol" of God, Griffiths, like some other Christian theologians, thus affirms that Christ is present in the other traditions.[13] Given his convictions regarding the universality of Christ and the limitations of the historical Jesus as a symbol of that Christ, Griffiths's position on the status of the Christ is closest to what is sometimes called a "universal Christology"—a position that has been described as follows: "On Christian grounds, it may be held that the divine person who appears in Jesus is not exhausted by that historical appearance. The symbols and myths of other religions may point to the one who Christians recognize as the Christ."[14]

In a 1992 reflection upon his use of the Jesus Prayer, Griffiths's Christology is clearly suggested:

> When I say, "Lord Jesus Christ, Son of God," I think of Jesus as the Word of God, embracing heaven and earth and revealing himself in different ways and under different names and forms to all humanity. I consider that this Word "enlightens everyone coming into the world," and though they may not recognise it, it is present to every human being in the depths of their soul.

Beyond word and thought, beyond all signs and symbols, this Word is being secretly spoken in every heart in every place and at every time. . . .

I believe that that Word took flesh in Jesus of Nazareth and in him we can find a personal form of the Word to whom we can pray and to whom we can relate in terms of love and intimacy, but I think that he makes himself known to others under different names and forms. What counts is not so much the name and the form as the response in the heart to the hidden mystery, which is present to each one of us in one way or another and awaits our response in faith and hope and love.[15]

While adopting this universal Christology, Griffiths nevertheless remains clear that, for him, Jesus Christ remains the fullest expression of that "divine person," of the Word of God.[16] In claiming first that Jesus is the Word known to others in different names and forms and second that Jesus is the fullest expression of that Word, is Griffiths being inconsistent and disclosing a persistent belief that Jesus does fulfill all other "real symbols"? The key qualification is that Jesus is "for him" the fullest expression of the divine mystery. Nevertheless, this tension lingers in Griffiths's later writings as will be discussed again in the next section.[17]

As noted in chapter 6, Griffiths claims that Jesus Christ is a unique symbol of the divine mystery in being a fully historical figure. In his writings, Griffiths also discusses the uniqueness of Jesus Christ as a symbol and his life story as a myth in terms of Jesus' particular experience of the divine mystery, an experience of intuitive insight into the divine nature and of his own status with respect to it—a status Griffiths characterizes as "identity in relationship" and "unity in duality."[18] In time, this unique experience of the divine mystery took on symbolic forms for the disciples, especially after Pentecost, and thus came to be expressed both in the story of Jesus' life itself and in the doctrines of the church. According to Griffiths, the actual events of Jesus' history as they are recalled in the Gospel narratives and the doctrinal formulations of the church, especially the Trinity, both constitute symbolic representations of Jesus' unique experience of God. It is through these representations that Jesus' followers then seek to realize a similar depth of relationship to the divine mystery in their own experience.

Through the deepening of his contemplative experience at Shantivanam, primarily through Christian symbols such as the Trinity,

Griffiths appears to come to a richer experience of the intuition expressed in Logos and Trinitarian theology which, in turn, informs his
understanding of Jesus' experience and of the Christ symbol.
Specifically, he describes the experiential resolution of the tension described in chapter 6 between the sacramental quality of all creation
(expounded in Hinduism and by some Christians) and the unique
symbolic efficacy of Christ as the Word of God. The Logos theology of
John's Gospel informs, and is confirmed by, Griffiths's experience
through the window of his hut. The vast diversity of creation, including the writer's own consciousness, is unified "in the light of the
Word" "through whom all things were made."[19] Christ, who as a "real
symbol" is identified with the Truth or Reality expressed in all religions, draws together the multiplicity of symbolic forms, uniting
them in their source. Griffiths's later experience of *advaita* will refine
this intuition.

Even after considering Griffiths's positions on the humanity of Jesus,
on the complementarity of religious symbols from different traditions,
and on Logos theology, one is still prompted to push Griffiths further
on the status of the symbol of Jesus Christ. In calling the church, with all
religions, to pass through the symbol to the "Reality," does Griffiths
suggest that one leaves Jesus Christ behind in order to experience fully
the mystery of God that he symbolizes?

For Griffiths, as a Christian seeks to approach the one mystery witnessed to by all the religions, he or she necessarily does so through the
particular symbolic mediations of the church—especially those provided by the Scriptures, the doctrines, and the liturgy, each of which reflects Jesus' experience. This starting point is significant not only in
defining the experiencer as a Christian but also in determining the kind
of experience that will result from "passing through" the symbol to the
Reality. In general terms, Griffiths argues, one may compare the experiences of the mystics of all traditions and find profound commonality;
all transcend to experience that which is beyond all images and concepts, named variously as Being, the Reality, God, and the One. But
while that which is experienced may be the same, the actual experience
of that will be quite different cross-culturally:

> The mystical experience . . . in each religion is an experience of
> God (the unconditioned) in the Spirit, that is, beyond image and
> thought, but in each religion the experience is conditioned by the
> images and thought patterns through which the experience is
> reached and necessarily seek expression through those same im-
> ages and thought patterns. Each person approaches God—the ul-
> timate reality—through the mental and moral conditions of his

religion, and these determine the mode of his experience. In other words mystical experience is always conditioned by the faith and the moral disposition of the believer.[20]

In this passage lies a significant, though relatively unexpressed, element of Griffiths's theory of religious symbols: The symbols through which the divine mystery has expressed itself in various traditions, though passed beyond in the experience of contemplation or "meditation," nevertheless shape to some degree the experience of the meditator.[21] Here is one part of Griffiths's response to the question of whether Jesus Christ as a symbol of the divine mystery is transcended when the Christian experiences the depths of meditation.

Rahner's implied response to the question of the relationship between the religious symbol and the experience of the divine mystery that it mediates further informs Griffiths's view. As the "real symbol" of God, Jesus Christ, in his divinity and his humanity, "contains" the reality of that which he symbolizes. No "going beyond" is either necessary or possible. For Rahner, to encounter fully the symbol of Jesus Christ *is* to encounter the divine mystery in a state of "mediated immediacy." Similarly, while for Griffiths the humanity of Jesus is transcended to experience the Logos who is Christ, that humanity nevertheless shapes the experience, as Jesus' Resurrection typifies.[22] In addition, what Griffiths has said regarding the complementary nature of the different great symbols found in the other religions implies that each mediates a somewhat different experience of the one "Reality," these differences corresponding to those between the symbols. Thus, in contrast to Rahner, Griffiths suggests that the totality of the divine mystery may be experienced in different ways corresponding to the different "real symbols." In Rahner's language, Griffiths contends that there is more than one mediation of immediacy, that is, the symbol is virtually transcended, and yet, it continues to shape the experience of the divine mystery.[23]

Griffiths's theory of religious symbols and the call to transcend all symbols in order to experience the silence of the divine mystery have important implications for speech about that mystery, that is, for theology in all traditions.

Symbolic Theology, Rethought in Terms of Mysticism

As a theologian, Griffiths accepted the mission given by Henri de Lubac to Jules Monchanin: "To rethink everything in terms of theology, and to rethink theology in terms of mysticism."[24] Essential to Griffiths's response to this call for a revision of theology was the recognition that all theological language is symbolic, that is, expressive of the divine mystery that is itself "Inexpressible":

> Without this basis in the Transcendent, the Inexpressible, all revelations would lose their meaning. They would become idols. Nothing can be spoken about God which does not become false if it is not referred to this transcendent Mystery. To say that God is good or wise or just, or even that he is Being, Truth or the Absolute, is simply untrue, if these words are used in their ordinary sense. They are signs which point beyond themselves to the Inexpressible. . . . The whole world is a sign of this Mystery, "from Brahma to a blade of grass." It is everywhere and nowhere. Everything speaks of it—the evil as well as the good, the pain and misery of life as well as the joy and the beauty—but it remains hidden. To speak of it is already to betray it; it is known in the silence of the world and of the self.

Nevertheless, just as the divine mystery must express itself in the Logos and through the Logos into the vast hierachy of symbols, so Griffiths concludes: "we must speak of it."[25]

Before examining Griffiths's understanding of the theological task, it is imperative, following de Lubac, to discuss the mystical basis of theology. Specifically, the relationship between the depths of mystical or contemplative experience and religious symbols must be developed further by means of two questions:

1. How do religious symbols originate in consciousness and therein make present the divine mystery they symbolize?

2. How do these symbols provide the means through which human beings may then experience the divine mystery?

Griffiths's answers to these two questions will be discussed in terms of symbolization, as the process through which symbols take form and are expressed in human consciousness, and self-transcendence, as the process by which symbols guide the mind through degrees of knowledge toward the contemplative state.[26]

A key prerequisite to these two processes is the mind's receptivity to the divine mystery through the spirit, as enhanced through contemplative practice, especially meditation. In order to become aware of symbolic processes as the basis of theology, one must experience one's own depth in which those processes occur:

This experience of God beyond image and concept in the depth of the human person is the source and goal of all theology. It is the source of theology, because all doctrine and sacrament, as at an earlier stage all myth and ritual, are an attempt to express in concept and image an experience which is originally beyond concept and image. Christian theology derives from the experience of Jesus, which like all genuine experience of God was strictly ineffable.[27]

The goal of all theology is to direct the mind back to the source of all such reflection, to the same depth of experience in which the divine mystery is known "beyond image and concept":

> The function of theology is to reflect on the terms in which the mystery of faith is expressed in the Scriptures and in the history of the Church in the light of the present experience of the Church and the world and so to renew the experience of the mystery of faith. Thus theology derives from a mystical experience and seeks continually to renew it by means of the words and images and thoughts through which that experience is expressed.[28]

The theological process thus interprets and further facilitates the mind's dual movements in response to religious symbols, from experience to expression (symbolization), and from expression to experience again (self-transcendence). Also apparent in Griffiths's view of the function of theology are the complementary roles of analytical reason ("to reflect") and intuitive awareness ("to renew the experience").

How is it that symbols originate in the depth of human consciousness and thereby make present the divine mystery? In the foreword to a text on Indian symbolism published in 1980, Griffiths explores from a psychological perspective the role of symbols in relation to the various depths of the human mind and their respective degrees of knowledge, advancing the earlier account described in chapter 3. In this foreword Griffiths begins with the image of what he calls "the primordial unity" or "the original darkness" within the evolving human psyche—suggesting parallels he would develop later between Oriental myth and the speculations of the so-called "new psychology."[29] Into this darkness and this unity breaks the light of consciousness as the human develops, bringing the differentiating awareness of self, other, world, and God. According to Griffiths, early on in this evolution the capacity to use symbols develops as a means to maintain harmony between that which consciousness divides.[30] As human awareness matures out of its primordial sense of unity with all that is, it becomes more and more fully conscious of the innumerable forms of life that have originated from the same "womb" of the unconscious as the human has.[31] Prior to the onset of the analytical abilities of the rational mind, the human expresses consciousness of this diversity of life through symbols within the imagination—what Thomas Aquinas called "the influence of spiritual substances" and "the subtle movements which are born in the imagination from the impressions of natural causes."[32] Griffiths describes such symbols by contrast with facts and concepts as follows:

> The symbol is not something static; it belongs not to the world of "fact"—of what has been done, which is finished and completed, which is also the world of death—but to the world of "actuality." A symbol is an "event." It is something which grows out of a situation, out of life itself. It has a life of its own, as every poet or artist knows. The rational, analytic mind separates the light from the darkness, the meaning from the event, and expresses itself in abstract concepts, which have a fixed meaning but no life. The symbol reunites meaning and event, understanding and life.[33]

Symbols are best conceived as "events" in consciousness that bridge the distance between subject and object, mental and physical, knowledge and life—or, "events" through which knowledge by identity or "connaturality" is realized.

In a religious context, symbols are events in human consciousness that mediate an experience of knowledge of the very ground of consciousness itself, the divine mystery, through a bridging or thinning of the separation between the spirit and the Spirit, the self and the Self. According to Griffiths, such events of what is called "meaning" are then expressed "in gesture and dance, speech and song, ritual and myth" in order to be shared and celebrated. Thus, symbols present the most effective entree into a religious tradition, for they represent not merely the concepts but the very "creative process . . . by which the ultimate meaning of life is discovered" in that tradition.[34]

The process of symbolization through which the self-expressions of the divine mystery take on forms in human consciousness and shape all thought and experience serves more than a private function; it is essential to the development of collective as well as individual consciousness. Particularly once enshrined in the myths and rituals of a religious tradition, the symbols or meaning-events of one person's experience may exhibit enduring power for mediating similar experiences for others. Here one may discern Griffiths's response to the question of how symbols guide others to experience the divine mystery. Symbols initiate a mental process, which Griffiths usually calls "intuition" or "self-transcendence," that is, the reverse of the gradual explication of the symbol within consciousness (symbolization). Religious symbols, as both expressions of the divine mystery and apprehensions of meaning, guide the mind's return to experience that same mystery.[35]

If the symbol is powerful enough and if the individual's awareness is highly receptive, experience of a symbol may draw the mind back through the various levels of consciousness to experience that ultimate point of receptivity, the spirit, through which the divine Spirit has originally expressed itself and been received. While poetry may evoke this kind of intuitive turn toward transcendence, Griffiths concludes that the symbols of the great revelations mediate this contemplative experience most fully.[36] Once one has become aware of the divine mystery through the mediation of the religious symbol, then one may verify through experience the further teaching that all of creation expresses and communicates its creator.

The problem arises in the West that for many people, including Christians, religious symbols do not hold the power to mediate the experience of the divine mystery in self-transcendence. Due to the rise and domination of the rational faculty over the imagination, according to Griffiths, access to the world opened up by religious symbols has become virtually blocked. He describes the plight of the West in terms of its inability to participate in symbolic expressions of the truth, that is, myths, and thereby to experience a depth of knowing not available through science:

> [T]he Western mind is prejudiced against myth. It is the defect of the scientific mind. The whole bent of science is to withdraw everything from the sphere of myth, to create a sphere of "fact" which can be observed and verified. This has its own value and is a necessary discipline of the mind. But it empties life of all meaning. . . . It is myth that opens the mind to these higher states of consciousness, while the scientist remains shut up in his little world of "facts."[37]

The scientist's "world of 'facts'" is the world "broken into pieces" described in the 1980 foreword that was just quoted. Griffiths's point is that no amount of theory can put all the pieces back together again; this is the role of symbol and myth. The situation created within Western cultures by the loss of the sense of symbol and openness to myth is dangerous:

> Man cannot live without myth; reason cannot live without the imagination. It creates a desert, within and without. It becomes the sword of destruction, bringing death wherever it goes, dividing man from nature, the individual from society, woman from

man, and man and woman from God. This is what the triumph of reason has done, and now we have to go back and recover the myth, return to the source, rediscover our roots, restore the wholeness to man and creation. The myth has to be reborn.[38]

Without an openness to the symbolic, self-transcendence cannot happen, leaving life fragmented and cut off from its source.

However, is the God that one encounters beyond all forms, concepts, and symbols still the God of the Christian revelation?

For Griffiths, the fundamental mystical experience in relation to which all theology must be "rethought" is the awakening to the divine mystery through and yet beyond all concepts and images, that is, all symbols. He supports this claim that theology be grounded in the mystical truth that God is transcendent mystery by turning to the biblical witness and to the example of the Church Fathers. Citing passages from both Testaments and from Clement of Alexandria, Origen, Dionysius the Areopagite, as well as from Aquinas, Griffiths affirms as orthodox the theological principle, based on mystical experience, that God is a mystery who transcends all names and all forms.[39] Nevertheless, one must speak about the experience of the transcendent mystery; however difficult, the attempt must be made to describe God using images, concepts, names, and forms. Furthermore, to attempt to convey the experience to others and recapture its holiness, one must resort to religious symbols. Yet, one should never forget, according to Griffiths, that all of these efforts to convey mystically realized truths result in imperfect reflections of the divine that are distorted by the mind. Griffiths finds a potent reminder of this principle of the transcendent nature of the divine mystery in the teaching of *neti, neti,* "not this, not this," found in the Upaniṣads and similar to Dionysius' negative theology.[40]

The contrast, as Griffiths sees it, between the degrees of self-consciousness with which Hindu and Christian theologians speak about God is based on their respective assumptions about the nature of religious symbols. Christianity is in need of recovering both its sense of mystery and its appreciation of symbols as mediators of the experience of that mystery. This need regularly arises in the history of all religions when the experiential inspiration supporting the use of symbols is lost; but the need is especially strong now in the West due to the dominance of rational ways of knowing:

The danger in every religion is, on the one hand, a slavish literalism, which clings to the letter or the outward form and loses the inner spirit, and, on the other hand, a crude rationalism, which empties the words and actions of all deeper meaning. The Bible and the Eucharist have both been subjected to this process continually.[41]

In other words, what has happened in Western Christianity, as in many religions before it, is the collective mistaking of the symbol for the reality, the *sacramentum* for the *res*, the image or concept for the truth by some, and by others the failure to recognize that the religious symbol is an expression and communication of the divine mystery itself rather than an arbitrary sign. The implications of these cultural habits for Christian theology are serious:

> In our Western tradition in theology we tend to translate experience into words and into thoughts and we begin to think that the words and the thoughts really are the object of our faith, but as a matter of fact it is not so. We do not believe in words or in doctrines, we believe in a mystery, the Mystery of Christ, the Word of God, that is beyond words and beyond thought. And so we have constantly to remind ourselves that we are using words and concepts to express a reality which is beyond words and concepts. . . . These words and concepts are symbols of something which is beyond and the whole movement of thought is to go beyond.[42]

The result of the church's failure to recognize the symbolic nature of its own theology, according to Griffiths, is that the Christian faith has become idenitified with assent to a body of dogmatic claims; dogmas themselves, like the Trinity and Incarnation, have become the objects of faith, rather than the living God, the divine mystery. In short, as Griffiths recognized while a monk in England, dogmas have not been understood as symbols, expressing and pointing to the mystery; the church has stopped short at the symbol and not gone beyond, with clear implications for its understanding of the theological task.[43]

What is needed, according to Griffiths, and what has already begun to be articulated by theologians such as Rahner, is a "new theology," which in fact is old by virtue of its Patristic foundations.[44] Such a theology is fully oriented to the divine mystery as its object of faith and is thus sensitively aware of the symbolic and analogical character of all theological language. Griffiths has taken seriously, and believes the church should as well, de Lubac's suggestion that all theology be rethought in terms of the mystical experience of the divine mystery that stands at the origin of all theological statements.[45]

This rethinking prompts the need within all religions for continual "demythologization" in order to free the symbols and myths from the extrinsic elements that become a focus of attachment rather than an aid to experiencing the mystery to which the symbols point.[46] According to Griffiths, even the historical symbols of the church, including Jesus Christ, stand in need of this kind of purification and renewal.

Implicit in Griffiths's account of the two processes of symbolization and self-transcendence is an understanding of how they correspond to the most fundamental symbols or dynamics within the Christian faith. Specifically, how symbols arise within human consciousness through encountering the divine mystery and are then expressed further in concrete forms is compared to incarnation. From the imagination, the symbols move into the forms of myth and ritual and thereby affect, and potentially transform, every aspect of human life. In other words, through this process of symbolic expression or explication, the divine mystery does indeed become incarnate in human life, though, as Griffiths so often says, in forms that both reveal and hide that mystery.[47]

In turn, the process to which the mind is subjected in transcending itself through the symbol to experience the divine mystery is compared by Griffiths to dying:

> This is the death we have to undergo, to go beyond the rational understanding, beyond the imagination and the senses, into the primeval darkness, where God, the divine mystery itself, is hidden. It is a return to the womb, to what the Chinese call the "uncarved Block," to the original darkness from which we came.

True to Christian symbolism, with this death comes a kind of resurrection, a new life in God, a new identity, a light of intuitive knowledge brought by grace alone:

> But now that darkness is filled with light, it is revealed as God. The senses, the imagination and reason by itself cannot pierce through that darkness, but when we die to ourselves, to the limitation of our mind which casts its shadow on the light, then the darkness is revealed as light, the soul discovers itself in the radiance of a pure intuition; it attains to self-knowledge.[48]

Such a "death," then, is a temporary dissolving of the dualistic mind as it awakens within the peace of the nondual experience symbolized by the Resurrection and lived by the *sannyāsi*.[49]

Theology, therefore, must undergo its own process of transformation powerfully symbolized as incarnation, death, and resurrection. Again and again, theologians must reflect upon the images and concepts through which the mystery of faith is communicated in the Scriptures, in worship, in doctrines, and in prayer in the light of the present experience of the community.[50] Such reflection must be based not upon rational analysis alone but also upon experience of the divine mystery beyond all images and concepts: "My patron St. Bede had a beautiful saying about theology: 'the only true theology is the contemplation of God'. . . . All theology should be leading to contemplation, to this realization of God."[51] Only from this mystical basis, for Griffiths, may one evaluate the viability of the intellectual and cultural forms given to the "real symbols."

At times, theology itself may need to enter into a kind of darkness or death in which the existing forms are let go and taken up into new symbolic expressions of the same essential truths that mediate experience of the divine mystery more fully for contemporary people. For Griffiths, interreligious dialogue played a significant role in this rethinking of theology. One key element from his experience of dialogue with Hinduism that he believed could serve to renew theology from its mystical origins is the symbol of *advaita*.

Christian Advaita

Griffiths's analysis of *advaita* as a philosophy and as an experience after his move to Shantivanam exhibits both continuity and development in comparison to his early writings from India. Enduring are the principles of relationship within the divine mystery, and between that mystery, the soul, and the world, and of realism regarding the soul and the world as God's creations. He continues to use the principles of relationship and realism to critique traditional Hindu interpretations of the nondual experience and to formulate what he calls a "Christian *advaita*."[52] Supporting both efforts are the doctrines of the Trinity, creation, and Incarnation, understood as symbolic expressions of fundamental spiritual experiences, that is, of the divine mystery and of that mystery's relationship to the world and to the soul, respectively. From 1968 on Griffiths's articulation of a Christian *advaita* and his experience of nonduality develop simultaneously.

In the third period of his life, Griffiths continued to propose that a Trinitarian model could best account for the nature of the divine mystery as experienced in mystical union.[53] The question is raised, How can one reconcile the experience of union with God as a bliss in which all distinctions are transcended with the experience of personal communion with a loving God?

It would seem that it is only the Christian doctrine of the Trinity, which is able to resolve this dilemma by conceiving the Godhead as absolute Being, one "without a second," infinitely transcendent, and at the same time having relations within itself, relations of knowledge and love, expressed in terms of a trinity of persons, who are one in essence (and therefore in no sense dual) and yet related by knowledge and love. The way is open therefore to communion within the Godhead; the Godhead is not simply being, knowledge and bliss, but also love and therefore communion.[54]

From a Christian viewpoint, it is equally correct to say that God is one, united with all manifestation, and that God is a communion of persons in which the soul may participate through love. The Trinity is the divine ground and model for the nonduality, the "unity in relationship," potential in the soul's relation to the divine.[55] The key passage in Griffiths's articulation of this principle of a Christian *advaita* is taken from Jesus' high priestly prayer in John's Gospel: "that they all may be one, as thou, Father, in me and I in thee, that they may be one in us" (17.20).[56]

In his Christian understanding of nonduality, Griffiths believes that the teaching of the Trinity, and by implication the contemplative experience supporting it, can shed light upon the Hindu experience and interpretation of *advaita*. The basic intuition that God is love, according to Griffiths, may be found in Hinduism as well, not only in the explicitly devotional sects but in the nondualist school as well.[57] Yet, the ability to articulate that intuition is hampered by the logical inconsistency in describing God both as "One 'without a second'" and as love, given that love always implies relationship—a problem that Griffiths also locates in other monotheistic faiths:

> The Hindu believes that God is love in a sense, and that you can love God but not that the Godhead Itself is love. There cannot be love without two. If God is a pure monad as He is in Islam, as He tends to be in Hinduism, He cannot be love in Himself. But in the Christian concept the Godhead Itself is love, is a communion of love. There is a distinction within the Godhead Itself, distinction beyond our comprehension which we crudely express in terms of person and relation. These are human terms pointing to the reality. The reality is that God is love, that there is something which corresponds to personal communion in love in the Godhead, and we are called to share in that communion of love.[58]

In terms of his theory of religious symbols, Griffiths suggests that the doctrine of the Trinity is an inexact way, as all religious symbols ultimately are, of communicating symbolically a fundamental spiritual experience, that God is self-surrendering love.[59] He further implies that the Christian symbols, however crudely based in metaphors from human experience, convey a richer understanding and a more intelligible account of what may be a similar experience of the divine mystery found in other religions.

Regarding the relation between the divine Spirit and the human soul (or *Paramātman* and *jīvātman*), Griffiths continues to apply the paradox of unity in relationship, characteristic of persons sharing through knowlege and love, in a way clearly analogous to the relationship between the "persons" of the Trinity. In support of the metaphor of the mirror image for this relationship between the divine mystery and the soul, Griffiths explores the parallels between the vision of the universe intuited by the "new science" and a nondualist view. One such parallel that is particularly important to Griffiths is the relationship between the whole and the part, especially as a vision of the ultimate state of realization alternative to the familiar metaphor of the drop merging and dissolving in the ocean found in the Upaniṣads. According to physical theorists such as Karl Pribram and David Bohm, it is clear from working with the hologram that not only is every part present in the whole, but the whole is also present in every part. Griffiths extrapolates as follows:

> In the ultimate state the individual is totally there, totally realized, but also in total communion with all the rest. There is the illustration, often used, of mirrors. There is one light and each mirror reflects the one light and reflects all the other mirrors. So it's diversified and yet it is all one.[60]

Thus, it is not a matter of the soul vanishing totally in the divine Spirit, the awakening to an always present unity that wipes away the "dream" of all individuality. Rather, the individual is transformed, taken up, aware of both his or her uniqueness and his or her oneness with the divine mystery. Again, for Griffiths, it is Jesus' experience that provides the model and evidence for these truths about the whole/part relationship. As conveyed in John's Gospel, Jesus' relationship to the Father is clearly nondual, not in the sense of an identity but a communion in love:

> If Jesus had been an *advaitin* he would have said, "I am the Father" or "I am God." Jesus never says that. In saying, "I am in the Father and the Father in me," "I know the Father and the Father knows me," "I love the Father, the Father loves me," Jesus is affirming total interpersonal relationship.[61]

As before, Griffiths is clearly implying that Jesus' path is exemplary and so is his realization. Through the divine or Holy Spirit, others may now participate in Jesus' unique experience of God, captured in his prayer of

Abba, described as "unity in relationship," and mediated through the symbols of the church.[62]

Griffiths also adapts the Platonic theory of "ideas" to answer the question of the relationship between the soul and the divine mystery. It is not a matter of one needing to achieve union with the divine mystery in order to create an intimacy that did not already exist:

> I think Maximus the Confessor expresses it the best I have ever found. He says that in moving towards God in knowledge and love, we are simply returning to our idea in Him. Even if I wander from God, our idea, that is the idea He has of each one of us, remains the same. Every person is a part of God, a *moira Theou*, "a part of God" to the extent that by his idea, his essence, he is eternally pre-existent in God.[63]

This view of each individual present "in God" as an "idea" is clearly an analogy, one that could be drawn out further to reflect upon the interrelationship between those "ideas" in the divine mind. Perhaps more revealing and more biblical is the similar analogy of the body of Christ.

Based upon the principle that the individual is not lost but rather taken up and transformed in union with God, Griffiths describes the mystical Body of Christ spoken of by Paul as a universal consciousness in which all persons are both distinct and united in the Person of Christ. What unites all persons in Christ is the very same love characteristic of the interpersonal life of the Trinity, that love in which all persons may participate through grace. Connecting the interpersonal communion or "coinherence" of the Trinity with the unity of all persons in the mystical Body of Christ, Griffiths writes:

> This concept of "co-inherence," of mutual indwelling of the Father in the Son and the Son in the Father through the Spirit of love, helps us to understand not only the nature of the godhead, but also the nature of human relationships within the godhead. When human nature is taken up by the Spirit into the knowledge and love of the Father and the Son, the human consciousness is opened up to the divine mode of consciousness. Each human consciousness is expanded so as to embrace all other spheres of consciousness, both of gods or angels and of men. There is mutual interpenetration at every level. Every being becomes transparent to every other being; each one mirrors the other and the whole.[64]

Far from being lost in the ocean of the Godhead, then, the soul, according to a Christian *advaita*, on realizing its fundamental nonduality with the divine Spirit, simultaneously experiences its "unity in relationship" with all other persons in a communion or wholeness symbolized as the mystical Body of Christ.

On the third central issue to be addressed in any theory of nonduality, Griffiths again employs the paradox of "unity in relationship" or in distinction as well as Plato's exemplarism in answering the question of how the world and the divine mystery are related. The principle that grounds insight into the relationship between the divine mystery and the world, as concerning the reality of the soul, is that of God's Word through whom all things were made and in whom all things continue to reside:

> [W]e have this coming forth of the Word from the Father, and the Word comes forth as distinct from the Father. All the distinctions in creation are found in principle in the Word. This is important because in the Hindu view you often hear that all differences disappear in the final state. We would say that those differences are eternally in the Word. There is the distinction between the Father and the Son which is the basis of the distinction of all creation from God, distinction and yet unity. The Son is really the principle of differentiation, and all the distinctions of the created order are contained in the Son as the Word or Logos.[65]

This is the vision of one who experiences the world unified in the light of Christ, an experience which, Griffiths implies, is quite different than that of the Hindu *advaitin* who claims that all distinctions are recognized as illusory in a nondual awareness. Such a vision comprehends the full meaning of the Christian symbol of Jerusalem, the City of God, where all is contained and united.[66]

Again turning to the theory of exemplarism, Griffiths explains the uncreated basis in the divine mind for the created world in terms of *ideas* and *archetypes:*

> The created world is a "reflection" of the uncreated archetypal world. Like an image in a mirror, it has only a relative existence. Its existence is constituted by this relation to God. It is in this sense that we can say with the Hindu school of Advaita, that God and the world are "not two" *(advaita)*. The created world adds nothing to God and takes nothing from him. Creation makes no change in him; change is in the creature.[67]

Due to its presence within the mind of God, the created world in its every detail and as a whole is indeed real and yet distinct from the reality of which it is a reflection.

It should be remembered that for Griffiths the nondual relationship between the world and God, between multiplicity and unity, between the many and the One, is potentially a reality of experience. It is because of the dualistic habits of most minds that the multiple world appears as fragmented and of uncertain relationship to its creator.[68] In meditation, however, through the experience of a different style of mind, the unity underlying the multiplicity becomes apparent. Griffiths is careful to assert that the multiplicity is not lost in this meditative experience of unity, nor is this vision of the many in the One restricted only to meditation. Potentially one may live in the world with this nondual awareness present along with the dualistic modes characteristic of sensory experience and rational activity, as "the view from his window" illustrates.[69]

Finally, Griffiths is convinced that the relationship between God and the world, unity and multiplicity, the One and the many, has been clearly intuited not only in Christian theology and in some Eastern mysticism, but also in modern science. The Christian theologian and scientist, Teilhard de Chardin, for instance, wrote that, "union differentiates" instead of removing all distinctions.[70] In Bohm's principle of the "implicate order," Griffiths finds a physical parallel for the total potentiality present in the unexpressed wholeness, for multiplicity in unity, with the added suggestion that the entire "implicate order" is present in every detail of matter and moment of consciousness.[71] Wilber's articulation of the dynamics necessarily present in any shift in consciousness (individual or collective) in terms of transcendence and integration also provides the basis for analogies between the physical, psychological, and spiritual realms that bear upon Griffiths's view of nonduality.[72]

Drawing the various parallels between Western science, Eastern mysticism, and Christian theology together, Griffiths identifies a common evolution of matter and consciousness from undifferentiated unity through various levels of differentiation to reach finally a fully differentiated unity that perfectly reflects the nondual being of the divine mystery:

> In the beginning the universe was undifferentiated. The original cosmos was an undifferentiated unity; the earliest human consciousness was an undifferentiated consciousness. We emerge through all the levels of consciousness, the physical, the vital, the emotional, the imaginative, the rational and the transrational until we reach a fully differentiated unity. The ultimate reality is a differentiated unity which transcends all categories of human thought, but in which all forms of being are integrated in a transcendent unity, which as far as it can be described in human terms is a communion of love, that is, of inter-personal relationship,

which recalls the description of the universe in modern physics as a "complicated web of interdependent relationships."[73]

Griffiths thereby affirms, in response to the question of the relationship between the multiple creation and the nondual divine mystery, that the world is indeed an "image," a symbol of God.[74]

As noted in his prior explorations of the same question, maintaining the reality of this world as well as of the soul and their relationship to God has practical as well as philosophical implications for Griffiths. In his view, a Christian *advaita* can uphold the eternal significance of the world, the person, and human history, knowing that it is in God "that we live and move and have our being" (Acts 17.28). Such an outlook will profoundly affect how human beings live out their day-to-day existence:

> If we think that the universe is ultimately unreal and that our own lives are unreal we will live accordingly. But it will make all the difference to how we live when we realise that this universe is created by God, that it has eternal value, that each one of us has an infinite eternal value in the sight of God and that we all form a unity which yet embraces all diversity.[75]

Such an appraisal of the creation would support the "organic understanding of nature" that Griffiths and others claim is replacing the mechanistic view prevalent in the West by enhancing "a sense of the cosmic whole" and of humanity's important role within that wholeness.[76]

In summary, by interpreting the nature of the divine mystery and its relationships to both the world and the human soul in terms of Christian doctrines (and thereby Jesus' own experience of nonduality), Griffiths believes that great clarity can be brought to the often misinterpreted truth of *advaita*. Careful to distinguish between Hindu and Christian experiences of the nondual reality, Griffiths claims that a Christian *advaita* has much to offer to the Hindu, just as Christianity has much to learn from Hinduism regarding spiritual methods for opening to a nondual experience. The key to a Christian *advaita* is the experience and the identification of a principle of differentiation within the Godhead itself that in turn grounds and unifies the diverse creation of that Godhead. On the basis of such a principle, an adequate account can be given for the nature of God as love, and for the enduring "unity in relationship" characteristic of the divine's relation to the human realm and to creation as a whole. That principle in Christian terminology is the Logos as revealed in the form of the supreme Person, Christ.[77]

Griffiths's account of the role of the Logos in the nondual reality that is God as well as his critique of the monistic and world-denying tendencies of Advaita Vedānta suggest an important third movement in the life of the symbol in human consciousness, completing the prior movements of symbolization and self-transcendence.

The Symbol's Reintegration as a Movement of Love

Griffiths defines the religious symbol as the means through which the divine mystery expresses and communicates itself to human consciousness. According to Rahner's ontology of the "real symbol," this expression and communication is based upon the inherent nature of being to know and love itself, a nature whose fulfillment is perfectly represented within the Godhead by its Trinitarian nature. As both Rahner and Griffiths assert, the supreme example of the "real symbol" is the Logos, the Word who serves as the object of the divine self-knowledge and love mediated by the Spirit. Besides its role within the Trinity, the Logos also serves as the image of God that draws together the vast diversity of the created world. Following two of the key analogies used by Griffiths, one can describe the Logos as the idea or archetype that contains all other ideas or archetypes representing the elements of creation within the mind of God; or, one can portray the Logos as the Person (or "Supreme Person," *Puruṣottama*) in whom all persons belong and realize their true nature. The Logos is the divine's eternal symbolization of itself and thus serves as the ultimate source and ground of all other symbols manifest in space and time. It is the special function of religious symbols to reverse this process of manifestation by pointing beyond themselves to that which they ultimately signify, the Logos.

As one who experiences and understands the divine mystery primarily through Christian symbols, Griffiths's most fundamental conviction is that God is love. Love is the mystery that the living and historical symbol of the Logos who is Jesus Christ made present under a specific, culturally conditioned form and continues to make present through the particular symbols of the Christian community. Among these symbols of the church are the doctrines of creation, Incarnation, and Trinity, each of which points to an aspect of the divine mystery who is love: Out of love, the divine mystery expresses and communicates itself in creating the world in its own image, the Logos, thus founding a nondual relationship between Creator and creation in which all distinctions are nonetheless preserved. Furthermore, it is compassionate love that is symbolized by the divine mystery becoming so fully present in a particular historical person, Jesus Christ, through whom all persons may return to a nondual relationship with their God.[78] Finally, the doctrine of the Trinity is the inspired way in which the church has sought to symbolize the mysterious love within the Godhead itself that is then made manifest in the creation and the Incarnation.

Extrapolating from Griffiths's theory of religious symbols, one also can describe that which moves the divine mystery to express and communicate itself in human consciousness (initiating the process of symbolization) and that which draws the mind toward its source through such "real symbols" (self-transcendence) as love, the very same love that moves and guides the relationships within the divine mystery itself. This dynamism found both within the divine mystery and in human consciousness is one love in two movements, a going out of the lover toward the beloved and a return of the beloved to the lover. A Christian *advaita* affirms that both in the divine mystery and in human consciousness these movements occur within the context of a nondual relationship between the lover and the beloved, who are thus "not-one" and "not-two." Griffiths, citing Rahner, asserts that these same two movements exist within the historical relationship between God and humanity.[79]

A close reading of Griffiths's later writings discloses what may be called "a third movement of love" both within the divine mystery and in human consciousness—a completion of the prior movements of symbolization and self-transcendence that is implied by his conviction that the soul and the world ultimately are realized as within the divine mystery. Griffiths suggests that the experience of what he sometimes calls "pure" *advaita* where all distinctions do disappear is an incomplete realization of the ultimate reality or divine mystery. In the experience of *samādhī* or "the 'still state' of *Brahman*," the world of differences is indeed lost, corresponding to that level of being known in Hindu cosmology as the *avyakta*, the unmanifest (or the imperishable). Citing Krishna's teachings in the *Gītā* as comparable to a Christian understanding, Griffiths claims that one must go beyond not only the physical and psychological realms but also this state of *samādhī* where the world of differences is lost in order to discover the Personal God, the Supreme Person (the *Puruṣottama* or "Christ"). Only when the Supreme Person is encountered does the realization of "distinction and yet unity" in the Logos who is that Person manifest itself.[80] Here again is an illustration of the principle from Wilber that at each stage of development in human consciousness the former stage is both transcended and integrated. In "the 'still state' of *Brahman*," the world of differences has been transcended, but it has not yet been reintegrated into a vison of the "unity in relationship" characteristic of the Logos. This third movement of reintegration appears clearly in Griffiths's interpretation of John Ruusbroec, the fourteenth-century Rhineland mystic and theologian.

For Ruusbroec, the soul as an eternal archetype within the *Logos* subsists in a relationship to the Godhead that is clearly nondual in the sense that Griffiths uses the term and in a way that is directly parallel to the nonduality of the Persons within the Trinity.[81] Griffiths also finds in Ruusbroec a rich account of the soul's participation in the inner life of the Trinity, one that engages the soul in an eternal going forth and return that correspond to the dual movements just described. Interpreting Ruusbroec's vision of a contemplative union with the Godhead, Griffiths writes:

> This is a coming back to the original unity. Everything comes forth from that original unity, from the Father, in the Son and the Spirit. We come forth in time and space with all our differences, all our conflicts, with all the sin and evil of the world, and then we are drawn back by the love of God. Love is drawing us out of our sin and out of the limitations of this world to the inner image, to the archetype within, and then in that image, in Spirit, we return through the Son to the Father and we reach unity again. We know ourselves in God, as God.[82]

Clearly similar between Ruusbroec and Griffiths's accounts of the common dynamism in the inner life of the Trinity and of the soul is the role of love as the underlying cause of movement.

For Ruusbroec, it is participation in the inner life of the Godhead that not only draws the soul back to a restful union within the Godhead but also then moves the contemplative, as divine love itself flows, back to serve the creaturely world.[83] This experience, reflecting Jesus' own, has been clearly expressed through the Christian doctrinal symbols relating love of God and love of neighbor. Similarly, in Griffiths's later thought, the contemplative encounter with God who is love is understood as leading one back into the world. Openness to God through the spirit simultaneously brings a renewed availability to be divine love for the entire creation. In this utter willingness to serve, Griffiths identifies a further depth of surrender, *sannyāsa*:

> You renounce all external attachments, all attachments to your own psyche, your own personality, and open up to God beyond, but when you encounter God, the infinite One at that point, you encounter love. You open on to a sphere of total inner freedom, and you're open now to humanity again. At each point you go in, and then as you find the deepest center, you open out on everybody and everything. This is the secret really. You discover the Holy Spirit as Love, and love is a dynamic power which sends you out.

And it may send you to live in a cave in the Himalayas. . . . But equally, you might be sent to the slums of Calcutta as a *sannyāsi*.[84]

The life of surrender, epitomized for Griffiths by the *sannyāsi*, entails more than a renunciation of the world but a return to it. The freedom that results from a full self-transcendence beyond "the world of signs" necessarily returns one to that "world" to serve either through silence or action. The soul that has realized its relationship to, and oneness with, the communion of love who is God, naturally moves out to re-create that communion in community. Griffiths is implying that love never remains static; it always seeks to include, to embrace more within its dynamic and nondual communion.

The return of the soul into the world of multiplicity, reflecting the eternal movement of love within the Trinity itself, also corresponds to a third stage in the life of the symbol within consciousness that has always been implicit in Griffiths's theory but that became more explicit as his experience and reflection deepened in the third period of his life. Griffiths named this third essential movement, which completes what have here been called "symbolization" and "self-transcendence," "integration" or "reintegration," perhaps drawing upon Wilber's principles guiding the transformation of consciousness. This third movement is symbolized historically by the Resurrection of Jesus Christ that completed his Incarnation and death.[85] It is fundamental to Christian doctrine that upon his death Jesus did not merely rejoin the Father in union. Rather, he returned to us through his Spirit to continue the transformation of the world, drawing all things to himself in love through the symbol of his Person as the Logos. Similarly, Griffiths comes to identify this third movement of the soul as the necessary completion of the life of the symbol within consciousness. Through having been transcended and then integrated into a transformed state of consciousness, the religious symbol, like the soul, is now thoroughly transparent—in Seyyed Hossein Nasr's terms, an *immediate symbol*—uniting and integrating the One and the many, the transcendent source and the world of multiplicity.[86] Here is the resolution of the tension just discussed between Griffiths's repeated call to "go beyond" the symbol to experience that which it symbolizes and Rahner's theory of the "real symbol" according to which such transcendence is neither necessary nor possible. Transcending the religious symbol is indeed an essential step toward experiencing the reintegration of that symbol in consciousness as an intrinsic self-expression of the divine mystery.

For Griffiths, then, the ultimate requirement for all who would fully know the divine mystery is that everything of this world, including all

symbols and myths, be surrendered. This requirement is itself symbolized, for Griffiths, in the ideal of *sannyāsa*.[87] The life of the *sannyāsi*,
which Griffiths himself followed almost since the beginning of his time
in India, is defined by him as a life in which "the world" in the biblical
sense and in the stricter sense of the world of appearances is fully renounced.[88] For Griffiths, as for the tradition of Christian *sannyāsis* of
which he was a part, such a life has important implications for the observance of one's religion, constituted as all religions are by symbolic expressions of the one Reality or divine mystery. Symbols belong to the
world of appearances or signs that the *sannyāsi* must renounce. Griffiths
elaborates the implications of this calling for the Christian as follows:

> The Church also belongs to this world of "signs." The doctrines
> and sacraments of the Church are human expressions or signs of
> the divine reality, which are likewise destined to pass away. So
> also Christ himself is the "sacrament" of God; he is a sign of God's
> grace and salvation, of God's presence among men, and this sign
> also will pass, when the Reality, the thing signified, is revealed.
> Finally God himself, in so far as he can be named, whether
> Yahweh or Allah or simply God, is a sign, a name for the ultimate
> Truth, which cannot be named. Thus the Sannyasi is called to go
> beyond all religion, beyond every human institution, beyond
> every scripture and creed, till he comes to that which every reli-
> gion and scripture and ritual signifies but can never name.[89]

The *sannyāsi* thus symbolizes the death with respect to symbols experienced in self-transcendence.

Griffiths is equally clear in his conviction, however, that to transcend
all religious myths and rituals is not to reject the value of symbols but
rather to engender an essential detachment toward them. In Griffiths's
own experience, the effect of living the life of a *sannyāsi* was that he felt
freer to appreciate the value and function of all religious symbols as
necessary means for approaching the divine mystery. The key to this
freedom is abandoning the habit of attachment to symbols that thereby
become idols. With the mind free, one may surrender to the attraction of
the mystery communicated through its own self-expression and also allow the symbols to be reintegrated into one's life as a *sannyāsi*. In the
following passage, Griffiths presents both the relativity and the necessity of religious symbols:

> To go beyond the sign is not to reject the sign, but to reach the thing
> signified. In the language of St. Thomas Aquinas, it is to pass from
> the *sacramentum* to the *res*. As long as we remain in this world we

need these signs, and the world today cannot survive unless it rediscovers the "signs" of faith, the "Myth," the "Symbol," in which the knowledge of reality is enshrined. But equally fatal is to stop at the sign, to mistake the sign for the ultimate reality. It is this that sets one religion against another and divides Christians from one another, from people of other religions and from the rest of the world. This is essentially idolatry. . . . The Sannyasi is one who is called to witness to this Truth of the Reality beyond the signs, to be a sign of that which is beyond signs.[90]

For Griffiths, the vocation of the *sannyāsi* to "go beyond" is a life of surrender, mirroring the life of the symbol in consciousness as it points beyond itself and eventually mediates its own transcendence by the mind. But this vocation is only completed when the *sannyāsi* also returns to the world of symbols. Ultimately, the *sannyāsi* is, for Griffiths, not only an ideal spiritual aspirant but also a model for the theologian who must move through and interpret the world of symbols with the same depths of detachment and freedom.

Griffiths's description of the *sannyāsi* suggests that these states of spiritual realization reflect a development of consciousness beyond a critical, analytical phase in which symbols lose their status as unquestioned mediators of revelation, are found opaque, and are set aside as inadequate representations of the truth. Having allowed the symbol to undergo a kind of death and the mind to transcend all images and concepts, the divine mystery is experienced. As death opens into the new life of Resurrection, the close relationship between the divine mystery and its almost infinite self-expressions in symbols becomes apparent, renewing the experiencer's appreciation of, and availability to, those symbols. In Wilber's language, what was transcended is now found integrated within the new state of realization. In this state may be the experiential basis for the renewed symbolic theology glimpsed by contemporary theorists. It is subject for further study whether such accounts of spiritual realization describe the path that someone who has undergone a critical awakening to the relativity of religious symbols necessarily must travel in order to experience what some have discerned as the required next step in Western cultures' tenuous relationship to the religious symbol.[91]

Awakening within the Nondual Reality

A significant catalyst for Griffiths's theological reflection upon *advaita* in his final years was the spiritual awakening that accompanied his stroke in January 1990. This awakening represented the culmination of his theoretical and experiential exploration of nonduality since the move to Shantivanam over twenty years before, and it set him upon a new direction during the three years before his death. The primary symbol through which he opened to a fuller experience and understanding of the divine mystery was the Trinity.[92] Specifically, it was through the symbol of the Trinity that his experience and understanding of self-transcendence as "the way of love" and of the divine mystery as an interpersonal "communion of love" deepened—a love that evoked, and responded to, his continuing surrender.

The parallel between the description of his own spiritual awakening and the following claim from a 1991 lecture is not mere coincidence but reflects his conviction that he had touched a reality toward which all (at least all Christians) are called:

[T]his is the experience of God which we have to seek, to transcend ourselves in a total self-giving in love and find ourselves taken up into an ocean of love, which is at once deeply personal and at the same time transcends all human limitations. It's deeply personal, and we must always keep that in our hearts; but it is also beyond anything we can conceive of person. It's like an ocean really. So the two aspects are there: It's a personal communion, a personal relationship, but it transcends all the limitations of a person and takes us into the depths of the divine being itself.[93]

It is into this "ocean of love" that is the interpersonal yet nondual life of the Godhead that Griffiths felt himself moving through the symbol of the Trinity.

As the sources for his reflection on *advaita* after the stroke, Griffiths relied heavily upon the New Testament as well as upon the Upaniṣads. A topic of examination throughout his life, the nature of the New Testament, and thus of Jesus himself, came more fully into focus in his final years. In the aftermath of the spiritual awakening that accompanied his stroke, he claimed ever more boldly that in Jesus' relationship to God one may discern a call to nonduality similar to that found in the Asian traditions.

Relying upon contemporary biblical scholars such as Raymond Brown and James Dunn, Griffiths speaks of the contrast between what Jesus actually taught and what the early churches soon organized into a religion. Griffiths finds great importance in the conclusion that Jesus left nothing behind him except his Spirit, that is, no words, no rituals, no offices, and no structures. One of the only exceptions is, perhaps, the Aramaic word Abba that above all expresses the intimacy of Jesus' relationship to God as Father. Significant for Griffiths in Jesus' use of this name for God is the striking contrast to the image of Yahweh that pervades the Old Testament and Judaism as a whole, an image that reinforces divine transcendence and the unbridgeable duality in the human's relationship to God. Griffiths speculates further that Abba may have served as a kind of mantra for Jesus, mediating and expressing his intimacy with God as Father, and moving him beyond the duality inherent in the Jews' relationship to Yahweh. Griffiths does not deny the validity of the Jewish experience as it is expressed in the Old Testament, but portrays it as a necessary stage beyond which Jesus and thus all of humanity must go, toward a nondual relationship with God.[94] While many Gospel passages record a Jesus conditioned by the dualistic tradition of his origin, Griffiths believes that Jesus' death on the cross marks his complete surrendering of all images of God, and thus of all duality, to be transformed into a being of total love in communion with the divine mystery. Once resurrected, Jesus comes to embody *advaita* beyond all limitations, that is, no longer "under the sign" of his historical identity ("Christ from a human point of view" [2 Cor. 5.16]), but as a very real and timeless presence.[95]

The New Testament witness to Jesus' passing beyond all the dualities characteristic of his Jewish heritage culminates for Griffiths in the seventeenth chapter of John's Gospel, "the summit of Christian religion." Griffiths's understanding of the key verse of this chapter for a Christian *advaita* (17.21) again reflects his experience of the deepening mystery of love into which he felt drawn:

> "May they all be one: as you, Father, are in me, and I in you, so also may they be in us." Here Jesus shows that he is totally one with the Father and yet he is not the Father. It is a nondual relationship. It is not one and it is not two. When two people unite in love they become one and yet keep their distinctiveness. Jesus and the Father had this total communion in love, and he asks us to become one with him as he is one with the Father: total oneness in the nondual being of the Godhead. It is the Christian calling, to recover this unity.[96]

For Griffiths, it is in John's Gospel that a full understanding of Jesus' realization of *advaita* and of the Christian vocation to open to God in a nonduality of love is found in a mature form.

According to Griffiths, it is the resurrected Jesus, not Jesus "from a human point of view," whom one meets in both the sacraments and in meditation. Yet Griffiths distinguishes between the sacramental presence of Christ in the Eucharist and the real presence of Christ encountered in the silence of meditation. The former has a value and plays a central role in the life of the church, but ultimately the church is called beyond to experience Jesus' Spirit directly in the heart through meditation.[97] In meditation one moves through the humanity of Jesus (the sign) to that which it signifies, the Father. More precisely, one moves in meditation through and beyond the mantric symbol, beyond the name and form, to experience the interpersonal and nondual "communion of love" who is God. Quoting what is significantly the most meaningful statement for him by John Main, Griffiths points to this Trinitarian experience as follows:

> Jesus reveals the Father as a source of infinite love, which he shares with the Father. It is the goal of Christian meditation, as Fr. John said, "to share in the stream of love which flows between Jesus and the Father and is the Holy Spirit."
>
> Christian meditation consists in entering into the "stream of love" in the intimacy of a personal union with the persons of the Trinity. Meditation leads us to that depth where the Holy Spirit is present and takes us into the inner mystery of God's life and love.[98]

As he said often, to "stop short" at the sign, whether it be the humanity of Jesus or the Eucharist or the mantra, instead of moving through them to the divine mystery they signify, is idolatry.[99]

Griffiths's experience of *advaita* in the early 1990s not only confirmed the truth behind Trinitarian doctrine, Jesus' spiritual transformation, and the identification of God as love, but also supported his conviction that such an experience of union with God does not entail leaving the world of dualities behind as so-called pure *advaitins* have claimed. Griffiths's account of his spiritual awakening implies that the unity he experienced is one that includes all multiplicity. By contemplating the nondual nature of the Godhead, he lived into a fuller appreciation that all multiplicity is not lost, but rather is contained, in the divine mystery—an intuition that guided his understanding of *advaita* from his earliest encounters with this philosophy in England.[100]

In the context of his 1991 lectures on Christian meditation, he elaborated upon this same point of "reintegration," weaving together his own experience and an interpretation of Mahāyāna Buddhism:

> My understanding of *advaita* is there is a unity which is beyond and within the whole universe. And if you concentrate on the beyond, then this universe may seem as nothing. But when you look more deeply, you see that all differences in this world and

you and I and every human being are integrated in the unity of the one. It's not a blank unity. Like the void of Mahāyāna Buddhism, it's not just emptiness. It's an emptiness which is totally full. And always when you get to that point you come to the world of paradox, that it's both empty and it is full. . . . *[N]irvāṇa* and *saṃsāra,* the way of the world, are one. It's a wonderful insight: You go to *nirvāṇa,* you leave the world behind and you enter this emptiness. And then you rediscover the whole multiplicity of the world in *nirvāṇa.* And that to me is the deepest insight. And that was my experience very much. When I had this break as it were, the mental faculties had rather collapsed; . . . unity was found; but everybody and everything was in the unity. And that's where I feel we have to move.[101]

The soul and the world are not illusory but real, yet in a way that is dependent upon the reality of the divine mystery. The relationship between the divine mystery, the soul, and the world has been experienced as nondual.

Here again is the familiar principle of transcendence and integration essential to Griffiths's understanding of evolution within all spheres of life: Like Jesus, one is called to transcend all of one's projections or images of God, only to receive the divine mystery ever more intimately. Letting go of the world of multiplicity *(saṃsāra)* entirely, one discovers it anew in the light of an underlying unity. Giving oneself completely in love, one finds oneself again "taken up into an ocean of love," not dissolved but distinct in the "not-one, not-two" relationship of the lover and the beloved. Forsaking all forms and symbols, one goes beyond them to experience reality as nondual, yet a nonduality in which all forms and symbols are somehow "integrated" or "contained."[102]

To the end of his life, Griffiths's spiritual experience and theological reflection continued to be closely interdependent. The fruit of his spiritual breakthrough was not a change of course but rather a confirmation of the insights he had received intuitively and gathered intellectually, especially in the third period of his life. Specifically, his early convictions regarding the nature of the divine mystery and its relationships to the soul and to the world were affirmed by his experience during and after the 1990 awakening. On the basis of his evolving experience, he felt qualified to critique other interpretations of *advaita,* including that of his predecessor at Shantivanam, Henri Le Saux or Abhishiktānanda. Griffiths concluded that Abhishiktānanda had not fully lived out the three necessary stages in one's relationship to the nondual mystery that is God. Specifically, he believed that his French predecessor failed to experience the final surrender in which all the distinctions lost through self-transcendence are reintegrated within the unity. Nevertheless, the similarities between the two Christian *sannyāsis* also aid an understanding of Griffiths's vocation in India.

For both writers, the momentum of surrender, deeply instilled by the vow of *sannyāsa*, carried them beyond even the symbols of Christ and the church, but did not undermine their conviction that these symbols are significant, "real symbols" of the divine mystery. Thus, neither Abhishiktānanda nor Griffiths left the church; having renounced renunciation itself, they lived within the church as a reminder of that which is beyond it. This is the deeper surrender of being in the world, though not of it. The position of the *sannyāsi* with respect to religion, then, is a tenuous one. It is not that the surrender calls one to adopt a kind of superreligion or a false view of neutrality toward all religions.[103] Rather, one is called to transcend religion altogether, a step that alone allows a legitimate, though completely unbinding, participation by the *sannyāsi* in a religious tradition. This call to self-transcendence must also be heard at the institutional level, according to Griffiths; and, according to Abhishiktānanda, it is in this call that the various traditions will eventually meet. Ultimately for both writers, the momentum of surrender moves one into the total self-giving in love that is symbolized by *advaita*.[104]

In spite of the commonality found in how Abhishiktānanda and Griffiths describe the *advaita* into which their respective observance of *sannyāsa* led them, there are clear differences, reflecting perhaps the different ways in which they felt called to fulfill that observance; for example, Abhishiktānanda and Griffiths provide different models of cross-cultural spirituality. In response to the question posed at the end of part two of whether one may fruitfully draw upon the spiritual riches of another tradition to foster one's own spiritual awakening, both Christian *sannyāsis* would have answered "yes." Both not only drew from the scriptural heritage of Hinduism in their theological reflection, they also engaged in spiritual practices derived from Indian sources. Nevertheless, while Abhishiktānanda "plunged" into the experience of *advaita* beyond all symbols with the abandon of radical faith, Griffiths always held onto the Jesus Prayer as a connection to Christ and to the tradition.[105] Some might argue as a result that Griffiths also succeeded more clearly in maintaining the integrity of his faith commitments even while immersed in cross-cultural practice.[106]

However one explains the divergence between Griffiths and Abhishiktānanda, it is true to the spirit of both writers to admit diverse ways in which the nondual reality may be realized and then expressed. From the admission of potential diversity of nondual realizations through the path of surrender there follows the related point that each *sannyāsi,* and in fact all persons, have a distinct mission. Here clarification of how Griffiths's own journey into *advaita* might effect the cultures around him may be found. While criticized by others, including Griffiths, for his "acosmism," Abhishiktānanda defended the role played by those few who removed themselves almost totally from society to pursue the highest spiritual ideal. Such persons, he said, may inspire others from a distance in the same way that the unattainable peaks of a beautiful mountain range do.[107] They remain symbols of that which goes beyond all cultures, however inexpressible that reality may be, and so draw others beyond their own cultural limitations in order to awaken to a new freedom within those same boundaries. Such persons (and Abhishiktānanda clearly approached this ideal), however, cannot be called culture-bearers in the sense discussed here because they do not bridge two worlds or ages (as Augustine and Griffiths did) as much as they stand as challenging representatives of another world or age in stark contrast to the "world of signs" in which most people live.

In contrast to Abhishiktānanda, it is clear that Griffiths's path of surrender was one that sought step-by-step to maintain the link between the world of *advaita* and the world of signs as two different levels of experience that may and must eventually be integrated. While taking perhaps a more cautious route, Griffiths felt called to bring Western Christian cultures, and to a lesser degree the cultures of the East, faithfully to the brink of their own self-transcendence. This caution enabled him to express more carefully, though some might say less charismatically, both the relationship and the radical distinction between the divine mystery and the symbols that guide the various cultures to experience that mystery. The path he was given thereby facilitated the eventual integration that he intuited from early on. Not having cast his multicultural sensitivity aside as he approached the mystery of nonduality, he was better able to chart the course that the cultures must themselves take in attaining their own self-transcendence and reintegration. Through his constant efforts to articulate the way of surrender and the realization of *advaita* in terms intelligible to the West he truly bore his culture of origin toward its transformation within himself.

That the transformation Griffiths sought through his exploration of nonduality was more than personal is illustrated through his deepening commitment to dialogue at many levels in the final period of his life.

Through Dialogue

In the first period of Griffiths's life, his experience of God in nature evoked a method for renewing and analyzing this experience through rational and nonrational means—representing two sides of himself and of his culture of origin that he perceived in conflict, rather than in dialogue, with one another. This independent, noninstitutional approach to truth encouraged a generally tolerant attitude toward all religious forms and teachers, while he remained committed to none of them. In the second period, as a result of his experience of conversion and monastic life, he sought to reconcile the exercise of reason with his commitment to Christian faith as a source of knowledge, eventually engendering a creative dialogue between the rational and nonrational, represented as "West" and "East" both within himself and in the world. This institutionally oriented and religiously committed approach to truth fostered an evaluation of non-Christian religions identifiable as the fulfillment theory. In the third period, Griffiths's context shifted to the contemplative orientation of Shantivanam, providing the opportunity for deeper meditative opening onto the realization that reality is nondual, *advaita*. The resulting recollection of the body and mental faculties in the spirit corresponded to a similar integration of various physical, intellectual, and spiritual means of inquiry, supporting a holistic vision of "the way of intuitive wisdom." It is as though the dialogue of the parts at all levels (intrapersonal, interpersonal, intercultural, interreligious, and cosmotheandric) was now seen from the viewpoint of the whole—a vision of nonduality brought through the practice of dialogue itself at these multiple levels. In turning to the evaluation of religions expressed in this third period, it is not surprising to find this move toward integration exemplified.

Evaluation of the Religions: Complementarity

What are the implications of Griffiths's increasing familiarity with *advaita* as an experience and philosophy for his view of the relationship between the religions? Do his descriptions of the contemplative method, with its transcending of rational consciousness and radical opening to the presence of Christ and the Spirit within, signal a growing openness to the Truth, who for him is Christ, within other religions? In other words, does his deepening contemplative experience, strengthened by the move to Shantivanam, bring about a subtle shift in his point of view, one from which the truth in other traditions was more apparent? If one may, with Griffiths, associate the activity of reason with making distinctions (analysis) and that of the intuition with discerning unity (synthesis), then it is not surprising that the increasing balance between his experience of these two mental styles resulted in a fuller appreciation of, and willingness to learn from, other religions. In time, his experience of intrareligious dialogue through contemplation and the spiritual life of the ashram directly affected his practice of, and his conclusions from, interreligious dialogue.[1]

In the writings published soon after the move to Shantivanam, Griffiths's position on other religions remains consistent with that described at the end of the second period. His dual task of affirming an ecumenical approach to other religions and of distinguishing what is unique to Christian teachings continues.[2] Thus, just as he strives to distinguish between Hindu and Christian contemplative experiences, so he articulates the differences between their respective positions on salvation, the Incarnation, and the nature of the personal God. During these years Griffiths mentions the principle of complementarity, suggested at the end of the previous period, as a more appropriate basis for evaluating other religions than the fulfillment theory. No longer is the "cosmic revelation" found in the Eastern religions seen as merely a preparation for the Hebrew-Christian revelation that fulfills them. Griffiths writes in a 1971 article that only when both revelations are taken together is a complete view of God and God's relation to creation made apparent, upholding both God's immanence in nature and in the human soul and God's transcendence beyond yet involved in history.[3] Writing in 1973, Griffiths clearly presents the principle of complementarity and the value of dialogue:

> The divine Mystery, the eternal Truth, has been revealing itself to all men from the beginning of history. Every people has received some insight into this divine mystery—which is the mystery of human existence—and every religion, from the most primitive to

the most advanced, has its own unique insight into the one Truth. These insights, insofar as they reflect the one Reality, are in principle complementary. Each has its own defects both of faith and practice, and each has to learn from others, so they may grow together to that unity in Truth which is the goal of human existence.[4]

Here, only a few years after the Second Vatican Council is a highly synthetic statement of the relationship between the diverse religions and a common "Truth," each religion being imperfect and thus in need of learning from the others.

It is already apparent in *Vedānta and Christian Faith* that the nondual awareness experienced through going beyond the rational mind has prompted Griffiths to search for the presence of such contemplative experience in all religions as a way of understanding what unites them— a pursuit that continued into the 1990s. At the end of this text he writes:

> There is a final transcendent state of being and consciousness, in which alone perfect bliss is to be found, to which every great religion bears witness. . . . [S]uch is the witness of every great religious tradition, in this Void, in this Darkness, in this Silence, all fullness, all light, all truth, all goodness, all love, all joy, all peace, all happiness is to be found. May our study of different traditions of religion lead us all to a deeper understanding of this divine mystery and to a share in a greater measure of this divine bliss![5]

In articles written from Shantivanam this bold position is reexpressed and interpreted in line with the ecumenical work of the post–Vatican II Church.

In an article on the work of the Secretariat for Non-Christians, he states the purpose of dialogue as being to understand individuals from other religions rather than to convert them. Furthermore, in recognition of the fact that divine grace is operative not only in Christianity but through the other great religions as well, one must, Griffiths argues, acknowledge that the Word of God has been spoken in other traditions— a Word to which Christians must listen if they are to open to the fullness of God's revelation. For the Christian, the Truth who is Christ may only be fully known if he is met in the wisdom of the other religions as well as in Christianity:

> We have to recognise that every religion, from the most primitive to the most advanced, throws a certain light on the one divine mystery, which is the object of all religious faith, and all are necessary to the full knowledge of Christ. It would seem that in time

to come it will become impossible to be a Christian in any complete sense, if one is ignorant of the treasures of wisdom and
knowledge to be found in the traditions of other religions. In this
way one can forsee a kind of convergence of the different religions
of the world on the one Truth, which is found in all and which for
a Christian is fully realised in Christ.[6]

In Griffiths's mind, interreligious dialogue has become not only an important new approach in Christian missions; it may someday be acknowledged as a spiritual duty of all Christians in order to know Christ
and to foster an "integral Catholicism."[7] Griffiths would later, in fact,
describe mission and dialogue as "indivisible" and envision the convergence of religions as part of God's plan.[8]

While acknowledging that such a theology of religions and the corresponding view of dialogue were not yet accepted generally within the
church in the mid–1970s, Griffiths did feel he was in line with the direction gradually being taken by the church.[9] Some in the church, however,
did not agree. In his journal reading he would meet negative estima-
tions of other religions and feel compelled to respond, criticizing the
theory he himself once held that Christianity fulfilled all other religions.
While *Christ* as the Truth may be said by Christians to be the fulfillment
of all religions, *Christianity* cannot, Griffiths argued.[10] This refinement of
his understanding of who Christ is in relation to Christianity and other
traditions is the key to his developing theory of complementarity and to
his vision of the church as "an open society in dialogue."[11]

Griffiths also began to find other Catholics criticizing in print his position on other religions, accusing him of ignoring important differences
between Christianity and all other traditions.[12] Aware of the potential
misinterpretation of his position, Griffiths often sought to distinguish
his stance from a facile syncretism. In an account of a Hindu-Christian
dialogue held at the ashram, attended by Monsignor Rossano from the
Secretariat for Non-Christians, Griffiths presents the ideals of the
ashram since its founding in 1950 as follows:

> We are not seeking a syncretism in which each religion will lose its
> own individuality, but an organic growth in which each religion
> has to purify itself and discover its own inmost depth and signifi-
> cance and then relate itself to the inner depth of the other tradi-
> tions. Perhaps it will never be finally achieved in this world, but
> it is the one way in which we can advance today towards that
> unity in truth, which is the ultimate goal of mankind.[13]

The ideal sought, then, through dialogue is not a mixing of religions but
mutual purification and exploration.

Perhaps in response to critiques of his vision of the complementary relationship between the Christian revelation and those of the great world
religions, Griffiths renewed his call for interreligious dialogue to be
grounded in the kind of experience that he and others in India had received: an intrareligious dialogue happening within one's own person
reaching to the very depths of contemplation. After describing the mystical experience of God as a "nameless Being," "known in the silence of
the faculties, in the interior depth of the soul (the 'cave of the heart'), beyond imagination and beyond thought," Griffiths concludes in a 1976 article: "It is important to emphasise that it is at this level of experience of
God beyond word and thought that the encounter of Hinduism and
Christianity has to take place. Anything else leaves the heart of Hinduism
untouched."[14] As noted before, in this experiment of in-depth dialogue
between Hinduism and Christianity, the ashram at Shantivanam served
as the perfect laboratory, attuned to the original vision of its founders and
Griffiths's own sense of vocation.[15] It is clear from Griffiths's writings that
the benefits of such an experiment in dialogue would touch not only
Indian Christianity but the church as a whole.[16]

The tendency to articulate common ground between all religions at
their mystical or contemplative depths is especially strong in *Return to
the Center* (1976), a text which, as already noted, is also emphatic in its
claims for the experience of *advaita*. Griffiths implies that the experience
of nonduality has brought the relationship between the One and the
many and thus the issue of sameness and differences between the various religions into a clearer light. There is one sacred Mystery to which
all religions point by means of their various names and signs, and into
which these religions provide access through contemplative or mystical
experiences—experiences that were the original inspiration for each
such tradition. The most urgent need in Christianity as in all religions is
to evaluate itself critically in order to distinguish clearly between what
is historical conditioning and what is the essential Truth. Such a renewal can best come through a return to the originating experience of
that which is beyond all images, concepts, and names. Then the "eternal
religion" that underlies all external ones will be discovered at the
source, the "center."[17]

The elements of Griffiths's position on the relationship between
Christianity and the other religions—complementarity, the avoidance
of syncretism, the significance and necessary depth of interreligious dialogue, the true basis of such dialogue in mystical experience, and the
suggestion that this experience in all traditions is essentially nondual—
are all reaffirmed in his later writing. Griffiths exhibits his growing ability to affirm the synthetic conclusions arising from the inspiration of the
intuitive mind while subjecting them as well to the analytical abilities of
the rational mind, drawing together the numerous individual insights

concerning the common elements and the clear differences between the various revelations. Repeatedly, he extols the virtues of each revelation, cites their limitations, and affirms their complementarity. Throughout such discussions, however, Griffiths's preference for what he sees as the completeness of the Christian revelation is apparent. In particular, he upholds the value given to creation, history, and the individual soul by the Incarnation—a value he believes is missing in most Eastern traditions and argues is essential to a complete spirituality.

In the 1980s, the scope of Griffiths's pursuit of dialogue deepened and broadened beyond his primary focus on the relationship between Hinduism and Christianity. In interviews and lectures he provided two useful analogies for understanding his approach to dialogue as it now came to be rooted in the experience of nonduality. The first analogy is that of surface and depths, illuminating here his perspective upon the key terms of *ecumenism, convergence,* and *syncretism.* In response to the question of whether there is anything in the spiritualities of the East and the West that cannot be "married," Griffiths answered as follows:

> At the deepest level I don't find anything incompatible. The deeper you go into Hinduism or Buddhism, the more you see how there's a fundamental unity with Christianity. On the surface there are many differences and contradictions, even below the surface there are still problems. But the deeper you go, you converge on this One. That is my vision of the future, that in each religion, as you go deeper into it, you converge on the original Source. We come forth from the One and we're returning to the One. But you can't mix on the surface. Syncretism is mixing on the surface—you take something of Buddhism, Hinduism, Christianity and you mix them. What we call Ecumenism is going beneath the surface to the convergence on the One, the Source. That is the real whole.[18]

Here again it is apparent how the experience of transcending dualities has shaped not only Griffiths's self-understanding of the mind and of his spiritual journey but also his evaluation of the religions. It is apparent as well from interviews in the early eighties that the type of dialogue that Griffiths envisions is at its early, "embryonic" stage in the West.[19] He contends further from his experience that there is little openness among Hindus and Muslims to true dialogue because in different ways they feel they already have the entire truth.[20]

As a second analogy for the relationship between the various religions, Griffiths adapts the image of white light and its diffraction into many colors. The following passage is also revealing in its identification of "faith" as representative of truth in its diverse expressions, in contrast to "wisdom" that represents truth in its unity or essence:

> Faith is reflected through the *manas,* which is the mind working through the senses and the feelings, and therefore through the whole cultural environment. This means that the same light of truth can shine in this man and that man, yet each will see it and interpret it and understand it in terms of his own culture. The one light of truth, the one reality, is shining through the whole of creation, through the whole of humanity and through every culture. Thus the one light of truth is broken up. A good image of this is to think of the one light and the many colours, where each culture is like a colour which reflects, as it were, a certain aspect of the one light.[21]

This image informs his view of intercultural dialogue as well.

In the 1980s and 1990s, Griffiths continued to meet with representatives of different religions as well as with Christians interested in dialogue, both at the ashram and on his travels in the West.[22] Using the language of the evolutionary perspective he received from sources as diverse as Teilhard de Chardin, Aurobindo, and Ken Wilber, he described the ongoing dialogue between Eastern and Western religions as "one of the focal points of human development today. . . . We have reached a point in evolution when we have to meet, we have to share, we have to discover one another."[23] As in the prior period, a sense of urgency remains behind his description of what such interreligious dialogue must be:

> The situation is extremely serious. . . . Everywhere religions are a source of conflict and violence. The only way we can overcome this is when we go beyond the limits of each religion and realize the transcendent mystery which is manifest in all of them.[24]

Late in his life, Griffiths's participation in interreligious dialogue lessened, though his conviction about its importance did not. In response to the persistent difficulties in pursuing meaningful dialogue with those of other religions, Griffiths maintained limited expectations for what can be accomplished in this age, even in this life.[25] The focus for Griffiths's own interreligious research, especially in his later years, was a comparative study of the scriptures of the major religions. *A New Vision of Reality: Western Science, Eastern Mysticism and Christian Faith* (1990) brings this ever-broadening research of the different major religions into conversation with the most recent insights of contemporary science. *Universal*

Wisdom: A Journey through the Sacred Wisdom of the World (1994) draws upon the evidence found in the Scriptures of Hinduism, Buddhism, Taoism, Sikhism, Islam, Judaism, and Christianity to establish the common mystical depths of these traditions.[26]

It is upon a mystical commonality, rather than upon any resolution of differences at the doctrinal level, that Griffiths rested his hopes for a meeting or convergence of different religions—a uniting which, like the experience of *advaita* itself, does not deny the importance of religious differences but rather upholds them. For Griffiths, a harmonization between different traditions based upon mutual recognition of their symbolic differences as well their common ground in *advaita* is a vitally important project for the world's future.[27] How he nuances these claims about commonality and convergence is significant, distinguishing him from more syncretistic approaches:

> What I am suggesting is that in each tradition there is an experience of transcendent reality, of the transcendent mystery, which is interpreted in terms of nonduality. It has different expressions in each tradition but basically they are the same.[28]

Griffiths is careful not to equate the actual experiences, shaped as these are by their respective symbolic mediations. It is "the transcendent mystery" to which the experiencer opens that is identified cross-culturally. Nevertheless, Griffiths finds that the dominating impression of nonduality permeates the diverse experiences, as well as the equally diverse interpretations of those experiences.

In the context of describing the symbols that mediate the experience of nonduality in the various traditions as disclosing complementary aspects of the same divine mystery, Griffiths continued to suggest on the basis of both his theological reflection and his contemplative experience that the Christian symbols, arising from Jesus Christ's own experience and expressed in church doctrines, mediate an understanding of the divine mystery as an interpersonal communion in love that is unique. Even if Griffiths's study of non-Christian traditions had become more comprehensive, it is likely that this conviction about the Christian experience of ultimate reality as an interpersonal communion would have remained firm.

Drawing together his insights concerning the presence of *advaita* in each major religion, Griffiths concludes:

> We can thus discern a basic pattern in all the great religious traditions. There is first of all the supreme Principle, the ultimate Truth, beyond name and form, the Nirguna Brahman of Hinduism, the

Nirvana and Sunyata of Buddhism, the Tao without a name of Chinese tradition, the Truth of Sikhism, the Reality—al Haqq—of Sufism, the Infinite En Sof of the Kabbala, the Godhead (as distinguished from God) in Christianity. There is then the manifestation of the hidden Reality, the Saguna Brahman of Hinduism, the Buddha or Tathagata of Buddhism, the Chinese Sage, the Sikh Guru, the personal God, Yahweh or Allah, of Judaism and Islam and the Christ of Christianity. Finally there is the Spirit, the "atman" of Hinduism, the "Compassion" of the Buddha, the Grace (Nadar) of Sikhism, the "Breath of the Merciful" in Islam, the "Ruah," the Spirit, in Judaism and the Pneuma in Christianity.[29]

Ultimately the wholeness ("the supreme Principle" or "hidden Reality") to which one opens through the various religious paths of self-transcendence is discovered to "contain" within itself both a principle of differentiation ("the manifestation of the hidden Reality") and an internal dynamism ("Spirit") through which that wholeness relates to all of its manifestations. It is to this basic, Trinitarian "pattern" of the nondual reality that each tradition has pointed with its own religious symbols and toward which those symbols guide the receptive aspirant.[30]

Griffiths follows Christian tradition in identifying the dynamism within the divine mystery as love, a power which, in turn, moves the journey of human consciousness toward full integration. While upholding the uniqueness of the Christian revelation of the divine mystery as an interpersonal communion of love, he also affirms that that which Christians call love is present as a guiding force in the other major religious traditions:

[T]here is one expression of the Spirit which is more meaningful than all others and that is love. Love is invisible, but it is the most powerful force in human nature. Jesus spoke of the Spirit, which he would send as Truth but also as Love. "If anyone loves me, my Father will love him and we will come to him and make our abode with him." This is the love, the *prema* and *bhakti,* which was proclaimed in the Bhagavad Gita, the compassion *(karuna)* of Buddha, the rapturous love of the Sufi saints. Ultimately a religion is tested by its capacity to awaken love in its followers, and, what is perhaps more difficult, to extend that love to all humanity. In the past religions have tended to confine their love to their own followers, but always there has been a movement to break through these barriers and attain to a universal love. The universal Wisdom is necessarily a message of universal Love.[31]

No doubt, some would evaluate Griffiths's claim that love is the essence and criterion of all major religions as nonetheless tradition-specific and thus symptomatic of a lingering inclusivism; clearly, he thought otherwise.[32]

Consonant with the theme and growing experience of this third period, Griffiths may have moved beyond a theory of complementarity where the different elements are seen as completing one another yet as independent. He eventually conceived the different religions as complementary parts of a whole in interdependent relation to one another, a position close to what has been called a "unitive pluralism."[33] In language intentionally reminiscent of Capra's and of his description of how reality is experienced from the highest level of consciousness, Griffiths claims that in the new age: "These different traditions will all be seen as interrelated and interdependent, each giving a particular and unique insight into ultimate truth and reality."[34] Griffiths's unspoken conclusion is that this vision of diversity in wholeness is the closest humanity can come in this life to the ultimate unity of religion to be found beyond death.

While capable of envisioning the nondual relationship between the religions from the point of view of the divine mystery, that is, the parts from the point of view of the whole, Griffiths nonetheless did not cease to remain committed to, and identified with, one of those religions, Christianity. While glimpsing that whole in relation to which interreligious dialogue comprises the creative interaction of parts, he maintained his role as a representative of one of those parts. He was, to the end, a *Christian* theologian, contemplative, and participant in dialogue.[35]

Implications of Awakening to the Nondual Mystery

Griffiths wrote informally in 1990 that he felt his life had entered a new stage. When asked for clarification of his meaning in relation to the three-part division of his life used to organize this study, he indicated that the third stage that he had signified by *advaita* actually culminated with the stroke that he had suffered at the beginning of 1990.[36] His verbal account of this experience indicates a profound change in his mental operations, a radical shaking of what he calls the rational mind, and a surrender to the feminine or more intuitive mode of consciousness. The result of this "death of the mind" was a pervasive awareness of the nondual reality that endured after the experience. One may easily interpret his account as a return to a unified state of mind, transcending and yet integrating the normal dualistic level of consciousness. All that he had glimpsed before in the third period as the consequences of experiencing *advaita* now appeared to have become permanent in his vision. He seemed to have moved through the dialogue of different mental faculties, of different religions and of cultures, even of Creator and creation, into a state where he identified more with the nondual relation of these dialogue partners than with specific partners themselves.

As he intuited almost forty years before, however, union with the divine mystery comes only at a cost, as the result of a complete self-surrender:

> This is the destiny of all humanity, to realize its essential unity in the Godhead, by whatever name it is known, to be one with the absolute Reality, the absolute Truth, the infinite, the eternal Life and Light.
>
> But this unity cannot be known without the pain of self-sacrifice; it demands "nothing less than all."[37]

Indeed in the sufferings of his final illness, "nothing less than all" seems to have been required of him. One can only wonder what the effects of his strokes in late 1992 and 1993 were upon his ongoing "surrender to the Mother," his awareness of the nonduality Reality revealed in Christ, and thus his ongoing experience of the creative dialogue between the many parts within that Reality.

Conclusion

———

Each of the three parts of this study have examined Bede Griffiths's life from three perspectives, attentive to his role as a culture bearer, to the interaction of psychological forces within him, and to his mystical experience of the sacred mystery through religious symbols. In the process, the discussion sequentially has sought understanding of three corresponding levels of self-transcendence in his life, the physical, the psychological, and the spiritual. Identified as the catalyst for this self-transcendence at each level has been a dialogue between diverse elements first encountered as opposites, then as partners in creative tension, and finally as complements within an encompassing whole. At the physical level, these elements were the cultures of England and India, generalized by him as "West" and "East," the eventual dialogue between which he conceived as a "marriage" essential to global survival. At the psychological level, the corresponding elements were the rational and the nonrational or intuitive forces or modes that he characterized as the two halves of his soul, the eventual integration of which was the fruit of both emigration and meditative practice. At the spiritual level, the elements in dialogue were human spirit and divine Spirit, the nondual relationship of which was glimpsed as early as the evening walk and was experienced with increasing clarity through the ensuing years, culminating in his final illness.

This study has further suggested that, according to Griffiths's self-understanding, what empowered dialogue at each of the three levels was surrender, a letting go of one's insistences and attachments cultivated by experience in nature, the Benedictine Rule, and the vow of *sannyāsa*. More fundamentally, however, what motivated Griffiths's lifelong surrender was love, love that is not simply an emotion but a symbol for the unity everpresent within the diverse elements in dialogue by virtue of their inherent nondual relationship—love that Griffiths near the end of his life would claim was "the basic principle of the whole universe."[1] With these principles in mind one may consistently sketch into the picture of this life in dialogue the difficult final months of illness, described

194

at the beginning of this study. One must resist bracketing them out as the lamentable conclusion to a remarkable life. Rather, one must attempt to understand the juxtaposed physical pain and bliss, mental confusion and clarity, and spiritual abandonment and awakening, as he would have, as the rhythms of a birth process.[2]

One may also use the criticisms that Griffiths evoked in order to focus the limitations of his life project in a way consistent with his role as a culture bearer and his theory of religious symbols.

Criticisms from Christians, Hindus, and Scholars of Religion

In charting the gradual development of Griffiths's culture critique, epistemology, mystical theology of symbols, and theology of religions, this study has noted some of the objections raised by those who believe that Griffiths moved too far or too quickly and thereby contradicted contemporary standards of orthodoxy, whether cultural or religious. Turning this criticism into an implied cause for praise, Griffiths's early companion in India Raimundo Panikkar eulogized his friend, in addition to his two French predecessors at Shantivanam, as "trespassers," each of whom risked misunderstanding by both fellow Christians and Hindus in order to fulfill their interreligious calling.[3] Nevertheless, how are we to assess the criticisms of Griffiths by Christians and Hindus, by theologians and academics?

In chapter 7 some objections by fellow Christians to Griffiths's efforts toward inculturation at his ashram and to the theological implications of his interreligious explorations were noted. It is significant that he never sought to distance himself from the Roman Catholic Church hierarchy in order to maintain his beliefs, even when the local Indian bishop criticized his efforts. Nor have his views been censured by Vatican authorities such as the Congregation for the Doctrine of the Faith that has in recent years criticized the works of other theologians engaged in dialogue with Hinduism such as Anthony de Mello, SJ and Jacques Dupuis, SJ. Griffiths sincerely understood his pursuit of inculturation and dialogue to be in accord with the directives of Vatican II and of subsequent papal statements. He thus understood criticisms from fellow Catholics as part of the necessary discernment process for charting the church's future course in response to the Second Vatican Council. Nevertheless, exemplifying the prophetic vocation discussed in earlier chapters of this study, he did not shy away from either criticizing some of the Vatican's positions nor from proposing changes within church structures.

Even if official church authorities have not openly censured his writings, can we judge whether he violated standards of Catholic orthodoxy? In response to this important and complex question, two points may be made. The first is that Griffiths believed he did remain in harmony with the official doctrines of his church to the end upholding the vital importance of maintaining orthodoxy in theory and practice.[4] The second is that his fidelity to key principles derived from the tradition concerning liturgy, theology, and doctrine led him to conclusions that some in the church judged were problematic. Certainly he was criticized as unorthodox by some fellow Catholics. His response to one such critic, an Indian priest, in 1976 who had taken him to task for both his helping to develop an Indian rite of the Mass and his methods of biblical interpretion is revealing:

> The question . . . between you and me is not whether what I say is according to the teaching of the Church, but whether it is according to your own peculiar opinion on the teaching of the Church. I have on my side the leading scholars and theologians of the Church; you have on your side a little group of ultra-conservative Catholics. . . . Will you never learn from the past? You clung fanatically to the Latin liturgy, until you were compelled to give up your opinions and admit that you were wrong. Now you have turned to theology and are clinging equally fanatically to an outdated theology, which you insist on regarding as the criterion of orthodoxy.[5]

Griffiths clearly identified himself with progressive elements within the Roman Catholic Church, those who were attempting to respond boldly to the calls for change voiced at Vatican II. Precisely who were "the leading scholars and theologians of the Church" that he believed were in support of his liturgical and theological efforts? As documented in this study, he consciously aligned himself with Patristic sources, with Aquinas, with the Maritains, with Avery Dulles, and especially with Karl Rahner. His interpretation of these authorities is not controversial. Nonetheless, his emphasis upon the symbolic nature of liturgy, theology, and doctrine, while firmly grounded in these authorities, had controversial implications, especially when applied to an interreligious context—implications that he was more daring than his authorities in explicating.

Also in chapter 7 some of the objections raised by Hindus regarding what appeared as deceptive missionary strategies were mentioned. Did Griffiths remain, either consciously or unconsciously, guilty of self-contradiction, claiming that he was not interested in converting Hindus to Christianity while at the same time developing Christian liturgical and spiritual practices that seemed to blur distinctions? In the same "open letter" to a Catholic detractor that was just quoted, Griffiths echoes clearly and perhaps more convincingly what he also expressed to Hindu critics such as those responsible for *Catholic Ashrams: Sannyasins or Swindlers?*

> Let me say that I have absolutely no claim to be a missionary and I did not come out to India to preach the Catholic faith. I am a contemplative monk, and I came out to India to found a contemplative monastery. In this work I have sought, following the teaching of the Vatican Council, to draw on all the riches and spiritual tradition of India, trying to assimilate in my Christian life and prayer "the spiritual and moral values, as well as the cultural and social values" of which the Council speaks, to be found in Hinduism and other religions.[6]

Given the legacy of British colonialism and of previous missionary efforts, as well as the contemporary reaction to this legacy among conservative Hindu political parties, the fact that projects such as Griffiths would be misunderstood is perhaps inevitable. To his credit, Griffiths did attempt to engage in dialogue with such Hindu critics, but with little if any positive results. By the final years of his life, he had quite despaired of productive dialogue with Hindus. His sense of mission seems to have become more clearly focused on communicating the fruits of his interreligious exploration with Western audiences and with the Indian Christian community, especially with the members of his ashram.

Acknowledging Griffiths's failed efforts to dialogue effectively with those Hindus who perceived missionary subterfuge in his interreligious exploration, we may still ask whether there is some truth in these criticisms. For example, by appropriating the Hindu concept of *advaita* in his theologizing and then by criticizing Hindu understandings of that concept was he, in fact, guilty of spiritual colonialism? Did he presume to take ideas, symbols, scriptures, and practices sacred to one tradition, praise their efficacy, but then "read" them through the Christian revelation and pronounce Hindu understanding of them deficient? If so, could one legitimately characterize his approach to interreligious relations as "dialogue," as a mutual interchange founded in respect for the integrity of the other?

In response to these questions, one must first recognize the reality of development within both Griffiths's view of non-Christian religions and the Catholic Church's. One may find plenty of evidence in the writings of the second period of his life to support the claim that he believed Christianity fulfills the Hindu religious quest. Nevertheless, building upon the dramatic opening initiated by the Second Vatican Council, he clearly, if gradually, changed his position to one that more strongly affirmed the efficacy of non-Christian religions. In his appropriation of aspects of Hinduism, Griffiths felt he was affirming the spiritual riches of this tradition as the Council encouraged, while at the same time maintaining his commitment to Christ—a delicate task that would inevitably offend those Christians and Hindus who evaluate differently the relation of other traditions to their own.

Secondly, Griffiths believed that there was significant common ground between the two traditions, both in the dynamics of the spiritual life and in theoretical reflection upon those dynamics. Eventually with the conviction born of direct experience in the third period of his life he believed it was possible and appropriate both to affirm the efficacy of Christian and Hindu spiritual paths, and also to criticize each tradition's interpretation of those paths. A Hindu cannot help but take offense unless he or she can affirm that such criticisms are accompanied by the kind of transformed consciousness that Hinduism more than most traditions upholds as a possible fruit of spiritual praxis. If one cannot in principle acknowledge the possibility of true spiritual authority in a non-Hindu, then Griffiths's critical appropriation of *advaita* will indeed seem an outrageous example of spiritual colonialism—as outrageous as Gandhi's praise and appropriation of Jesus and the way of the cross, coupled with his scathing criticism of Christianity.

Finally, one must set Griffiths's use of Hindu ideas, symbols, scriptures, and practices in the context of his entire life. As this study has shown, his first spiritual awakening and an accompanying intimation of nonduality preceded his conversion to Christianity. While he would later reinterpret his early spiritual quest in relation to Christian symbols, he found he could also use Hindu ones. It is this enduring sense of the relativity of religious symbols, while not lapsing into relativism (because "real symbols" do exist), that informs his appropriation of *advaita* and other aspects of Hinduism. It is perhaps surprising that some Hindus would not recognize a sense of symbolism close to their own; but it is not surprising that, given the triumphalist attitudes of most Christians they have met toward the symbols of Christ and the church, Hindus would not expect a Christian to relate to symbols in a way like their own and would distrust someone who said they did.

Criticisms from another direction should also be anticipated, those from Western academics who are likely to object both to Griffiths's comparative methodology and his highly synthetic conclusions. The scholar of religion who examines Griffiths's treatment of Hindu thought, and even more his discussion of other non-Christian religions, will be unsatisfied with an apparent lack of rigor in the Oxford graduate's methods. His use of rather popular translations of Asian texts, his emphasis upon Vedānta in its various schools as the authoritative voices for a dauntingly complex set of traditions known as "Hinduism," and his enduring use of Christian categories to interpret and evaluate non-Christian traditions violate accepted scholarly standards for the comparative study of religions. In response, one can only agree by acknowledging that Griffiths did not write for the academy nor within the field of the history of religions. He was a theologian and a mystic—two roles that in themselves can often be found at odds. This characterization should not suggest that he not be held up to the standards of reasoned inquiry; as discussed throughout this study, he held himself to such standards, but not always as interpreted by scholars of religion. Quite simply, he spoke to a different audience.

Regarding his interreligious conclusions, Shirley du Boulay has insightfully summarized in her biography of Griffiths both their strength and their potential weakness:

> His great gift was for the overarching synthesis, his vision spanning many different disciplines in search of the truth he was seeking. This, though considered impressive, even breathtaking, by many, has been dismissed as superficial by others.[7]

His basic categories of "East" and "West," associated with the correlates of feminine and masculine, intuitive and rational that are in need of being "married," no doubt strike many as radically simplistic. In response, one may suggest that such categories functioned for Griffiths more as symbols, in the sense of "events" that draw together diverse elements into provocative unities, than as the ciphers of objective theory. He seemed called to voice vast syntheses in a prophetic fashion, provoking criticism and refinement by others. Is this a legitimate function in fields, such as comparative study and interreligious dialogue where careful analysis of differences is essential to seeing the religious "other" clearly? It is correct to say this is a risk-laden strategy, provoking legitimate concerns.[8] However, the academic study of religion would be much poorer without visionary synthesizers, "trespassers," and provocateurs such as Griffiths—those who seek to remain linguistically in contact with accepted scholarly standards while at the same time challenging the boundaries set by those standards.[9]

The weaknesses in Griffiths's methodology and conclusions that have been identified by Christians, Hindus, and scholars of religion serve to clarify what he was and was not able to accomplish within the

inevitable limitations of a single life. Clarity is also brought by returning to the model of the culture bearer.

The Vocation of the Culture Bearer

Objections could also be raised by those who find that Griffiths did not
move far enough or quickly enough in his intercultural and interreligious conclusions. In chapter 7, a relevant theme within Griffiths's self-
understanding was identified: his sense of vocation to integrate each
new step of his experience and thought within the Catholic church's
and (one could add) his culture's self-understanding. Some may suggest that the price of maintaining this connection with orthodoxy, that
is, the reigning cultural and religious paradigms, and thus with the
standards, methods, and symbols of contemporary Western Christian
culture, was too high. In the interest of remaining orthodox, in both a
cultural and religious sense, did Griffiths fail to live up to the "new vision of reality" that he espoused?

Did Griffiths's incessant effort to balance rational and nonrational
means for gaining knowledge compromise his ability to explore the
depths of wisdom he calls "contemplative?"[10] Did his attempt to subject
all knowledge to the criteria set by a culture primarily receptive only to
the fruits of scientific inquiry limit his grasp and his expression of what
he himself identifies as an intuitive knowledge that cannot be understood by the dualistic mind? Did his enthusiasm about the "new science" distract him from holding to the prophetic conviction that "a
deliberate break with the whole system," of which science is the foundation, is needed?[11] Even while immersed in an Eastern culture, through
continued adherence to the epistemological principles instilled through
education did Griffiths remain subtly bound to his culture of origin that,
by his own admission, threatens to undermine the spiritual heritage of
countries like India?

In reference to Griffiths's relationship to Christianity, similar doubts
about his consistency with his "new vision of reality" may be expressed. Was he able to live up to his self-description as a *sannyāsi*, defined by him as "one who is called to witness to this Truth of the Reality
beyond the signs, to be a sign of that which is beyond signs," especially
in relation to the "signs" or symbols of his own tradition?[12] Or did the
need to remain orthodox subtly bind him to the symbols and the worldview of Catholic Christianity, undermining his claim, for instance, to
embrace a position of complementarity with regard to other religions?
Did his enduring preference for the Christian symbols of Christ, death-

resurrection, Trinity, communion, and love reveal a failure to transcend these fully to experience a "Truth" or "Reality" or "Mystery" to which no tradition can claim superior access?[13]

Each of these questions is based on doubts about Griffiths's ability to transcend fully, before then reintegrating, the cultural and religious paradigms into which he was born. Such doubts may be addressed by investigating the reasons behind his desire to incorporate his experience and insights into the self-understanding of his culture and the Catholic church.

There are a number of possible reasons behind Griffiths's expressed need to remain in contact with the reigning paradigms and standards of orthodoxy, both cultural and religious, in which his thought originated. First, one might propose that he felt at an unconscious emotional level the need to be accepted by his culture of origin and his religion. Second, it may be that his intentions were practical. By maintaining an orthodox foundation for his life's work, both his writing and the ashram would be assured a more enduring acceptance by his church and by his primarily Western audience. Third, in spite of his commitment to *sannyāsa*, he might have been unable to go fully beyond the ideal of his culture, reflected in scientific methodology and the symbols of his religious tradition, and so he remained cryptically or unconsciously attached to them. (As a corollarly, the *sannyāsi*'s goal of going beyond and then integrating one's culture and religion, as Griffiths understands that goal, may not be possible in this life.) In part through personal contact with Griffiths and in part through this study's approximation of an "integral understanding" of his life's work, these reasons for Griffiths's desire to integrate his insights and experience into the self-understanding of his culture and religion have been rejected.[14] In their place, the thesis of the culture bearer has been developed.

To defend the proposal that Griffiths's contact with the reigning cultural and religious paradigms is consonant with a prophetic role toward his culture and with the transcendence of religious symbols characteristic of *sannyāsa*, one must probe the dynamics of his life more deeply. First, one must recall that Griffiths's roles with respect to Western cultures and the Christian religion were understood by him as vocations, callings that were given in the context of an ever-deepening surrender to God. The sense that his experience was somehow not for himself alone but for others as well was, by his own claim, not contrived or desired. Second, contact with the predominant cultural and religious paradigms is essential to the vocation of the culture bearer who serves as a "bridge" between two ages. In Griffiths's case, this "bridge" is based upon his ability to connect two selves as well as two cultural and religious worldviews.[15]

It is a significant attribute of innovators like Augustine and Griffiths that they maintain a continuity between their old selves and their converted selves in order to facilitate the transition between paradigms and ages. Although conversion by definition demands a radical shift in perspective that necessarily breaks continuity, the culture bearer later builds a "bridge" in order that others, even the culture as a whole, may follow into a similarly new sense of self. As Karl Joachim Weintraub observes, one significant way in which Augustine achieved this connection between his old and converted selves, and thus between the classical and the medieval ages, was through writing his autobiography. More fundamentally, one can say that it is through language, and thus through symbols (both secular and religious), that a "bridge" may be built between two selves, two cultural and religious paradigms, and two ages.

In bridging two cultural paradigms through words, the culture bearer's use of language can facilitate not only linguistic continuity but also a revision of the fundamental epistemological assumptions of the prior paradigm implicit in that language. Thus Griffiths employs terms available in his culture of origin such as *reason* and *intuition* that are intelligible and are supported by a tradition of interpretation. Nevertheless, the epistemological assumptions in the language are taken up and transformed, even as the terms and syntax remain consistent. This is the proper context for understanding Griffiths's rethinking of the respective roles of reason and intuition. The intended result of his exploration of Indian as well as Western intellectual frameworks, then, was a rebalancing of Western methods of inquiry, the impact upon Indian methods being appropriately a lesser priority.

Similarly, as Griffiths's ongoing appropriation of Christian symbols in the context of interreligious exploration exemplifies, part of the culture bearer's work in connecting two selves and two ages is the reinterpretation and reviving of the key symbols of the predominant religious paradigm. The clearest example of Griffiths's renewal of key religious symbols is his work on articulating a Christian *advaita* in which the traditional symbols of the Trinity, Christ and Logos, communion, and love are recast in light of a contemplative vision, a reshaping that brings these symbols into creative dialogue with the spiritual philosophies of the Eastern religions. In this way, the old symbols are revived within a new religious paradigm in which interreligious dialogue is accepted as a powerful method for disclosing what is true.[16] While there is thus symbolic continuity between one paradigm and the next, the interpretation of those symbols may be transformed and their power to mediate the knowledge and experience of the sacred mystery renewed.

Thus through words, the culture bearer may revise the epistemological assumptions inherent in a particular language and may reshape the religious symbol system within which she or he operates in response to its prior inadequacies. However, there is always the possibility that she or he will appear to be speaking the same old language and upholding the older cultural and religious paradigms. This is part of the risk that an innovator takes in order to articulate the semblance of continuity between old and converted selves, between outdated and revolutionary paradigms, and thus between two ages. Remaining orthodox both culturally and religiously through employing the established language and religious symbols is one of the limitations that the culture bearer assumes as part of his or her calling. Although it may legitimately be the vocation of others to break with a language or religious symbol system or to stretch their intelligibility and thus take relative leave of concern for maintaining orthodoxy, the culture bearer must sustain contact through the language and symbols of the current age, even while transforming their interpretation.[17]

Surrendering to the Limitations of Symbols

To fault Griffiths for continuing to rely primarily upon Christian symbols and to defend their uniqueness, or to criticize his attempt to balance intuitive exploration with reasoned assessment is, in part, to misconstrue his mission as a culture bearer. Such criticism may also reflect an inadequate or partial understanding of what it means to be human, a flaw in judgment that can be addressed by means of his theory of religious symbols and *advaita*.

According to Griffiths, the particularity of the religious symbol is essential; its power to mediate what is universal depends upon its very limitations. Nor is this particularity something that is finally transcended and forever lost. Rather, a complete realization of the universal includes the awareness of how all particularity, all limitation, is integrated within that wholeness. Religious symbols, then, are not means that are rejected once the end is reached; rather, they are aspects of the end itself through which one has been drawn toward participation in that end; in Karl Rahner's language, they are "real symbols." The "real symbol" is not an accidental or temporary reflection of the symbolized; it is an expression and communication intrinsic to the symbolized, a self-disclosure of the reality to which it as a symbol points and toward which it draws the receptive human consciousness. For Griffiths, the range of what may qualify to stand in this nondual relationship to the divine mystery (the symbolized) is broad, including ultimately all persons, even all creation. His theory thus suggests that each human being is, in a sense described by Rahner's theology, a "real symbol" of the divine mystery, both particular and universal, limited and unlimited, human and divine.[18]

The challenge in understanding the nature of being human is to sustain a vision in which both dimensions of the person, the limited and the unlimited, are recognized at once. Interestingly, this is precisely the type of seeing that supports Griffiths's understanding of nonduality, the taking up of reason and intuition into a pure awareness. Such a state of mind integrates both the analytical and synthetic functions, the dualistic and unitive ways of knowing. The human and the divine mystery, as part and whole, are not-one and not-two. Similarly, each human, like each significant religious symbol, each culture, and each symbol system or religion, represents a complementary aspect of the divine mystery *and* is a hologram or "real symbol" that "contains" the wholeness of that mystery. In its silence, each complement can know its nondual relationship to that wholeness. But once moved to expression, to symbolization, to incarnation, the limited aspect of every complement necessarily comes to life. As Griffiths expressed this paradox, every mystical experience where the divine mystery is known consists of both unconditioned and conditioned elements.[19]

One may respond to the conjectured criticism that Griffiths did not move quickly enough or far enough in his revision of cultural and religious orthodoxy as follows: To fault a complement for expressing itself as a complement and not as the whole is to misunderstand the paradox of nonduality in a way directly parallel to the so-called pure *advaitins* who claim that all differentiation finally disappears in Brahman. One may experience the transcendence and integration of one's particular language and symbol system, of the cultural and religious assumptions they embody, and thus of one's own limitations as a symbol or "idea" within the wholeness of the divine mystery. Nevertheless when one speaks, one's silence must move into expression through particular words, symbols, and assumptions that are inherently limited. This is the limitation accepted not only by the culture bearer but also by the sensitive participant in interreligious and intercultural dialogue, as Griffiths realized. It is only through the humble and self-conscious appropriation of limitation that the unlimited may express itself effectively.

John A. T. Robinson, in his own response to Indian thought, makes an acknowledgment that fits Griffiths's own stance as a practitioner of dialogue:

> We must speak from where we are, looking out on the world from our vision of it, demeaning neither our centre nor that of the other person. But always it will be for the sake of that creative tension-within-unity which, I am convinced, lies at the heart of truth and

indeed of reality itself. For truth is two-eyed, if not many-eyed. Indeed, as Kierkegaard said, it is all eyes—and it looks at us, searchingly, as we so myopically are looking at it.[20]

However "pancultural" a person may become or however profound one's "multireligious experience" might be, one must always undergo experiencing, thinking, and speaking through cultural and religious limitations, through language and through symbols.

Griffiths's life and his self-understanding of that life reflect his self-appropriation as a culture bearer and his acceptance of the limits of his vocation as a practioner of interreligious and intercultural dialogue. As a *sannyāsi* embracing and transcending these same limits with detachment, he points beyond them to the mystery of nonduality in which all limitations are integrated in a fully differentiated wholeness. Being himself a rich and complex living symbol, he points beyond himself and beckons all to embrace and move through their own limitations as incarnate beings to experience the freedom found in surrender. In opening through religious symbols to the Spirit, "the *advaita* of God," Griffiths allowed a cultural transformation to happen within his own body, mind, and spirit, thereby rendering it somehow easier for others to be transformed as well.

The Relationship between Individual and Cultural Transformation

What is the role of the individual in the changing of cultures? Karl Joachim Weintraub's presentation of Augustine suggests a cause-and-effect relationship whereby the creative efforts of one individual influence the culture for centuries, for instance, through autobiography. The metaphor of synchrony is both less presuming and more provocative an image. For example, rather than seeing Griffiths as a quiet but nonetheless potent cause of changes evident in Western cultures, it is more consistent, especially with the goal of surrender, to recognize in him forces of change that are beginning to express themselves in his culture of origin and perhaps in others. He then becomes not a solitary confronter of contemporary cultural ideals but a highly focused example or instantiation of what is beginning to happen throughout the culture. But how may one reconcile such an image with the inevitably idiosyncratic features of any one person's journey? How does one explain that some individuals serve this role earlier and more potently than others? How is the individual's influence transmitted to the collective consciousness?

Through his contact late in life with scientist philosophers such as Fritjof Capra, Rupert Sheldrake, Ken Wilber, and David Bohm, Griffiths embraced the image of the universe as "a complex web of interdependent relationships." Importantly, this physical image is homomorphic with his vision of the divine mystery as "the exemplar of all interrelationship and the unity of all being in love," the love into which he felt himself taken up in the aftermath of his 1990 stroke.[21] In reference to the role of an individual in cultural change, these images suggest that each person, through and not in spite of her or his individuality, influences every other in the ongoing life of the whole.

Nevertheless, a discussion of changes happening in a culture as well as in an individual, necessarily raises the issue of causality. In the modern Western mind-set, which may in fact be part of the problem, it is still difficult to understand an event—personal, cultural, or global—without pinning down a cause for that event. Does one, then, invoke God or the Spirit as the ultimate guide for the transformation happening in individuals such as Griffiths, as well as in the cultures surrounding him? Or, does one propose a vague and profane cause such as Evolution or Fate or History? Or, does one opt for a purely human, though admittedly complex, cause comprised of the accumulated effects of all the individuals? In this light, is there any place for the principle that "the whole is greater than the sum of the parts," that is, an organic model?

Do the answers to such questions about the causes of individual, cultural, and global changes evade explanation because the questions, and the minds that think them, are somehow misguided, seeing only part of the picture, the thought world of Western cultures' own making? Griffiths's life experiment in dialogue between Western and Eastern ways of seeing and knowing suggests that the answer is "yes." In seeking the other half of his soul through encountering Indian religion and culture, Griffiths sought to expand his own vision and way of knowing. By integrating the active and the receptive dimensions of his psyche and by employing both rational and nonrational means for gaining knowledge, he broadened the horizon or thought world within which meaningful questions can be asked and answers recognized. Having diagnosed in his culture of origin and in his own habits of thinking the inadequacy of the modern Western cultural ideal based primarily in the scientific method of reasoned analysis, Griffiths reoriented himself through decades of dialogue with Asia, forging thereby a new ideal based in the integration of the aspects of his own pysche he found reflected in "West" and "East." By articulating this integration in his later works, he offers that renewed ideal to the culture, simultaneously expressing a change already taking place within the "complex web of interdependent relationships" that is that culture.

Within the transformed thought world from which Griffiths spoke by the end of his life, the question of causality for individual and cultural change does not arise. Using the language of Christianity and his understanding of symbols, the following account of the relationship between individual spiritual transformation and cultural change is suggested by his writings and by his role as a culture bearer: Those individuals who through grace are deeply transparent to the Spirit give voice to ideas that express the loving will of that Spirit for humanity as a whole. These ideas, in turn, serve as symbols, drawing the minds of others toward their common source in the ground of consciousness, for some effecting a spiritual transformation that reflects the changes needed throughout the culture. The essential attribute that such individuals embody, then, is the very same to which Griffiths often returned in his self-understanding: surrender. Through surrendering ever more thoroughly to the Spirit within, the individual may become a more concrete expression of the change being stirred in a culture by that Spirit. Such persons not only express symbols that mediate cultural change, they themselves become living symbols who through their transparency allow the healing light of the Spirit to touch the culture. Here is the lasting witness of Griffiths's life: that true spiritual surrender brings transformation not only in the individual but also through that individual in the world; and that such surrender demands our being fully the limited life-as-symbol that we were created to be:

> We experience the divine itself but in different ways. And maybe even in the ultimate state in heaven, we bring with us our particular tradition; we experience God in a unique way—each one. . . . That's why we were created, to have a distinct experience of the One. Each of us is a distinct revelation of God; the One is totally there in you and me, but in a unique way in each one. "[E]ach of us is an idea in the mind of God." And the aim of our life is to coincide with that idea in God which is eternal and is God in a sense, but God knowing himself in that particular idea, in me and in you.[22]

Notes

―――

Introduction

1. See Kathryn Spink, *A Sense of the Sacred: A Biography of Bede Griffiths* (Maryknoll, NY: Orbis, 1989; and Shirley du Boulay, *Beyond the Darkness: A Biography of Bede Griffiths* (New York: Doubleday, 1998).

2. Joachim Wach, *The Comparative Study of Religions* (New York: Columbia University Press, 1958), 11. See also William Cenkner, "Understanding the Religious Personality," *Horizons* 5/1 (1978): 1–16.

3. Fr. John Killian, Attica, NY, letter to friends, May 10, 1993.

4. Fr. Douglas Conlan, remarks made at a Memorial Service held at the 1993 World's Parliament of Religions, Chicago.

5. For two similar accounts of this experience, see Bede Griffiths, *The New Creation in Christ: Christian Meditation and Community*, eds. Robert Kiely and Laurence Freeman (Springfield, IL: Templegate, 1994), 103–104; and John Swindells, ed., *A Human Search: Bede Griffiths Reflects on His Life* (Liguori, MO: Triumph, 1997), 88–90. This experience will be discussed in greater detail in part III.

6. Swindells, *Human Search*, 9.

7. Ibid., 89; see also Griffiths, *New Creation in Christ*, 104.

8. Griffiths, interview by Christopher Venning, January 21, 1993, quoted in du Boulay, *Beyond the Darkness*, 257, 258.

9. Russill Paul D'Silva, Shantivanam, letter to friends, April 1993.

10. Bro. John Martin, OSB Cam., remarks made at a Memorial Service held at the 1993 World's Parliament of Religions, Chicago.

11.　Andrew Harvey, interview by Shirley du Boulay, quoted in du Boulay, *Beyond the Darkness,* 261.

12.　Russill Paul D'Silva, Shantivanam, letter to friends, April 1993.

13.　Russill Paul D'Silva, quoted in du Boulay, *Beyond the Darkness,* 260.

14.　*Śvetāśvatara Upaniṣad* 3.8, 10 (adapted from Juan Mascaro's translation, one often used by Griffiths).

15.　Du Boulay, *Beyond the Darkness,*263.

16.　I am indebted to correspondence by Fr. John Killian and Russill Paul D'Silva, to Bro. John Martin and Fr. Douglas Conlan's remarks at a Memorial Service held at the 1993 World's Parliament of Religions, Chicago, and to du Boulay's *Beyond the Darkness* (chap. 20) for the general sense and content of this account of Griffiths's final months.

17.　Griffiths, *The Golden String: An Autobiography* (Springfield, IL: Templegate, 1954, 1980), 187–88. The theme of surrender is also found in his discussion of *sannyāsa,* the vow of renunciation that he appropriated from Indian spirituality. See especially his *The Marriage of East and West: A Sequel to The Golden String* (Springfield, IL: Templegate, 1982), 42–44.

18.　Griffiths, interview by the author, tape recording, Shantivanam, India, January 1989. To my knowledge, Griffiths never expressed this threefold schematization of his life in print. Cf. William LaFleur's discussion of "self-structuring" in his article "The Death and 'Lives' of the Poet-Monk Saigyo," in *The Biographical Process: Studies in the History and Psychology of Religion,* eds. Frank E. Reynolds and Donald Capps (The Hague: Mouton, 1976), 344.

19.　Griffiths, *A New Vision of Reality: Western Science, Eastern Mysticism and Christian Faith,* ed. Felicity Edwards (Springfield, IL: Templegate, 1990), 41, 55, 93. He found clear articulation of this principle in the work of the transpersonal psychologist Ken Wilber, *Up From Eden: A Transpersonal View of Human Evolution* (Boston: Shambhala, 1981), 310.

20.　In his discussion of this principle of explication, Griffiths drew upon the contemporary physicist David Bohm's *Wholeness and the Implicate Order* (London: Ark Paperbacks, 1980). For an application of a similar principle by Griffiths to his own life, see Swindells, *Human Search,* 27.

21.　Griffiths, *Golden String,* 56.

22.　E.g., Griffiths, *New Vision of Reality,* 204, 220–23.

23.　Griffiths, *Golden String,* 12–14. For Griffiths, these "others" whose rediscovery of religion was grounded in direct experience included especially Romantic poets such as Wordsworth, Coleridge, and Keats. Cf. various contemporary and liberation theologians who emphasize praxis in relation to theory.

24. Griffiths, *Marriage of East and West,* 58. Griffiths finds this threefold division of the human person in 1 Thess. 5.23, as well as in Irenaeus and Origen.

25. See the many works of Raimundo Panikkar on dialogue, especially his *The Intrareligious Dialogue* (New York: Paulist, 1978). "Cosmotheandric" is Panikkar's comprehensive adjective for describing the interrelationship of cosmic, divine, and human realities.

26. Griffiths, *Marriage of East and West,* 25.

27. Griffiths, Shantivanam, India, letter to the author, May 31, 1988.

28. Wayne Robert Teasdale discusses Griffiths's reversal of the British approach to India—from oppressive ruler to humble student—in his article "Bede Griffiths as Mystic and Icon of Reversal," *America* 173/9 (September 30, 1995): 22–23.

29. Karl Joachim Weintraub, *The Value of the Individual: Self and Circumstance in Autobiography* (Chicago: University of Chicago Press, 1978), 43. See the author's "Bede Griffiths as a Culture Bearer: An Exploration of the Relationship between Spiritual Transformation and Cultural Change," *American Benedictine Review* 47/3 (September 1996): 260–83. Having reviewed the author's use of this thesis, Griffiths affirmed its applicability to his life. Cf. William James's discussion of "religious geniuses" and "sick souls" in *The Varieties of Religious Experience: A Study in Human Nature* (New York: Collier, 1961), 37, 78–143; and Erik Erikson's portrayal of ideological innovators in *Young Man Luther: A Study in Psychoanalysis and History* (New York: W. W. Norton, 1958), 48.

30. Panikkar, *Intrareligious Dialogue,* 12.

31. Cf. James Redington, "The Hindu-Christian Dialogue and the Interior Dialogue," *Theological Studies* 44 (1983): 596.

32. I am indebted to an anonymous reader of this manuscript for the general shape of these three questions raised by Griffiths's life experiment.

33. Swindells, *Human Search,* 100.

34. Griffiths, *New Creation in Christ,* 104.

An Evening Walk

1. Griffiths, *Golden String,* 9, 12. The metaphor of the "golden string" is taken from William Blake's poem "Jerusalem."

2. Ibid., 9.

3. Griffiths, "A Pilgrim to Jerusalem," *Pax* 28 (1938): 7.

4. Swindells, *Human Search,* 26–27. Note I have taken the liberty of re-punctuating the transcript in the final sentence to clarify Griffiths's meaning. For both the sense and content of this description of these key experiences I

have relied upon the first two chapters of Swindells's "oral history" as well as the prologue and first two chapters of Griffiths's *Golden String*.

Chapter 1: *The Romantic Explorer of English Countryside*

1. Griffiths, *Golden String*, 19.

2. Swindells, *Human Search*, 5.

3. Ibid., 9.

4. Ibid., 15–16.

5. Griffiths, *Golden String*, 23.

6. Ibid., 26.

7. Ibid., 28.

8. Ibid., 10.

9. Ibid. Griffiths concludes that his experience of heightened awareness was not unusual or uncommon. For many, however, the transformed vision does not endure; the veil again falls; "old habits of thought reassert themselves" (11).

10. Ibid., 13.

11. Ibid., 12.

12. Ibid.

13. Ibid., 13.

14. Griffiths's pessimism was supported by his reading of Oswald Spengler's *Decline of the West* that portrayed the history of civilization in terms of cycles of growth and decay. Later in his life in England, Griffiths found in the writing of Christopher Dawson a theory of civilization which, like his own, argued for the foundational role of religion (*Golden String*, 31, 170).

15. Ibid., 42–43.

16. According to one Griffiths biographer, Kathryn Spink, part of Lewis's intention in suggesting a stiff regimen of reading in Western philosophy was to support his efforts in shedding critical light upon Griffiths's ardent romanticism and anti-intellectualism. Spink states that Lewis himself, by the time Griffiths began studying with him, had moved through a similar transition from romanticism and atheism to a more balanced philosophical position that included belief in a Universal Spirit (Spink, *Sense of the Sacred*, 57–58).

17. Griffiths, *Golden String*, 56.

18. Ibid., 64. Griffiths later wrote a commentary on the first of these texts entitled *River of Compassion: A Christian Commentary on the Bhagavad Gītā* (Warwick, NY: Amity House, 1987; reprint, New York: Continuum, 1995).

19.   Griffiths, *Golden String*, 66.

20.   Griffiths, letter to Martyn Skinner, December 19, 1955, quoted in du Boulay, *Beyond the Darkness*, 30.

21.   Spink characterizes the closeness of Griffiths and Lewis's relationship during these years as follows: "After Alan left Oxford in 1929 they continued to correspond and to meet at intervals and between that time and 1932 when they were both undergoing a conversion to the Christian faith, Alan was probably closer to C. S. Lewis than anyone else was" (Spink, *Sense of the Sacred*, 62). Clive Staples Lewis corroborates this close companionship in his own autobiography of his early life, *Surprised by Joy: The Shape of My Early Life* (New York: Harcourt, Brace & World, Inc., 1955), 234—a book that Lewis dedicated to Griffiths.

22.   Griffiths, *Golden String*, 56.

23.   Swindells, *Human Search*, 18.

Chapter 2: Reconciling Reason and Imagination

1.   Griffiths, *Golden String*, 27; Swindells, *Human Search*, 7.

2.   Griffiths, *The Golden String*, 11.

3.   Ibid., 34. Wordsworth's own description of the state of mystical silence is found in the poem, "Lines Written above Tintern Abbey." Interestingly, this poem, influential upon Griffiths, was written to commemorate one of the poet's own walks in the English countryside. The passage from this poem used as an epigraph at the beginning of part I of this study is quoted by Griffiths during a filmed interview near the end of his life. See Swindells, *Human Search*, 16.

4.   See Griffiths's account of Mary Webb's nature mysticism, reminiscent of his own, as "the reaching out of the soul still immersed in the impressions of the senses towards the reality of God" (Griffiths, "The Mysticism of Mary Webb," *Pax* 28 [October 1938]: 162). See also du Boulay, *Beyond the Darkness*, 13, 28–29 on Griffiths's "longing for direct firsthand experience."

5.   For Aquinas's discussion of the various faculties, see *Summa Theologiae* (New York: McGraw-Hill, 1964–76), 1, qq. 77–82.

6.   Griffiths, *Golden String*, 56.

7.   This distinction is found in Griffiths's earliest writings, three unpublished articles composed in the 1930s. In "The Process of Knowledge," Griffiths quotes D. H. Lawrence in support of the value of knowledge gained by "intuition," as opposed to "reason," lamenting that "rational consciousness" with its ability to think abstractly and logically has largely eclipsed non-rational sources of knowing, photocopy from Griffiths's typewritten unpublished man-

uscript, 7–8. In general, by "rational" Griffiths means analytical, discriminative, and based on the exercise of discursive reason. "Intuitive" or "nonrational" denotes what is nonconceptual, synthetic, unitive, and based in the exercise of faculties other than reason, such as the senses and the imagination.

8.   Griffiths, *Golden String*, 35. Again Griffiths recalls the influence of Lawrence in recognizing the nature of "the unconscious," especially "its deep instinctive feelings and its power of intuition," and the habitual repression of the unconscious throughout his life and education (44–45). See also Griffiths, *Pathways to the Supreme: The Personal Notebook of Bede Griffiths*, ed. Roland Ropers (London: HarperCollins, 1995), 31–33, where Lawrence is quoted.

9.   Griffiths, *Golden String*, 38. See also his later account of the relationship between the "rational mind" and the "poetic mind" in his *Pathways to the Supreme*, viii–ix.

10.   Griffiths, *Golden String*, 55. See also Griffiths's assessment of Lewis's difficulties in reconciling reason and imagination in the former's "Light on C.S. Lewis," *Month* 35/6 [June 1966]: 338. See also Spink, *Sense of the Sacred*, 60–62.

11.   Griffiths, *Golden String*, 50.

12.   Ibid., 50–51; see also Swindells, *Human Search*, 31.

13.   In light of the discussion of different types of knowing to follow, it is interesting to note that Spinoza, although Griffiths does not mention the fact, actually articulated four such means for gaining knowledge: perception, imagination, reason, and intuition, the last being "the highest virtue of the mind." See the last book of Benedict de Spinoza's *Ethics*, trans. R. H. M. Elwes (New York: Dover Publications, 1951), vol. 2, *The Chief Works of Benedict de Spinoza*, xl n. 2, a text that Griffiths has said was of "incalculable significance to me" (Griffiths, *Golden String*, 50).

14.   Ibid., 53. Griffiths notes three works by Samuel Taylor Coleridge recommended by Lewis that influenced him during this time of reading philosophy in the late 1920s: *Aids to Reflection*, *The Friend*, and *Biographia Literaria*, especially the chapter on imagination (Griffiths, *Golden String*, 54–55).

15.   Coleridge, *The Collected Works of Samuel Taylor Coleridge*, no. 7, *Biographia Literaria*, vol. 1, eds. James Engell and W. Jackson Bate (Princeton: Princeton University Press, 1983), lxxxi, 254–55. See also Griffiths, "The Power of the Imagination," photocopy from Griffiths's typewritten unpublished manuscript, 1930s, 1; idem, *Universal Wisdom: A Journey Through the Sacred Wisdom of the World*, ed. Roland Ropers (San Francisco: HarperCollins, 1994), 14, 33.

Spinoza's "intuition" and Coleridge's "imagination" are similar. During this first period, Griffiths appears to have preferred the term *imagination* for this nonrational capacity of the mind to know things in themselves and thus to gain true knowledge.

16.   Coleridge, *Biographia Literaria*, 1:263; see also 174, 295.

17.   Griffiths, *Golden String*, 56.

18. Ibid., 34.

19. Ibid., 78, 86.

20. Ibid., 87, 88–89. One must suppose that Griffiths includes here even the broad sense of philosophy just discussed in Coleridge. Cf. Coleridge, *Biographia Literaria*, 1:281.

21. Griffiths, *Golden String*, 91.

22. Ibid., 56.

Chapter 3: God through the Symbol of Nature

1. Griffiths, "The Power of the Imagination," photocopy of Griffiths's typewritten unpublished manuscript, 1930s, 1, 3. Recall that for Griffiths "mind" and "soul" are synonymous. On the relation of body, soul or mind, and spirit, see the introduction.

2. Ibid., 4.

3. Ibid., 6.

4. Griffiths, *Golden String*, 33–35. As Griffiths puts it, the Romantic poets became the "prophets" of a "new religion" based upon this sense of the "spirit of nature."

5. Griffiths, "The Mysticism of Mary Webb," *Pax* 28 (October 1938): 161–65. Cf. idem, *The Cosmic Revelation: The Hindu Way to God* (Springfield, IL: Templegate, 1983), 31; and idem, *Marriage of East and West*, 46–47.

6. Griffiths, *Golden String*, 53–56.

7. Ibid., 55. See also Griffiths, "The Process of Knowledge," 9: "The image, whether myth or idol, really represents, that is makes present, the mystery which it signifies and is charged with all the mysterious power of nature and the subconscious life."

8. Coleridge, *Collected Works of Samuel Taylor Coleridge*, no. 7, 1:xciv (editors' introduction), and 241–42.

9. Cf. the claim by some physicists (e.g., on the basis of holographic research) that the whole of reality is present in every part. See Griffiths, *New Vision of Reality*, 174–75.

10. Imprecision in Griffiths's use of the terms *sign, symbol,* and *sacrament* must be noted. To clarify, one might safely say that for Griffiths symbols, as those images or words that actually make present (to varying degrees) that which they symbolize, are a subset of signs, things that point to other things according to convention. Sacraments are a subset of symbols; that which they make present is not just any reality but the mystery of God who transcends the

world of all other significations. Whether something (e.g., bread) functions as a merely conventional sign, a presentational symbol, or a sacrament to a large degree depends upon the openness of the experiencer to the divine mystery rather than upon the nature of the thing itself.

11.   Owen Barfield, *Poetic Diction,* 3d ed. (Middletown, CT: Wesleyan University Press, 1973), 80–81. Cf. Griffiths, *Marriage of East and West,* 49–50.

12.   Griffiths, *Marriage of East and West,* 50. Griffiths's view of primitive culture here reflects the influence of his reading of other scholars such as Mircea Eliade and Jacques Maritain. See the quotations from these authors he recorded in his notebooks in "The Way of the Cosmic Revelation," part 1 of his *Pathways to the Supreme,* 1–19. Griffiths has linked the original multivalent sense of a word or symbol and the collective process of revealing the multiple meanings to David Bohm's "implicate" and "explicate orders" (Interview by the author, August 1991, tape recording, Trappist, KY).

13.   Griffiths, *Golden String,* 28–29.

14.   Ibid., 34. This is an excerpt from Wordsworth's "Lines Composed a Few Miles above Tintern Abbey." See also Griffiths's analysis of an earlier portion of the same poem in his *Marriage of East and West,* 157–58.

15.   Griffiths, *Golden String,* 34.

16.   Swindells, *Human Search,* 18.

17.   Griffiths, *Golden String,* 35.

18.   Those familiar with Indian philosophy may associate the term *advaita* more strictly with Śankara's school of thought, Advaita Vedānta, where nonduality is usually characterized in a more monistic sense than Griffiths's account. Note that when Griffiths applies this term for nonduality to the third stage of his life, he is employing it in a highly general, cross-traditional sense that will be developed later in the book—a sense that he explicitly distinguishes from the usual monistic interpretation of Śankara.

19.   Griffiths, *Golden String,* 34.

20.   Ibid., 11.

21.   Swindells, *Human Search,* 5, 9. For a comprehensive study of Griffiths's lifelong relationship to nature and its implications for his theory of nonduality, see J. Samuel Savio, "The Principle of Relatedness in the Ecological Ethic of Bede Griffiths" (Doctor of Sacred Theology diss., Catholic University of America, 2000).

22.   The term *connaturality* is derived by Griffiths from the writings of Thomas Aquinas to be discussed in chap. 6. Griffiths began his study of Aquinas just after his year-long experiment living in the countryside in 1931 and thus prior to his conversion.

23.   Griffiths, "Process of Knowledge," 1, 12, 14.

24.   Griffiths, *Golden String*, 90–91.

25.   Griffiths, Shantivanam, India, to the author, June 6, 1990.

The Conditions for Dialogue

1.   For an honest assessment of Griffiths's ability to consider viewpoints other than his own at this stage in his life, see du Boulay, *Beyond the Darkness*, chap. 4.

2.   Griffiths, *Golden String*, 64.

3.   Ibid., 13–14.

4.   Swindells, *Human Search*, 17.

5.   Ibid., 16. Here is a clear example of Griffiths living out the principle he recognized in Ken Wilber's work that at any stage of evolution the earlier stages must not simply be left behind but integrated. See the introduction. For a comparison of the pattern of paradise-exile-self-conscious-return suggested here in Griffiths's understanding to Paul Ricoeur's account of a "second naïveté," see the author's "The Mutual Transformation of Self and Symbol: Bede Griffiths and the Jesus Prayer," *Horizons* 23/2 (Fall 1996): 215–41.

Night of Conversion

1.   Griffiths, *Golden String*, 104.

2.   Swindells, *Human Search*, 53.

3.   Ps. 119.10, 18, as quoted in Griffiths, *Golden String*, 107.

4.   Ibid., 108.

5.   Quoted in ibid.

Chapter 4: The Benedictine in England and India

1.   Griffiths, *Golden String*, 63.

2.   Ibid., 102.

3.   Ibid., 103, 117:

Each renunciation had been dragged out of me painfully against my own will. I had struggled against it and felt it as an invasion of my being by an alien power.

There was indeed something terrifying in this power which had entered into my life and which would not be refused. It had revealed itself to me as love, but I knew now that it was a love which demanded everything, and which was a torment if it was resisted. Once the surrender had been made, that power took over the direction of my life.

4.   Ibid., 115.

5.   Ibid., 132.

6.   Ibid., 16–17:

I know now that God is present not only in the life of nature and in the mind of man, but in a still more wonderful way in the souls of those who have been formed in his image by his grace. I had sought him in the solitude of nature and in the labour of my mind, but I found him in the society of his Church and in the Spirit of Charity.

7.   Ibid., 130.

8.   Ibid., 162, 179. Contrast his earlier stated intention in pursuing the monastic life in a 1933 letter: "I am hoping by retiring into a monastery to withdraw my mind altogether from the wisdom of this world, and to give myself up to the contemplation of heavenly things" (quoted in du Boulay, *Beyond the Darkness*, 69).

9.   Spink, *Sense of the Sacred*, 103. This prayer, usually associated with Orthodox Christianity, customarily involves the silent, mental repetition of the phrase: "Lord Jesus Christ, Son of God, have mercy on me, a sinner," or a variation thereof.

10.   Griffiths, *Golden String*, 174. Griffiths's interest in India was "revived" through meeting in London an early disciple of Carl Jung, Toni Sussman, who shared her own experience of Yoga and her understanding of Eastern philosophy with him (Swindells, *Human Search*, 68).

11.   First mention of this phrase is found in Griffiths's early article, "The Incarnation and the East," which first appeared in *The Commonweal* 59/12 (December 25, 1953) and was then republished in *Christ in India: Essays Towards a Hindu-Christian Dialogue* (Springfield, IL: Templegate, 1966; 1984). Scholars may take legitimate objection to Griffiths's highly generalized concepts of "East" and "West." Even after his sense of these labels was informed by years of living in India, he chose to continue to use them—more with the intent of prophetic urgency than scholarly precision.

12.   Spink, *Sense of the Sacred*, 108. See also du Boulay, *Beyond the Darkness*, 105.

13.   Griffiths, *Christ in India*, 21. An early companion in this cultural exploration was Raimundo Panikkar, himself a Catholic priest, born of a Spanish Catholic mother and a Hindu father, and raised in Europe. Panikkar

was to become a well-known scholar and author, teaching for many years at the University of California at Berkeley, and publishing numerous articles and books, some of which are cited by Griffiths in his own works. Panikkar was a regular visitor to Griffiths's Saccidananda Ashram in South India.

14.   Griffiths, *Marriage of East and West*, 10, 15.

15.   Griffiths, *Christ in India*, 19–22; idem, *Marriage of East and West*, 8, 12–18; Swindells, *Human Search*, 69–71.

16.   A reevaluation of his early experience in nature was thus prompted by his move to India:

> I have said that since my coming to India I have been led in a strange way to re-trace the path of the Golden String. My awakening to the mystery of existence had come to me through the experience of the beauty of nature, which I have described in the opening chapter of *The Golden String*, and this experience had been ex-pressed and interpreted for me in the writings of the Romantic poets. . . .
>
> But when I came to India these ideas took on a new life. I discovered that what in Europe had been the inspired intuition of a few poets, had been the common faith of India for countless centuries. That power which pervades the universe and the mind of man had been revealed with marvellous insight in the Vedas centuries before the birth of Christ. (Griffiths, *Marriage of East and West*, 46–47)

17.   He attended, and sometimes gave talks at, the annual meetings of the Union for the Study of Great Religions, a group founded by the Indian president and philosopher, Sarvepalli Radhakrishnan. In addition, he joined in the regular gatherings of a group of Christians of various denominations who were reading and comparing the Bible and the Upaniṣads (Spink, *Sense of the Sacred*, 120–21).

18.   Griffiths's first encounter with the two French priests and their ashram came through his reading of their book, *An Indian Benedictine Ashram* (published in 1951, in England in 1964, but now out of print), while he was a monk in Scotland.

The most important secondary source on Monchanin is *In Quest of the Absolute: The Life and Works of Jules Monchanin*, trans. and ed. Joseph G. Weber (Kalamazoo, MI: Cistercian Publications, 1977). On Le Saux, see Marie-Madeleine Davy's *Henri Le Saux—Swami Abhishiktānanda: le passeur entre deux rives* (Paris: Le Cerf, 1981); Emmanuel Vattakuzhy's *Indian Christian Sannyāsa and Swami Abhishiktānanda* (Bangalore, India: Theological Publications in India, 1981); and a biography by James Stuart, *Swami Abhishiktānanda: His Life Told Through His Letters* (Delhi: International Society for the Propagation of Christian Knowledge, 1989).

19.   Roberto de Nobili (1577–1656) was an Italian Jesuit whose early vo-cation as a missionary guided him to India in 1605. He quickly learned the ob-stacles to presenting the Gospel there and decided to adopt the dress, diet, and life-style of a "renunicant" or *sannyāsi*, becoming the first Christian to do so. He

was also the first Christian to read the Hindu Scriptures in Sanskrit. He was thus able to enter into dialogue with the priestly class in an effort to lead them to Christ. See Vincent Cronin's *A Pearl to India: The Life of Roberto de Nobili* (New York: Dutton, 1959).

Brahmabandhab Upadhyay (1861–1907) was a Brahmin convert to Catholicism who was influential in the struggle for independence and in the adaptation of Christian monastic life to the Indian tradition of *sannyāsa*. He was also an inspired and prolific writer whose essays contain some of the key ideas later taken up and developed by Monchanin and Le Saux as well as by Griffiths. These insights include the identification of the Trinity with the Hindu *saccidānanda*, the potential value of Vedānta philosophy in general for Indian Christianity, and the conviction that Christ completed or fulfilled Vedānta. Upadhyay also founded a monastery in the model of the Hindu ashram in 1900, but its life was brief due to ecclesiastical opposition. When Monchanin and Le Saux founded their own ashram fifty years later, they did so in conscious relation to, and gratitude for, Upadhyay's earlier attempt. See B. Animananda's *The Blade: The Life and Work of Brahmabandhab Upadhyay* (Calcutta: Roy & Son, 1945); and Julius Lipner, *Brahmabandhab Upadhyay: The Life and Thought of a Revolutionary* (Delhi: Oxford University Press, 1999).

20.   E.g., "For a Hindu Catholicism," *Tablet* 205/6000 (May 21, 1955): 494–95; "Fulfillment for the East," *Commonweal* 63/3 (October 21, 1955): 55–58; and "The Missionary Today," *Commonweal* 64/4 (April 27, 1956): 90–92.

21.   Griffiths, *Marriage of East and West*, 18.

22.   Griffiths, *Christ In India*, 53.

23.   Griffiths was particularly sensitive to "the extremely Western character of our Latin Catholicism" as one cause for "the comparative failure of the Church to take root in the Far East"—as discussed in "Catholicism and the East," in *Christ in India*, 94–103. Other relevant works published during these years on this subject include the following articles by Griffiths: "Liturgy and the Missions," *Asia* 12 (1960): 148–54; "The Language of a Mission," *Blackfriars* 41/478 (January–February 1960): 20–27; "Liturgy and Culture," *Tablet* 218/6471 (May 30, 1964): 602–3; "Background to Bombay," *Month* 32/6 (December 1964): 313–18; "The Ecumenical Approach in the Missions," *India* 15 (1964): 64–67; and, "India after the Pope," *Commonweal* 81/20 (February 12, 1965): 641–42. For a discussion of the nature and value of the Syrian tradition of Christianity, see idem, *Marriage of East and West*, 20–22.

24.   Griffiths reflects upon the Sarvodaya movement, its relationship to the Gospel, and his meeting with Vinoba Bhave in "Walking With Vinoba," in *Christ in India* (126–33). See also his "Vinoba Bhave," *Blackfriars* 38/443 (February 1957): 66–71. Griffiths was impressed enough by what he had heard and seen of the Sarvodaya movement, and its devotion to the renewal of Indian society, to travel and meet with Bhave in 1960. While joining in Vinoba's walk from village to village, Griffiths proposed the foundation of a Sarvodaya center based upon Christian principles. Though deeply respecting Vinoba's work in

the villages, Griffiths was at that time uncertain about the movement's practice of common prayers and readings, a practice that seemed to ignore religious differences and was thus unacceptable to most Christians. (Given the practice of reading from various religious Scriptures in the context of worship he instituted at Saccidananda Ashram, Griffiths may have later had a somewhat more tolerant attitude toward the principles of this movement.) During this walk, Vinoba agreed that Christians involved in the work of Sarvodaya would not be expected to participate in the common prayers and could conduct their own. This accord removed the obstacles in Griffiths's mind to setting up a Sarvodaya center in a village of the Madura district, a center to be placed in the care of an Indian oblate. This project prompted a letter to the oblates of Prinknash Abbey at home in England asking them to contribute to this important social work. In the conclusion to this appeal, Griffiths wrote:

> When I first came out to India I had no idea in mind except to help to establish a contemplative monastery in India. By the grace of God I can say that this aim has now been accomplished [i.e., Kurisumala Ashram]. . . . But though I am happy that we have been able to accomplish so much, yet my experience of India has made me feel that the contemplative life alone is not enough. The poverty in India is so great, and the need to help the poor so urgent, that I feel that we ought to do something in this direction. ("A Letter from India," *Life of the Spirit* 15/172 [October 1960]: 181–82).

The Christian Sarvodaya center that Griffiths envisioned was never actualized.

25. E.g., Griffiths, "Meeting at Rajpur," in *Christ in India*, 199. Experience of India evoked further expressions of Griffiths's ambivalence toward his culture of origin as well. For a discussion of his views on the perennial question for him of the value of industrialization and modernity in general based on letters at this time, see du Boulay, *Beyond the Darkness*, 135–37.

26. These lectures were published in the United States by Dawn Horse Press in Los Angeles in 1973 and reprinted in their entirety (except for a 1973 preface by Griffiths) in 1991 with additional texts by Griffiths, Abhishiktānanda, and Swami Paramānanda. (Unless noted otherwise, the 1991 edition is cited here.)

27. E.g., Griffiths, "The Vatican Council," *Star of the East* 25 (1964): 9–12; idem, "The Dialogue with Hinduism," *New Blackfriars* 46/538 (April 1965): 404–10; and his interpretation of the Second Vatican Council's "Declaration on the Relation of the Church to Non-Christian Religions" *(Nostra Aetate)*, idem, "The Church and Non-Christian Religions: Salvation Outside the Church," *Tablet* 219/6552 (December 18, 1965): 1409–10. See also du Boulay, *Beyond the Darkness*, chap. 11.

28. Spink, *Sense of the Sacred*, 146–47. Griffiths discusses *Kuṇḍalinī* Yoga and the related topic of tantrism in "Interview: Father Bede Griffiths, O.S.B.," interview by Johannes Agaard and Neil Duddy (Europe, Summer 1984), *Update* 9 (1985): 22–36; and in *New Vision of Reality*, 193–98.

29.   Both Spink and du Boulay also describe some interpersonal tensions arising from Mahieu's reluctance to share his authority as a cause contributing to Griffiths's eventual departure from Kurisumala (Spink, *Sense of the Sacred*, 148; du Boulay, *Beyond the Darkness*, 144–45). A further sign of surrender, Griffiths was prepared to return to England in order to allow Fr. Mahieu to have clearer authority over Kurisumala. It was then that the invitation from Fr. Le Saux to take over Saccidananda Ashram came.

30.   Griffiths, *Marriage of East and West*, 7.

31.   Ibid., 7–8.

32.   Weintraub, *Value of the Individual*, 24. Using Augustine as one example, Weintraub describes how autobiography orients the author and offers reorientation for the culture.

33.   See also Antony Kalliath, "Inward Transcendence: A Study on the Encounter of Western Consciousness with Indian Interiority Based on the Works of Fr. Bede Griffiths" (masters thesis, Dharmaram Pontifical Institute, 1986), 2: "Fr. Bede Griffiths, both in his life and in his visions, epitomizes the disillusionment and agony of the western civilization. All the same he is the symbol of hope, of a new vision and realization of that new vision for the west in its pilgrimage for greater authenticity and profundity in the experience of Reality."

Chapter 5: *Faith as a Way of Knowing*

1.   Griffiths, *Golden String*, 103–104.

2.   Ibid., 104.

3.   Ibid.

4.   Griffiths defines "faith" more clearly in later texts as "the awakening to the light of truth in our own minds" and "an illumination of the mind from the Supreme" (Griffiths, *River of Compassion*, 290). Capturing even more clearly the dynamism of his early experience, Griffiths also defines faith as "the opening of the inner heart, the inner spirit, to the Reality of God. Faith is precisely that movement beyond to the transcendent Mystery" (idem, "Contemplative Life in the Church Today," side 1, *Christian Meditation: The Evolving Tradition*. Chevy Chase, MD: John Main Institute, 1991). These lectures and discussions have been edited and published as *The New Creation in Christ: Christian Meditation and Community*. See also idem, "On Poverty and Simplicity: Views of a Post-Industrial Christian Sage," interview by Renee Weber, *ReVision* 6/2 (Fall 1983): 29 (reprinted in Renee Weber, *Dialogues with Scientists and Sages: The Search for Unity* [New York: Routledge & Kegan Paul, 1986, 157–80]), quoted in the next section.

5.   Griffiths, *Golden String*, 132.

6. Ibid., 89, 116–17.

7. Jacques Maritain, *Distinguish to Unite, or The Degrees of Knowledge* (New York: Scribner, 1959), 259: "[F]aith, even though it does reach God according to His very inwardness and His proper life . . . reaches Him thus only at a distance and remains a mediate knowledge, enigmatic, in the word of St. Paul; in the sense that . . . faith has to make use of formal means, proportionate to our natural mode of knowing—concepts and conceptual formulas, analogical or rather superanalogical notions." (This text was originally published in 1932 and is cited by Griffiths in *Golden String*, 169.)

8. Jacques Maritain, *Distinguish to Unite*, 252.

9. Griffiths, *Golden String*, 187. Cf. idem, "In Jesus' Name," *Tablet* 246/7915–16 (April 18, 25, 1992): 499.

10. Griffiths, "The Power of Intuition," photocopy from Griffiths's typewritten unpublished manuscript, 1930s, 9.

11. Griffiths, "The Divine Office as a Method of Prayer," *Life of the Spirit* 6/62–63 (August–September 1951): 84; idem, "Liturgical Formation in the Spiritual Life," *Life of the Spirit* 6/69 (March 1952): 368. The relevant passage in Aquinas's *Summa Theologiae* is 2–2, q. 45, a. 2, just quoted as an epigraph for this part.

12. Griffiths, "Liturgical Formation in the Spiritual Life," 368.

13. Ibid., 365.

14. Griffiths, *Golden String*, 187, just quoted. See Aquinas, *Summa Theologiae* 2–2, q. 45, a. 1, ad 2.

15. Jacques Maritain, *Creative Intuition in Art and Poetry* (New York: Pantheon, 1953), 3. A similarly broad sense to poetry is found in Raissa and Jacques Maritain's *Situation of Poetry: Four Essays on the Relations between Poetry, Mysticism, Magic, and Knowledge*, trans. Marshall Suther (New York: Philosophical Library, 1955), 44. In conversation Griffiths affirmed the influence of Raissa Maritain's article, contained in the latter text, on "Magic, Poetry, and Mysticism," 23–36, as well as the former text. See also Griffiths, *Marriage of East and West*, 215.

16. Raissa and Jacques Maritain, *Situation of Poetry*, 47; Jacques Maritain, *Creative Intuition in Art and Poetry*, 94.

17. Jacques Maritain, *Creative Intuition in Art and Poetry*, 118–20. See also Raissa and Jacques Maritain, *Situation of Poetry*, 64–65. Cf. Griffiths, "Divine Office as a Method of Prayer," 84–85.

18. Raissa and Jacques Maritain, *Situation of Poetry*, 64.

19. The differentiation between these two types of "knowledge by connaturality" is found in both of the Maritains' texts. See Raissa Maritain's article, "Magic, Poetry, and Mysticism" (ibid., 23–36); Jacques Maritain's more

philosophical treatment in the same volume (64–68); and *Creative Intuition in Art and Poetry* (123, nn. 234–36).

20.   In articles written in the 1930s Griffiths interpreted this distinction in ways revealing of how he might then have looked upon his own early experience of God's presence in nature. In his citation of Raissa Maritain's account of "the natural mystical experience" where God is found as the ground of one's existence, and in his critique of Mary Webb's "natural mysticism," Griffiths reaffirms the existence of a higher mysticism whose object and source are supernatural. See "Power of Intuition," 6–7; and idem, "Mysticism of Mary Webb," 162. In the copy obtained of the former article, it is interesting to note that Griffiths has written at some unknown time in the margin next to his description of Christian mysticism as being of "another order altogether" in comparison to the "natural mystical experience" of the Eastern religions the following remark: "I would not now express the division of the natural and supernatural orders in this way."

21.   Jacques Maritain, *Distinguish to Unite*, 264–65.

22.   Ibid., 260–64.

23.   Jacques Maritain, *Creative Intuition in Art and Poetry*, 118.

24.   In the passage from Aquinas just cited (*Summa Theologiae* 2–2, q. 45, a. 2), reason is praised as a means for gaining wisdom whose perfection leads to a kind of knowledge of divine things and right judgments. Jacques Maritain is equally clear that reason holds an important place in the healthy mind, including the mind of the poet. Some degree of rationality is essential to the successful expression of what the poet experiences in a nonrational way. On the other hand, some measure of nonrational or intuitive knowledge is vital to the success of all speculative knowledge, including science and philosophy (Jacques Maritain, *Creative Intuition in Art and Poetry*, 76). Both ways of knowing are necessary and already at work in the broad range of human inquiry. Consciously adverting to them both is what is missing in Western culture, according to this critique by Griffiths and Maritain.

25.   Griffiths, "The Transcendent Unity of Religions," *Downside Review* 72/229 (July 1954): 269.

26.   M. Frithjof Schuon, *The Transcendent Unity of Religions* (Wheaton, IL: Theosophical Publishing House, 1984), xxix–xxx.

27.   Griffiths, "Transcendent Unity of Religions," 271. The citation of Aquinas here is *Summa Theologiae* 1, q. 94, a. 3, ad 1.

28.   Ibid., 273.

29.   Ibid., 271–72. Griffiths obscures the discussion in this article by not defining what he means by faith as a mode of knowledge in juxtaposition to Schuon's text. Griffiths thus allows the perennial philosopher to determine the meaning of faith being debated. Schuon describes "faith" as "an indirect and

passive participation" while "intellectual intuition" is "a direct and active participation in divine Knowledge," one that is more certain than other sources of knowledge "because of the identity between the knower and the known in the Intellect" (Schuon, *Transcendent Unity of Religions,* xxx). One wonders if what Griffiths means by faith and Schuon's description are really that similar. Nevertheless, Griffiths's reticence on this matter in the article being discussed implies at least that faith is a knowledge that is "inferior" in its mode because it is mediated; it takes place in a relationship to the divine not in a strict identity with God. Such knowledge, however, is ultimately superior for Griffiths because the mediator of it is Christ and his Body, the church, whose origin is supernatural.

30. The distinction thus drawn between the metaphysic underlying all religions, according to the "perennial philosophy," and Christian teaching, naturally corresponds to, and supports, Griffiths's position at this time (just before his departure for India in 1955) on the relationship of Christianity to other religions. The natural/supernatural distinction that underlies Griffiths's position with regard to both the different types of knowing and the different traditions of knowledge is central to Jacques Maritain's own treatment of the same issues. See *Distinguish to Unite,* 265–83. On Gregory's principle, found also in Griffiths's account of knowledge, that love exceeds all other ways of knowing, see Griffiths, "Transcendent Unity of Religions," 273.

31.   Griffiths, "Incarnation and the East," 74.

32.   Griffiths, *Golden String,* 167.

33.   Griffiths, "Fulfillment for the East," in *Christ in India,* 80.

34.   Ibid., 81. The relevant passages from Aquinas are *Summa Theologiae* 2–2, q. 45, a. 2; and, q. 45, a. 1, ad 2. *Patiens divina* is a quotation from Dionysius (*Divine Names* 2.9).

35.   Ibid., 80. Cf. Aquinas, *Summa Theologiae* 2–2, q. 45, a. 1, ad 2; and, q. 45, a. 3, ad 1.

36. Ibid.: "We cannot enter into the Eastern tradition unless we are prepared to meet its representatives on the level of contemplation. It is union with God—beyond images and concepts—in the ground of the soul that the true meeting must take place. This means that we have to recover our own contemplative tradition. . . ."

37.   Griffiths, "Kerala," in *Christ in India,* 53.

38.   This critique of Latin theology and liturgy is found especially in Griffiths, "Liturgy and Culture," 602–3.

39.   Griffiths, "Church Universal," in *Christ in India,* 239.

40.   Griffiths, *Marriage of East and West,* 21.

41.   Griffiths, "The Church and Hinduism," in *Christ in India,* 182.

42.   During a 1983 interview, Griffiths said:

[F]aith is simply a preliminary stage for knowledge, knowledge in the deep sense of *jnana*. In fact, faith in the strict tradition is an illumination of the mind. It's an opening of the mind to the transcendent reality, but like a seed it's just an opening, a beginning, and faith has to grow into experience. Actually you know the Middle Ages talk of *fides quaerens intellectum*, faith in search of intellect—knowledge. But I would rather say *fides quaerens experientiam*, faith looking towards experience. Perhaps one of the great differences in the Christian tradition since the Middle Ages is that we've tended to concentrate on intellectual knowledge, theology, faith becoming theology, but not on faith becoming *experience*. (Griffiths, "On Poverty and Simplicity," 29)

43.   Griffiths, *Return to the Center* (Springfield, IL: Templegate, 1976), 73; idem, *Marriage of East and West*, 75, 102, 199; idem, *River of Compassion*, 289–91.

Chapter 6:   *God through the Symbols of Bible, Liturgy, and Prayer*

1.   Griffiths, *Golden String*, 130.

2.   Griffiths, letter to Martyn Skinner, undated (quoted in du Boulay, *Beyond the Darkness*, 63): "Thoughts are all turned inward now, for it is there and not in nature that I believe the kingdom of heaven is to be found."

3.   Griffiths, *Golden String*, 116–17. As discussed in chap. 3, Griffiths also wrote of the "centre of the soul" in a similar way in his earliest articles, "Power of the Imagination" and "Power of the Intuition." In his later writings, Griffiths will more often use the term *spirit* to refer to this center.

4.   Jacques Maritain, "Concerning Poetic Knowledge," in *Situation of Poetry*, 68. Maritain cites Aquinas's 1 *Sent.*, prol., q. 1, a. 5, ad 3.

5.   Raissa Maritain, "Sense and Non-Sense in Poetry," in *Situation of Poetry*, 19–20. The quotation from Aquinas is a translation of *Summa Theologiae*, 2–2, q. 172, a. 1, ad 1.

6.   Jacques Maritain, *Creative Intuition in Art and Poetry*, 92.

7.   Ibid., 94.

8.   Griffiths, "The Platonic Tradition and the Liturgy," *Eastern Churches Quarterly* 4/1 (January 1940): 5–8. Cf. his later criticisms of some forms of Indian spirituality based, he felt, upon an inadequate philosophy of the relationship between God and the world.

9.   Ibid., 7–8.

10.   Griffiths, "The Priesthood and Contemplation," *Orate Fratres* 25/8 (July 1951): 347, 352, 353 (reprinted in *The Life of the Spirit* 5 [April 1951]: 439–46).

11.   Griffiths, "Liturgical Formation in the Spiritual Life," *Life of the Spirit* 6/69 (March 1952): 364.

12.   Griffiths, "The Divine Office as a Method of Prayer," *Life of the Spirit* 6/62–63 (August–September 1951): 77–85; idem, "The Mystery of the Scriptures," *Life of the Spirit* 7/74–75 (August–September 1952): 67–75.

13.   Griffiths, "St. Benedict in the Modern World," *Pax* 59 (1969): 77–79. The editor notes that this article is reprinted from *Church and People* "nearly twenty years ago."

14.   Griffiths, "Priesthood and Contemplation," 349. For a similarly comprehensive statement, see idem, "Divine Office as a Method of Prayer," 84; and idem, "Process of Knowledge," 10–11: "[T]he human mind desires to know reality not merely by an image or likeness, but as it is in itself: this is the impulse which underlies the whole quest of knowledge. Nor will it be satisfied merely with concepts: for the concept also, however abstract and universal it may become, still remains a sign. It gives us knowledge of things but still by means of a sign which can never adequately represent them. We can never know anything, still less any person, by means of a concept, so as to possess them completely, to share their existence and make them our own. To attain this we have to pass beyond both images and concepts." Cf. idem, *Marriage of East and West*, 27.

15.   Griffiths, "Divine Office as a Method of Prayer," 79.

16.   Griffiths, "Liturgical Formation in the Spiritual Life," 365. See also idem, *Golden String*, 158–60.

17.   Griffiths, "Liturgical Formation in the Spiritual Life," 366–67. See also idem, *Golden String*, 160–63.

18.   Griffiths, "The Cloud of the Tabernacle," *Life of the Spirit* 7/83 (May 1953): 478–86; idem, "Mystery of the Scriptures," 71–72.

19.   Griffiths, "The Enigma of Simone Weil," *Blackfriars* 34/398 (May 1953): 236. One wonders, as in the case of the earlier article on Mary Webb, whether Griffiths recognizes in Weil's attitude toward dogma an obstacle to embracing the church fully that he himself had difficulty in crossing. Griffiths specifies that the doctrines of the Trinity, the Incarnation, and the Eucharist are "signs of a mystery which cannot be expressed" (Griffiths, *Golden String*, 186).

20.   Griffiths, *Golden String*, 186. See also idem, "Christian Existentialism," *Pax* 43 (1953): 144; and idem, "Process of Knowledge," 4, 10–11.

21.   Griffiths, "Cloud on the Tabernacle," 486.

22.   Griffiths, "St. Benedict in the Modern World," 79. See also idem, *Golden String*, 181.

23.   Griffiths, "Divine Office as a Method of Prayer," 83; idem, *Golden String*, 183, 187.

24.   Griffiths, "Mystery of the Scriptures," 70–71. Cf. idem, "Symbolism and Cult," in *Indian Culture and the Fullness of Christ* (Madras, India: Madras Cultural Academy, 1957), 60. Griffiths's position on the greater efficacy of "historical symbols" is based on the assumption that religions whose primary sense of time is cyclic rather than linear thereby devalue the created world that is repeatedly destroyed and human history that seems to move toward no definitive goal.

25.   Griffiths, "Divine Office as a Method of Prayer," 85. See also idem, "Mystery of the Scriptures," 71; idem, "Liturgical Formation in the Spiritual Life," 363.

26.   Griffiths, *Golden String*, 186. See also idem, "Process of Knowledge," 10–11; and much later, idem, *New Vision of Reality*, 245–47.

27.   Griffiths, "Priesthood and Contemplation," 350. He quotes Weil's *Attente de Dieu*.

28.   Griffiths, "Mystery of the Scriptures," 68.

29.   Griffiths, "Liturgical Formation in the Spiritual Life," 367, 368.

30.   Griffiths, "Process of Knowledge," 9. He cites Coleridge, D. H. Lawrence (*Apocalypse and the Writings on Revelation*), and Jacques Maritain (especially "Sign and Symbol in Redeeming the Time").

31.   Griffiths, "Power of the Imagination," 5.

32.   Ibid., 6. Compare to Griffiths's later statement that "the language of the imagination is part of the process of incarnation" (idem, *Marriage of East and West*, 103).

33.   Karl Rahner, "The Theology of the Symbol," in *Theological Investigations*, trans. Kevin Smyth (Baltimore: Helicon Press, 1966), 4:225. Griffiths speculates that one reason for the profoundness of Rahner's insight and his ability to facilitate our understanding of Eastern traditions (though he knew little about them) was that he had what Griffiths calls "mystical intuition," a clear sense of the mystery that transcends all words and concepts (Interview by the author, January 1989). Griffiths was impressed by the interpretation of Rahner's theology offered in Joseph H. P. Wong's *Logos-Symbol in the Christology of Karl Rahner* (Rome: Libreria Ateneo Salesiano, 1984).

Mircea Eliade is also among the relatively few authors on symbolism that Griffiths cites in his writing (Griffiths, *Christ in India*, 175–76, 194–95; and idem, *Marriage of East and West*, 206).

34.   Ibid., 227.

35.   Ibid., 225, 230–31.

36.   Ibid., 236.

37.   Ibid., 239.

38. Ibid., 240.

39. Ibid, 242.

40. Ibid., 239.

41. Ibid, 244. Griffiths's implicit interpretation of Rahner's concept of "mediated immediacy" is discussed in chapter 9. For Rahner's own understanding of the concept, see his *Foundations of Christian Faith: An Introduction to the Idea of Christianity* (New York: Crossroad, 1986), 83–84.

42. Rahner's primary modes of spiritual experience (according to Joseph H. P. Wong, *Logos-Symbol in the Christology of Karl Rahner* [Rome: Libreria Ateneo Sqlesiano, 1984], 74) were the Ignatian "Exercises" and devotion to the Sacred Heart of Jesus, both of which focus upon the humanity of Christ. Griffiths's spirituality, even at this time is more contemplative and will increasingly tend toward the apophatic (in the sense he found in Gregory of Nyssa's "darkness" and in Dionysius), that is, Griffiths's path is more focused upon transcending all supports. The issue resolves to the question of whether "the humanity of Christ" is a symbol inherent within the Trinitarian experience of the Godhead or a symbol that must be transcended in order for that experience to dawn most fully.

43. Griffiths, *Christ in India*, 19–29, 115–25; idem, *Marriage of East and West*, 7–15; idem, "Village Religion in India," *Tablet* 230/7098 (July 24, 1976): 726–27.

44. Griffiths, *Christ in India*, 21.

45. Griffiths, *Marriage of East and West*, 46.

46. Griffiths, *Vedanta and Christian Faith* (Clearlake, CA: Dawn Horse Press, 1973, 1991), 104. See also similar imagery of the veil in idem, *Golden String*, 11.

47. Griffiths, *Vedanta and Christian Faith*, 146.

48. Griffiths, *Marriage of East and West*, 15.

49. Ibid., 174; idem, *Christ in India*, 175; idem, "Symbolism and Cult," 52–61.

50. Griffiths, *Christ in India*, 21.

51. Ibid., 176; cf. idem, *Marriage of East and West*, 15.

52. Griffiths, *Christ in India*, 101–102. Griffiths calls for such a recovery throughout his time in India, as evidenced in the following articles: "Symbolism and Cult," 59; idem, "Catholicism and the East," in *Christ in India*, 94–103; idem, "The Sacred Cow," *Commonweal* 85/17 (February 3, 1967): 484; idem, "Village Religion in India," 727; idem, "The Advaitic Experience and the Personal God in the Upanishads and the Bhagavad Gita," *Indian Theological Studies* 15 (1978): 71–72, 76; and idem, "A Symbolic Theology," *New Blackfriars* 69/817 (June 1988): 294.

53.   Griffiths, "Symbolism and Cult," 57.

54.   As evidenced in Griffiths's generally positive appraisal of biblical criticism, his call for a recovery of a sense of symbolism is *not* a suggestion that Western intellectual culture return (even if it were possible) to some primitive, naive immersion in the world of symbols but rather to a postcritical appropriation of the symbolic and the sacred.

55.   Some may object to characterizing Christ as a symbol, taking "symbol" to mean something that stands for, but does not necessarily have an intimate relationship with, something else. When Griffiths speaks of Christ as a symbol, it is in the sense articulated by Rahner. For Rahner and for Griffiths, Christ, the Logos, is the supreme symbol, that is, the intrinsic expression and complete self-presentation, of the Godhead.

56.   Griffiths, "Symbolism and Cult," 52–56.

57.   Ibid., 52–53. The Vedic tradition would make a similar claim for their own rituals, based as these are in the revealed portion of their Scriptures (*śruti*). The crux of the matter is, then, what Griffiths calls "the authority of Christ."

58.   Ibid., 58.

59.   Ibid., 60; see also 34–35. Cf. idem, *New Vision of Reality*, chaps. 6–7.

60.   Griffiths, *Christ in India*, 111. See also idem, "Indian Spirituality and the Eucharist," in *India and the Eucharist*, ed. Bede Griffiths and Co. (Ernakulam, India: Lumen Institute, 1964), 9–18.

61.   Because the Hindu sense of time is cyclical as opposed to linear, symbols are generally understood as transhistorical and of relatively equal merit as windows onto the timeless dimension of absolute reality. This understanding when applied to the symbols of other religions supports, for example, the belief that Jesus is an *avatāra* just like Rāma and Krishna. On the inability of the Hindu to take religious differences, including differences between religious symbols, seriously, leading to syncretism, see "Walking with Vinoba," in *Christ in India*, 130–33.

62.   Griffiths, "Symbolism and Cult," 53. See also idem, "Language of a Mission," 20–27, where he endorses efforts to introduce the vernacular language and some native customs into the rites in various places. Griffiths participated in a number of meetings of Catholic clergy during the late 1950s and early 1960s on the topic of an Indian rite of the Mass. Within such deliberations there was a wide diversity of views concerning just how Indian such a rite should be, given the close interweaving of Indian culture and the Hindu religion. Finally, in the late 1960s, the bishops of India endorsed a rite of the Mass that did incorporate a number of ingredients from Indian culture. It is this rite that Griffiths would later use at Shantivanam.

63.   Griffiths, *Christ in India*, 165. Cf. the Catholic theologian Avery Dulles's distinction between "real" and "secondary" symbols in his *Models of*

Revelation (Garden City, NY: Doubleday, 1985), 258—a text Griffiths would later read and admire.

64. Griffiths, "Symbolism and Cult," 58.

65. Griffiths, *Christ in India,* 184. No reference for Maritain is given.

66. Griffiths, "Placing Indian Religion," *Blackfriars* 44/521 (November 1963): 478–79. In this article Griffiths is responding to Zaehner's *Convergent Spirit* from which the quotations are taken (without page references). For a full treatment of this comparison of views, see Albano Fernandes, "The Hindu Mystical Experience according to R. C. Zaehner and Bede Griffiths: A Philosophical Study" (Ph.D. diss., Gregorian Pontifical University, 1993).

67. Griffiths, *Christ in India,* 35–36, 185.

68. Ibid., 184; idem, "Placing Indian Religion, 480.

69. Griffiths, "Indian Spirituality and the Eucharist," 11–12; idem, "Dialogue with Hinduism," 406–7; idem, "Monastic Life in India Today," *Monastic Studies* 4 (Advent 1966): 128–30; idem, "Meeting at Rajpur," in *Christ in India,* 202–205, 212–15—for early interpretations of Śankara's philosophy. For an even earlier critique of Śankara that follows along the same lines, see Griffiths, *Golden String,* 172. In this last text, Griffiths cites Fr. Pierre Johanns and his book *To Christ Through the Vedanta* that must have been one of Griffiths's first influences in interpreting Śankara. Later, once he had reached India, Griffiths recalls, he encountered Dr. T. M. P. Mahadevan, then chair of the Philosophy Department at the University of Madras, whom Griffiths describes as a "pure *advaitin*" who advocated this particular nonrealist or acosmic interpretation of Śankara (cf. Griffiths, *Cosmic Revelation,* 71). Griffiths does note that Śankara's position on the relative reality of the world can be exaggerated by some interpreters. Nevertheless, a basic disagreement persists between how Hindus and Christians experience nonduality.

70. For the details of Griffiths's response to these other two schools, a response that remained unchanged, see his "Dialogue with Hinduism," 406–9; idem, "Monastic Life in India Today," 129–30; and, as a later version, idem, *New Vision of Reality,* 153–54. While Rāmānuja upholds the personal nature of the absolute reality, his theology, according to Griffiths, verges on pantheism because the absolute is qualified by the world, being in relation to it as the soul is to the body. In maintaining a strict duality between God and world, Madhva claimed that the world and souls were also eternal, thus compromising God's transcendence. In *New Vision of Reality,* Griffiths critiques several other schools of Indian philosophy on this same fundamental issue of how God, the world, and the soul are related.

71. Griffiths, *Christ in India,* 214. For Griffiths's assessment of Aurobindo's philosophy, see also idem, *Return to the Center,* 137; idem, *Cosmic Revelation,* 114; idem, *New Vision of Reality,* 92–94; idem, "Father Bede Griffiths," interview by Malcolm Tillis [Shantivanam, India, January 27, 1981], in *Turning*

East: New Lives in India: Twenty Westerners and Their Spiritual Quests, eds. Malcolm Tillis and Cynthia Giles [New York: Paragon House, 1989], 124; and idem, *A Follower of Christ and a Disciple of Sri Aurobindo* (correspondence between Bede Griffiths and K. D. Sethna [Amil Kiran]) (USA: Integral Life Foundation, 1996).

72. Griffiths, *Christ in India*, 36 (1965 introduction); see also 201.

73. E.g., ibid., 44, 47; idem, "On Poverty and Simplicity," 26; idem, *Cosmic Revelation*, 130. Griffiths is careful to note that, given the diversity of interpretations within Vedānta itself, there are multiple positions among Hindus regarding the relationship between God and the soul. Nevertheless, he concludes that the extreme "pure *advaita*" attributed to Śankara predominates (idem, "Indian Spirituality and the Eucharist," 13). It is for this reason that much of Griffiths's attention in critiquing Hindu understandings of *advaita* is directed at Śankara. Compare his *New Vision of Reality*, 153, where this position is nuanced.

74. Griffiths, *Christ in India*, 186.

75. See also Griffiths, *Cosmic Revelation*, 118; idem, *River of Compassion*, 93.

76. As Griffiths argues repeatedly in his writings, Jesus never said: "I am the Father," or "I am God." Even in John's Gospel he always spoke of himself in relationship to God, as in "I and the Father are one." See Griffiths, "The Christian Doctrine of Grace and Freewill," *Mountain Path* (April 197): 127; and idem, "Indian Spirituality and the Eucharist," 16.

77. Griffiths, *Christ in India*, 211; idem, *Golden String*, 172; idem, "Indian Spirituality and the Eucharist," 14–17.

78. Griffiths, *Christ in India*, 205.

79. Ibid., 204. See also Abhishiktānanda, *Hindu-Christian Meeting Point: Within the Cave of the Heart*, rev. ed. (Delhi: ISPCK, 1976), 22–23.

80. Griffiths, *Christ in India*, 205.

81. Griffiths, "Christian Witness in India: Ways of Knowing God," transcript of "The Catholic Hour," radio program (November 10, 1963), (Washington, DC: NCCM, 1963):

> [T]his is where the Hindu mind needs to discover Christ. We have to show the Hindu in the light of our faith, that in this ultimate experience of God, the absolute being, the world and the soul are not lost, nor is the personal being of God absorbed in the impersonal Godhead. It is in this ground of our being, in the real Self, that in our Christian experience there is a mystery of personal relationship even in the ultimate depth of the Godhead. The abyss of the Godhead as it exists beyond all human conception, is not merely absolute Being; it is a mystery of knowledge and love, of personal intercommunion of an incomprehensible kind, of which human knowledge and love is a faint shadow. In the same way, our faith in the

Incarnation teaches us that the human and the divine nature are united in the Person of Christ in such a way that the human is not absorbed in the divine, and in the mystical Body of Christ, Christians are united to God and to one another in a personal relationship of knowledge and love, in which, while sharing in the divine nature, in the divine being, knowledge and bliss, they yet remain distinct in themselves, each a unique reflection of the Being of God.

See also idem, "Process of Knowledge," 14.

82. Swindells, *Human Search*, 53; cf. Griffiths, *Golden String*, 108.

83. Griffiths, *Golden String*, 186.

Into Dialogue

1. Griffiths, *Golden String*, 64.

2. Griffiths, "St. Justin's 'Apology,'" *Pax* 27 (March 1937): 289–93.

3. An early use of the term and concept *fulfillment* for understanding the relationship of Christianity to Hinduism may be found in the work of J. N. Farquhar (1861–1929) whose most significant work is *The Crown of Hinduism* (Oxford: Oxford University Press, 1913).

4. Griffiths, "St. Justin's 'Apology,'" 293. The quote is Griffiths's paraphrase of a thesis found in Pierre Johanns's *Hinduism*. Fr. Johanns is later described by Griffiths as a great Sanskrit scholar who with another Jesuit, G. Dandoy, published a periodical in India in the 1920s entitled *The Light of the East*. Especially helpful to Griffiths were Johanns's regular articles in this periodical over the course of twenty years called "To Christ Through the Vedānta." These articles were later collected and published in one volume of the same title. Griffiths found in Johanns's writing the idea that what Hinduism lacked and what would resolve a number of troubling philosophical problems in the Vedāntic view of the relationship of God to the world was a theory of divine creation ex nihilo. See Griffiths, "Incarnation and the East," 60–61.

5. Griffiths, "St. Justin's 'Apology,'" 293. A similar optimism about the contact between Christianity and Indian ideas is expressed in the 1954 article already discussed, "Transcendent Unity of Religions," 264, 275; idem, *Golden String*, 174; and idem, "For a Hindu Catholicism," *Tablet* 205/6000 (May 21, 1955): 494–95.

6. Griffiths, "Catholicism To-day," *Pax* 40 (1950): 13, 14.

7. Griffiths, "Transcendent Unity of Religions," 273, 275.

8. Griffiths, *Golden String*, 174–75.

9. Ibid., 176–77.

10.   Griffiths, "Incarnation and the East," 73–74. Evident in this passage is Griffiths's familiarity with the thought of Carl Jung.

11.   Ibid., 74.

12.   Griffiths, "Fulfillment for the East," 82.

13.   Griffiths, "Missionary Today," 92.

14.   Ibid., 90–92; idem, "Catholicism and the East," 96. Cf. the Second Vatican Council's "Decree on the Church's Missionary Activity" (*Ad Gentes*, 9 [1965]).

15.   Griffiths, "Catholicism and the East," 98. Within both the church and Griffiths's position the issue naturally arose in the years after Vatican II regarding the relationship between dialogue and missions. For Griffiths's resolution of this tension, see his response to A. K. Saran in "Further Towards a Hindu-Christian Dialogue," *The Clergy Monthly* 32/5 (May 1968): 220.

16.   Griffiths, "Catholicism and the East," 100. See also idem, "Kurisumala Ashram," in *Christ in India*, 46.

17.   Griffiths, "Walking with Vinoba," in *Christ in India*, 131.

18.   This term is suggested in a number of Griffiths's articles during the 1960s, including "Ecumenical Approach to Non-Christian Religions," 305–10. Using such an approach, the Christian strives to "enter with sympathy" into the way of thinking found in the other religion in order to grasp its "inner core of truth" and then relate it to the Christian revelation (308). Cf. Griffiths, "Liturgy and Culture," 603.

19.   Griffiths, "Kurisumala Ashram," in *Christ in India*, 46–47. Cf. idem, "Experiment in Monastic Life," *Commonweal* 68/26 (September 26, 1958): 636. See also idem, "Monastic Life in India Today," 132–33.

20.   Griffiths, "Monastic Life in India Today," 133, 135. See also idem, "The Church and Hinduism," in *Christ and India*, 187.

21.   For an early mention of "complementarity" by Griffiths, see "Dialogue with Hinduism," 405. After comparing the primarily "mystical" and "prophetic" characters of the Eastern and Western religions respectively, Griffiths states that "these religions are essentially complementary, representing the two sides of all genuine religion."

The View from His Window

1.   Swindells, *Human Search*, 79.

2.   Ibid., 84. Griffiths identifies this "rhythm" as the Tao.

3.   Griffiths, *Return to the Center*, 35, 35–36.

4.   Ibid., 34. In a letter written soon after the move to Shantivanam, Griffiths elaborates:

> What I am discovering is the intimate relation between nature and God. God is *present* in nature, in every created thing. . . . Nature comes into being in the Word and expresses the mind of God to us, and nature is moved by the Spirit, which brings all things to maturity in Christ. This creation is in evolution towards the new creation, and man is the mediator, the high priest, who unites nature with God. (Letter to Martyn Skinner, December 25, 1968, quoted in du Boulay, *Beyond the Darkness*, 148–49)

5.   Griffiths, *Return to the Center*, 37.

Chapter 7: *The Guide of Shantivanam and Prophet of Dialogue*

1.   Spink, *Sense of the Sacred*, 149.

2.   Griffiths, *Marriage of East and West*, 23. See also Spink, *Sense of the Sacred*, 149–64; and du Boulay, *Beyond the Darkness*, 146.

3.   Griffiths, *Marriage of East and West*, 22–23.

4.   In addition to the first chapter of *Marriage of East and West*, Griffiths published a number of articles about the purpose and daily life of Shantivanam and about Christian ashrams in general: "Forest of Peace in South India," *Tablet* 223/6716 (February 8, 1969): 130–32; "Shantivanam: A New Beginning," in *Kurisumala: A Symposium on Ashram Life*, ed. Francis Mahieu (Bangalore, India: Asian Trading Corp., 1974), 75–76; "Shantivanam," *Spirit and Life* 70 (1975): 24–27; "A Christian Ashram," *Vaidikamitram* 9 (1976): 14–20; "Shantivanam: An Explanation," *Vaidikamitram* 9 (1976): 44–48; "Christian Monastic Life in India," *Journal of Dharma* 3/2 (April–June 1978): 122–35; "The Monastic Order and the Ashram," *American Benedictine Review* 30/2 (June 1979): 134–45; "Christian Ashrams," *Word and Worship* 17 (1984): 150–52; "Benedictine Ashram: An Experiment in Hindu-Christian Community," *Laughing Man* 5/3 (1984): 34–37; "The Ashram and Monastic Life," *Monastic Studies* 15 (Advent 1984): 117–23 (reprinted in *In Christo* 22 [1984]: 217–22); "The Christian Ashram," *Examiner* 139 (December 17, 1988): 1235; "The Meaning and Purpose of an Ashram," in *Saccidananda Ashram: A Garland of Letters* (Tiruchirappalli, India: Saccidananda Ashram, 1988), 4–9; and "A Benedictine Ashram," in *Saccidananda Ashram: A Garland of Letters* (Tiruchirappalli, India: Saccidananda Ashram, 1989), 3–5.

For a thorough study and evaluation of the Christian ashram movement in India that focuses upon the problematic role of the Christian guru (including Griffiths), see Catherine Cornille's *Guru in Indian Catholicism: Ambiguity or Opportunity for Inculturation?* (Louvain, Belgium: Peeters Press, 1991).

5.   When asked whether the move to Shantivanam had brought this type of change in his life, Griffiths responded as follows: "Yes, very much. I've

always been into the liturgy, the Latin liturgy and then the Syriac. It was only when I came here that . . . [he paused] Liturgy is still important. But the mystical tradition was far more important. And it's the meditation morning and evening that is to me the center of it" (Interview by the author, January 1989). See also Griffiths, "Forest of Peace in South India," 130–32. Perhaps the most striking witness to the change in his life brought about by the move to Shantivanam is the book *Return to the Center,* handwritten in the mid-1970s and published without any changes.

6. Spink, *Sense of the Sacred,* 156–58. Concerning the contrast between Griffiths and Abhishiktānanda in their respective approaches to dialogue, see Wayne Teasdale, *Toward a Christian Vedanta: The Encounter of Hinduism and Christianity according to Bede Griffiths* (Bangalore, India: Asian Trading Corp., 1987), 125–28; and the author's "Two Models of Christian Dialogue with Hinduism: Bede Griffiths and Abhishiktānanda," *Vidyajyoti* 60/2–4 (February–April, 1996): 101–10, 183–91, 243–54.

7. Founded by St. Romuald in the eleventh century, the Camaldolese order balances a solitary and community life with openness to the world. Griffiths's contact with the community occurred in Italy, and in 1980 he became affiliated with the order. In 1982, the ashram was formally received into the Camaldolese community; and four years later, the two Indian monks who had helped Griffiths establish the ashram were ordained as priests in this order. These two events brought a status and recognition in the church that eased relations with the local bishop as well as with the Vatican (cf. Swindells, *Human Search,* 82–83). In addition, these developments brought a deep personal satisfaction to Griffiths and a new ease and peace of spirit. Drawing from conversations with the two newly ordained priests, Amaldas and Christudas, Spink records that they found Griffiths weeping with joy in his hut the night of their ordination—a rare and thus telling display of emotion (Spink, *Sense of the Sacred,* 199).

8. In his writing and lectures throughout the 1980s, Griffiths was consciously influenced by the thought of scientific theorists like Fritjof Capra, whose book, *The Tao of Physics: An Exploration of the Parallels between Modern Physics and Eastern Mysticism* (New York: Bantam Books, 1975), is cited in the second autobiography. In 1982 Griffiths met Capra and other exponents of the so-called new science at a conference on Western science and Eastern wisdom in Bombay—an experience that would help to shape his perspective and thus his writing, especially on intercultural change.

9. Griffiths, *Marriage of East and West,* 27–28. In other contexts, Griffiths has adopted from "the new science" the term *paradigm shift* for the cultural changes he foresees.

10. Spink, *Sense of the Sacred,* 197. See also Griffiths, "On Poverty and Simplicity," 22.

11. In quotations are the subtitles of Griffiths's *River of Compassion* and *New Vision of Reality*. Following these are descriptions of his lecture series, *Christian Meditation: The Evolving Tradition*, later published as *The New Creation in Christ*, and his anthology, *Universal Wisdom*.

12. The details of these controversies with the local bishop are reported in Spink, *Sense of the Sacred*, 161–64; in Swindells, *Human Search*, 81–83; and in du Boulay, *Beyond the Darkness*, chap. 16.

13. Cornille, *Guru in Indian Catholicism*, 193.

14. Jose Pereira, "Christian Theosophists?" *Dilip* (November–December 1990): 11–19.

15. Robert Fastiggi and Pereira, "The Swami from Oxford," *Crisis* (March 1991): 25. In further response to such criticisms, Griffiths would compare his own theological explorations to the efforts of the early Church Fathers to articulate Christian theology in the terms of Greek philosophy (e.g., Griffiths, *Christ in India*, 24). As further defenses of his interpretation of the church's call for inculturation, see his "Indianisation," *Examiner* 126/19 (May 10, 1975): 233; and idem, "Dialogue and Inculturation," *Examiner* 137/33 (August 16, 1986): 777–78. Contrast Pereira and Fastiggi's assessment to Teasale's positive evaluation of Griffiths's efforts toward inculturation and dialogue based upon the integrity and unique value of the Christian tradition (Wayne Teasdale, "Bede Griffiths and the Uniqueness of Christianity," *Communio* 9/2 [Spring 1984]: 177–86).

16. Fastiggi and Pereira, "Swami from Oxford," 24. See Griffiths, "The Church of the Future," *Tablet* 236/7396–97 (April 10, 17, 1982): 364–66; idem, "The Church of Rome and Reunion," *New Blackfriars* 66/783 (September 1985): 389–92; and idem, *New Vision of Reality*, 287–96. See also his article on the magisterium ("The M-word," *Tablet* 244/7830 [August 11, 1990]: 1002), and "For Those Without Sin" (*National Catholic Reporter* 28/36 [August 14, 1992]: 20) where the church's attitude toward sexual misconduct is discussed.

17. Sita Ram Goel, ed., *Catholic Ashrams: Sannyasins or Swindlers?* (New Delhi: Voice of India, 1988, 1994), 167.

18. Ibid., 78, 129. An evaluation of these criticisms by Hindus as well as Christians is given in the conclusion of this book. See also du Boulay, *Beyond the Darkness*, chap. 16.

19. See du Boulay, *Beyond the Darkness*, chap. 19. Raimundo Panikkar describes and interprets Griffiths's travels in 1992 as follows: "[T]he rousing success of Bede Griffiths in Europe, Australia and the United States this year, at the age of 85, when thousands of people came to hear him, shows how profound are the changes of the spiritual geography of our times, and how widespread is the thirst for spiritual masters" (Panikkar, "The Wider Ecumenism: An Explorer Crosses the Borders," Review of *River of Compassion*, by Bede Griffiths. *Tablet* 246/7938 [September 26, 1992]: 1192).

20.   Undated letter, quoted in du Boulay, *Beyond the Darkness*, 237. Du Boulay suggests Griffiths's close friendship with D'Silva and his wife that preceded the stroke may have contributed to the 1990 breakthrough to the feminine (236–37).

21.   Spink, *Sense of the Sacred*, 205.

22.   Griffiths, *Golden String*, 9, 10, 11, 12, 16.

23.   Griffiths, *Cosmic Revelation*, 7.

24.   Griffiths, *Golden String*, 16–17.

25.   Griffiths, *Marriage of East and West*, 16.

26.   Griffiths, *Golden String*, 26, 38.

27.   Ibid., 28. See also du Boulay, *Beyond the Darkness*, 177–78.

28.   This subtle tension appears in Griffiths's attempt to uphold both an evolutionary perspective (exemplified by the writing of Pierre Teilhard de Chardin and Ken Wilber) and the myth of return (Griffiths, *New Vision of Reality*, 92–99). Indicative of the continual development in his thinking, Griffiths in 1991 stated that his interpretation of the biblical Fall had recently changed. While at first disagreeing with Wilber's positive assessment of that symbolic event as a valuable step in the upward movement of human evolution, Griffiths affirmed that Eden does represent a stage out of which humanity needed to mature:

> The original state was not, as St. Thomas Aquinas [said], . . . original man, perfect wisdom and knowledge. . . . It was on the contrary this global consciousness; nothing had emerged into rational consciousness at all. It was just above the animal where you're one with nature, one with everybody else, and you don't become individual. . . . And then the eating of the tree of knowledge was this awakening to individual, rational consciousness. And in one way, it upsets things and is the cause of all the conflict. And in another way, it's the path to transcendence and discovery. . . . So it's ambivalent in that way. On the one hand, it breaks up the unity which you experience. But it's also the pathway to a new unity beyond. And therefore it is a growth process. So Wilber is right; it's "up from Eden." (Interview by the author, tape recording, Trappist, KY, August 1991)

29.   Griffiths, *New Vision of Reality*, 11, 202–3. In articulating this paradox, Griffiths is dependent upon the writings of Wilber, especially *The Spectrum of Consciousness* (Wheaton, IL: Theosophical Publishing House, 1977) and *Up From Eden*. Wilber outlines three major stages in human evolution that clarify Griffiths's changed position on the Fall: the prepersonal and subconscious stage (the state of uniformity symbolized by Eden), the personal and self-conscious stage (the state of individuation that results from the Fall), and the transpersonal and superconscious stage (representing the state of unity or fully differentiated wholeness to which the mystics of many traditions attest we "return" (Wilber, *Up from Eden*, 8).

30. Griffiths, *New Vision of Reality*, 11.

31. Griffiths, *Marriage of East and West*, 27.

32. Compare Griffiths's discussion of *sannyāsa* in *Marriage of East and West* (42–44) to Abhishiktānanda's essay, "Sannyāsa," in his *Further Shore* (Delhi: ISPCK, 1975), 1–56.

Chapter 8: The Way of Intuitive Wisdom

1. Cf. chap. 6. In a conversation about this change in interpretation, Griffiths acknowledged the influence of two Catholic scholars who were working on Śankara's writings in India: Richard De Smet, SJ (1916–97) and Sara Grant, RSCJ.

2. Griffiths, *Vedanta and Christian Faith*, 146; cf. idem, *Golden String*, 116.

3. Griffiths, *Vedanta and Christian Faith*, 147.

4. Ibid., 150–51. Griffiths cites the following sections from the *Summa Theologiae* in support of his comparisons: 1, q. 3, a. 1–8 ("On the Simplicity of God"); and 1, q. 15 ("On Ideas"). Aquinas declared on the basis of Plato and Augustine that the "ideas" of all things exist in the mind and essence of their Creator. Thus God knows all things in knowing God's own essence, that is, through identity. Griffiths claims that a similar knowledge dawns in the experience of *advaita* in which one knows all things in God through oneness with God. Griffiths notes the distinction between the two traditions that while Hindu philosophy contends that such complete knowledge is possible in this life, Christian authorities believe that such perfection is not realizeable until after death (Griffiths, *Vedanta and Christian Faith*, 149).

5. Griffiths, *Vedanta and Christian Faith*, 151–52.

6. Griffiths tends to use the term *meditation* in this text for what he has elsewhere spoken of as *contemplation,* a nondiscursive method of prayer for transcending thoughts to experience the spirit or center of the soul, what he begins to also call the "ground of consciousness." While "contemplation" is also referred to as a depth of experience available through various means (including liturgy, reading the Scripture, even manual labor), meditation retains for Griffiths a more narrow connotation as a nondiscursive method of prayer. Griffiths's primary method of meditation remains "the prayer of the heart" or Jesus Prayer, informed by yogic teachings on the importance of posture, breath, and mental state.

7. Griffiths, *Return to the Center*, 35–36.

8. Ibid., 37–38.

9. Griffiths, *New Creation in Christ*, 44. In the Yoga tradition, the breath is spoken of as the link between the body and the mind, between the physical and the nonphysical. The movement of the breath, and with it one's attention,

from the head to the heart is a common instruction in the Eastern Orthodox teaching of the Jesus Prayer. See also Griffiths, "Interview: Father Bede Griffiths, O.S.B.," interview by Johannes Agaard and Neil Duddy, 24–27.

10.   Griffiths, "In Jesus' Name," 498–99. See also the author's "Mutual Transformation of Self and Symbol," 215–41. See also du Boulay, *Beyond the Darkness*, 173–74; and Griffiths, "Eastern Religious Experience," *Monastic Studies* 9 (Autumn 1972): 158, 159.

11.   Griffiths, *New Creation in Christ*, 39–57.

12.   Ibid., 41.

13.   Griffiths, *Vedanta and Christian Faith*, 124–25.

14.   Ibid., 109, 162–63. Griffiths relates the Christian doctrine of original sin to "the fact that man has fallen from the state of intuitive wisdom and communication with God into its present state of dependence on sense and reason" (139). One is reminded of the principle that further development or evolution in human knowledge will necessitate, for Griffiths, a return to an original state.

15.   Griffiths, "Indian Christian Contemplation," *Clergy Monthly* 35/7 (August 1971): 278. The scriptural quotation is from Rom. 5:5. See also idem, "Interview: Father Bede Griffiths, O.S.B.," 27; and idem, *New Creation in Christ*, 43.

16.   Griffiths, "Indian Christian Contemplation," 279. The citation from Paul is Eph. 3.19. It is significant and not surprising that Griffiths understands the purpose of a Christian ashram like Shantivanam in terms similar to those just used to distinguish Christian contemplation; it is a place where this kind of experience of God, which fulfills the goal of "Self-realization" sought by many from various religions, can happen. Congruent with his lingering sense of the superiority of the Christian revelation, Griffiths writes in 1971 that a Christian ashram can potentially provide this contemplative dimension more completely than those of other traditions: "An ashram is a place which should be open to all such seekers of God, or seekers of Self-realization, whatever their religion or without any religion. The Church in India has an urgent call to answer this need. At present most people go to Hindu ashrams or Buddhist monasteries or schools of Yoga. But a Christian ashram should be able to answer this need no less effectively, and to lead on to a deeper experience of God than may be found elsewhere" (Griffiths, "Indian Christian Contemplation," 280).

17.   Griffiths, *Marriage of East and West*, 91.

18.   Ibid., 91–92. Cf. idem, *Return to the Center*, 29.

19.   Griffiths, *Return to the Center*, 16. Cf. idem, *Golden String*, 38.

20.   Griffiths, *Return to the Center*, 18.

21.   Ibid., 19.

22.   Griffiths, *Marriage of East and West*, 8, 151–52, 164–66; and idem, "Incarnation and the East," 74.

23. Griffiths, *Marriage of East and West*, 153. See also idem, "Power of Intuition," 1; idem, *Universal Wisdom*, 19.

24. Griffiths, *Marriage of East and West*, 154. The image of intuition as arising from "beneath the sunlit surface" of the mind is quoted by Griffiths from Jacques Maritain (*Creative Intuition in Art and Poetry*, 94).
There are obvious similarities between this theory of the mind and those offered by Western psychology, especially Freud's theory of the unconscious. Griffiths seeks to distinguish his own view from that of Freud by saying that the unconscious is not just the vast collection of impressions from repressed experiences, desires, and fears but is an actual state or level (or "field") of consciousness that opens not only onto the total range of past impressions but also onto the "mystery of being," the transcendent reality. Griffiths follows Jacques Maritain in making this distinction (Jacques Maritain, *Creative Intuition in Art and Poetry*, 94).
Griffiths also compares and contrasts his own view with that of Jung by affirming the existence of "archetypes" in the mind but locating them not in an "unconscious" but in those levels of consciousness that are "subliminal" or "beneath the surface" of the mind (Griffiths, *Marriage of East and West*, 162).

25. Griffiths, *Vedanta and Christian Faith*, 108.

26. Griffiths, *Marriage of East and West*, 155. Cf. Aquinas, *Summa Theologiae* 1, q. 79, a. 2–3. In his discussion of intuitive knowing it is clear that Griffiths has drawn not only upon Western sources like the Maritains and Aquinas, but also upon Vedānta philosophy (71). Griffiths later concludes that the important distinction between the active intellect (*manas* or *ratio*) and the passive intellect (*buddhi* or *intellectus*) can be identified in principle in all advanced languages (Griffiths, *Universal Wisdom*, 13).

27. Griffiths, *Marriage of East and West*, 156.

28. Ibid, 157. See also idem, "Power of Intuition," 5.

29. Griffiths, *Marriage of East and West*, 157–59. Cf. idem, "Process of Knowledge," 3.

30. Griffiths, *Marriage of East and West*, 160–62.

31. Ibid., 162–65.

32. Ibid., 165.

33. Ibid., 166.

34. Ibid., 157. Cf. *Muṇḍaka Upaniṣad* 3.1.

35. Griffiths, *Marriage of East and West*, 166. See idem, *Return to the Center*, 41.

36. Griffiths, *Marriage of East and West*, 199.

37. Ibid., 167.

38. Ibid., 167–69.

39. Ibid., 170.

40. Capra, *Tao of Physics*, 14.

41. Ken Wilber, *The Spectrum of Consciousness* (Wheaton, IL: Theosophical Publishing House, 1977), 43, n. 30. See also Wilber's *Eye to Eye: The Quest for the New Paradigm*, expanded ed. (Boston: Shambhala, 1990), 2–7.

42. Bohm, *Wholeness and the Implicate Order*, 64.

43. Griffiths, *River of Compassion*, 161–62, 91. See idem, *New Vision of Reality*, 233.

44. Griffiths, *New Vision of Reality*, 39.

45. See Karl Jaspers's *Origin and Goal of History*, cited in Griffiths, *Marriage of East and West*, 59–61, and idem, *Universal Wisdom*, 8–9, 18.

46. Griffiths, *New Vision of Reality*, 41.

47. Ibid., 48.

48. Ibid., 100; cf. idem, *Vedanta and Christian Faith*, 146.

49. Griffiths, *New Vision of Reality*, 136. See also idem, "Symbolic Theology," 293.

50. Griffiths, *New Vision of Reality*, 106. Capra's phrase is from his *Tao of Physics*.

51. Griffiths emphasizes the importance of meditation in general as a means for experiencing what lies "beyond" the dualistic mind: "Unless you get into meditation, you don't transcend your rational mind. And the whole art of meditation is precisely to let it [i.e., the rational mind] become quiet and calm, and then this awareness of the beyond emerges simply" (Interview by the author, January 1989).

52. Griffiths, *New Vision of Reality*, 140, 143, 182, 244, 251. This kind of "supraconceptual knowledge" that Griffiths finds in the writings of mystics of many traditions, while clear in the Church Fathers, is ignored, in his view, by the official church's current view of meditation. This opinion is expressed by Griffiths in his criticism of the Doctrinal Congregation's 1989 document, "Some Aspects of Christian Meditation" (*Origins* 19/30 [December 28, 1989]: 492–98). Griffiths finds the document's estimation of the value of Eastern meditation practices for the Christian "disappointing" and its presentation of Christian prayer "inadequate." See his "Monk's Response to the Document on Christian Prayer from the Congregation for the Doctrine of the Faith," *NABEWD Bulletin* (1990): 11. (This journal is published by the Benedictine Order's North American Board for East-West Dialogue, available from Fr. James Conner, OCSO, Abbey of Gethsemani, Trappist, KY 40051.)

53. Griffiths, *New Vision of Reality*, 41; cf. Wilber, *Up From Eden*, 310.

54. Griffiths, *Marriage of East and West*, 60.

55. Griffiths, *New Vision of Reality*, 267.

56. Ibid., 266.

57. Griffiths, *New Creation in Christ*, 103. See also Swindells, *Human Search*, 88; du Boulay, *Beyond the Darkness*, 227–28. In conversation, he added: "It knocked out my mind completely. And since then the nondual reality is the only reality to me. . . . [T]his total oneness is there now. And I've never lost it since" (Interview by the author, November 1990).

58. Griffiths, *New Creation in Christ*, 103–4. See also Swindells, *Human Search*, 88–90; du Boulay, *Beyond the Darkness*, 229–31. It was significant for Griffiths that the stroke was felt on the left side of the head, the side of the brain associated with rational thinking, the type of mental activity associated by some with the masculine aspect of the psyche. At the end of his account of the experience at the John Main Seminar, Griffiths jokingly remarks: "I think it was the woman in me who came and hit me on the head! But then she came back to me as a loving mother. When you let the feminine open and your unconscious lets her come up, then she is the loving mother and in coming back to you she transforms you" (idem, *New Creation in Christ*, 104). Cf. Griffiths's 1971 letter to John Moffitt quoted in the latter's *Journey to Gorakhpur: An Encounter with Christ beyond Christianity* (New York: Holt, 1972), 264.

59. Cf. Kevin Joyce, "A Study of the Higher States of Consciousness and Their Interpretation according to Teresa of Avila and Maharishi Mahesh Yogi" (Ph.D. diss., Catholic University of America, 1991) a manuscript that was studied by Griffiths with keen interest. Specifically, Griffiths affirmed the accuracy of Maharishi's account of "cosmic consciousness" as very similar to his own experience of "this awareness of the supreme Reality all the time in the background" (Interview by the author, August 1991). Note that neither in Maharishi nor Teresa's system is the state of cosmic consciousness or the parallel state of "the prayer of union" the final one. In Maharishi's schema, the individual in cosmic consciousness matures farther through devotion to the personal God to experience an ever-deepening oneness with the creation of that God. In Teresa's understanding, the soul moves toward spiritual betrothal and then toward marriage with the divine spouse.

Chapter 9: God beyond the Symbols of the Religions

1. Griffiths, *Return to the Center*, 76. See also idem, "The Mystical Dimension in Theology," *Indian Theological Studies* 14 (1977): 229–46.

2. Griffiths, *Return to the Center*, 38, 73.

3. Ibid., 57. See the following by Griffiths: "Erroneous Beliefs and Unauthorised Rites," *Tablet* 227/6928 (April 14, 1973): 356; "The One Mystery," *Tablet* 228/6975 (March 9, 1974): 223; "The Universal Truth," *Tablet* 229/7022 (February 1, 1975): 101–2; "Dialogue with Hinduism," *Impact* 11 (1976): 152–57; "The Mystical Tradition in Indian Theology," *Monastic Studies* 13 (Autumn 1982): 161–62; "On Poverty and Simplicity," 19; "Transcending Dualism: An Eastern Approach to the Semitic Religions," ed. Wayne Teasdale, *Cistercian Studies* 20/2 (1985): 85–86; "Emerging Consciousness for a New Humankind," *Examiner* 136 (February 9, 1985): 125, 128.

4. Griffiths, *Return to the Center*, 71.

5. Ibid., 74.

6. On the controversies raised by Griffiths's efforts at inculturation, see chap. 7.

7. Cf. Griffiths, "Mystical Tradition in Indian Theology," 171.

8. Griffiths deals with the question of the divinity of Jesus Christ in *Marriage of East and West*, 186–87. See also excerpts from an unpublished article by Griffiths, "In What Sense Is Jesus Called God?" quoted by Teasdale in *Towards a Christian Vedanta*, 140–41.

9. Griffiths, *Return to the Center*, 57–58. See also idem, *Vedanta and Christian Faith*, 141. Cf. Aquinas's principle that God is beyond all names and forms (e.g., *Summa Theologiae* 1, q. 3).

10. Griffiths, *Return to the Center*, 86–87.

11. Ibid., 71.

12. Ibid., 74.

13. Griffiths would, like Avery Dulles, reject "an extreme 'archetype Christology'" in which Jesus' life is seen as the instantiation in time and place of an archetype that may be found working everywhere. Both theologians would assert, however, that one may legitimately conceive of the Logos expressing itself (in the Rahnerian sense) "to other peoples through other religious symbols" (Dulles, *Models of Revelation*, 190; see also Lucien Richard, *What Are They Saying about Christ and the World Religions?* [New York: Paulist Press, 1981], 66–67.) While one might characterize some of Griffiths's accounts of Christ as reflecting an "archetype Christology," he is clear that the incarnation was a unique historical event, revealing an unprecedented dimension of the Godhead (explicated in Trinitarian doctrine) and of the human's relation to the divine (expressed in Jesus' *Abba*). In other words, the Christ as "the archetypal ideal" is, for Griffiths, focused in a "unique way in a particular individual at the same time" (Richard, *What Are They Saying about Christ and the World Religions?*, 67).

14. Dulles, *Models of Revelation,* 190. See also Paul Knitter, *No Other Name? A Critical Survey of Christian Attitudes Toward the World Religions* (Maryknoll, NY: Orbis, 1985), 154–57. Dulles and Knitter both attribute a "universal Christology" to Panikkar. See Panikkar's *The Trinity and the Religious Experience of Man* (Maryknoll, NY: Orbis, 1973), 53–54.

15. Griffiths, "In Jesus' Name," 498.

16. Cf. "Interview with a Spiritual Master: The Trinity," interview by Teasdale (Shantivanam, India, December 1986), *Living Prayer* 21/3 (May–June 1988): 25. Here Griffiths speaks of Jesus as "the culmination" of the process begun in other holy persons, and as "the ultimate expression of the Word."

17. For one resolution of this apparent contradiction, see Seyyed Hossein Nasr's "relative absolute" discussed in a text that was important to Griffiths, Nasr's *Knowledge and the Sacred* (New York: Crossroad, 1981), chap. 9.

18. Griffiths, *Vedanta and Christian Faith,* 141; idem, *Return to the Center,* 58; idem, *Marriage of East and West,* 189.

19. Griffiths, *Return to the Center,* 34, quoted above in "The View from His Window."

20. Griffiths, "Mystical Dimension in Theology," 243. See also idem, *Marriage of East and West,* 178–79.

21. Griffiths confirmed this point in conversation, claiming that all "coloration" by one's religious conditioning does not disappear even in the contemplative state beyond all symbols: "I think as long as we remain in this world those conditional elements will always [endure]. We experience the divine itself but in different ways" (Interview by the author, August 1991).

22. Griffiths distinguished his view from that of Advaita Vedānta in which all differentiations are left behind in encountering the divine mystery: "To me it's Jesus of Nazareth . . . you go deeper and deeper into his reality, and you find you don't lose him. He's found in the depths of his being which is the being of creation, which is the being of God. You go in and with him to the supreme. You don't leave him" (Interview by the author, August 1991). This account is clearly consistent with Rahner's sense of "mediated immediacy." See also du Boulay, *Beyond the Darkness,* 174.

23. Cf. Dulles, *Models of Revelation,* 148–49; and Nasr, *Knowledge and the Sacred,* 200–201.

24. Quoted by Griffiths in "Mystical Tradition in Indian Theology," 159; and idem, *Cosmic Revelation,* 85. See Weber, *In Quest of the Absolute,* 25.

25. Griffiths, *Return to the Center,* 26–27.

26. *Symbolization* is not a term original to Griffiths but rather is taken from Susanne Langer's *Philosophy in a New Key: A Study in the Symbolism of Reason, Rite, and Art* (Cambridge: Harvard University Press, 1942), 24, 42, a text

that he suggested in conversation bore close affinities with his own view of symbols. Langer defines "symbolization" as the fundamental ("prerationative") and "constructive" response of the human mind to the data of experience whereby that experience is transformed (interpreted) in terms of a few "elementary ideas" (ideas here in the broad sense including images as well as concepts) known as symbols. Note that given their different methological assumptions, logical versus theological, Langer does not address the possibility of divine agency in the process, while Griffiths does.

27.   Griffiths, "Mystical Dimension in Theology," 242; see also 231, where the same thesis is applied to all religions.

28.   Ibid., 244.

29.   Griffiths, Foreword to *Child and the Serpent: Reflections on Popular Indian Symbols*, by Jyoti Sahi (Boston: Routledge & Kegan Paul, 1980), xi; idem, *Marriage of East and West*, 69; idem, *New Vision of Reality*, chap. 2.

30.   Griffiths, Foreword to *Child and the Serpent*, xi: "The word symbol comes from the Greek word *symballein* meaning to 'throw together.' The idea behind it is that the world has been broken into pieces and the function of the symbols is to put these pieces together." See also idem, *New Vision of Reality*, 37–39.

31.   Griffiths's understanding of the term *the unconscious* is related to, but distinct from, how Jung used it (Griffiths, *Marriage of East and West*, 153–54, 162). Clearly, Griffiths's view of symbols, particularly in how they arise within the deeper recesses of what he prefers to call "the subliminal depths of consciousness," bears a resemblance that he acknowledges with Jung's "archetypes." Both terms refer to basic forms or images (Langer's "elementary ideas") that are general to human consciousness and shape (Langer's "transform") the mind's spontaneous interpretation of life events.

32.   *Summa Theologiae* 2–2, q. 172, a.1, ad 1; see chap. 6.

33.   Griffiths, foreword to *Child and the Serpent*, xii. See also idem, *Marriage of East and West*, 59–61, 170.

34.   Griffiths, foreword to *Child and the Serpent*, xii. On the relationship between the human and the divine that is the basis of the process of symbolization, Griffiths wrote:

> I am clearer now that, as Jung says, symbols arise originally in the unconscious and these symbolic structures are reflections in the human psyche of the eternal archetypes or patterns of reality. This is where the link between the human and the divine occurs. Naturally, the symbolic expression is largely determined by the conditioning of the individual consciousness, which varies immensely. Some have only confused images in their dreams; in a great poet or prophet the symbols may come very close to the original archetype. The archetype of "God," for instance, can vary from the "dream-time" figures of the Australian aborigines to the figure of Krishna in the Gita or of Christ in the New Testament. (Shantivanam, India, to the author, June 15, 1990). See also idem, "Process of Knowledge," 5.

35. Griffiths, "Emerging Consciousness and the Mystical Traditions of Asia," in *Emerging Consciousness for a New Humankind: Asian Interreligious Concern,* ed. Michael von Bruck (Bangalore, India: Asian Trading Corp., 1985), 53: "What then is consciousness? Consciousness, as Susanne Langer has explained, is essentially the process of symbolisation. A symbol is a sign by which something becomes present to consciousness. The human organism is part of the whole organism of nature and is subject to innumerable waves of energy which are continually working upon it. But it has the capacity to structure these waves (in the manner of a hologram) into a form which makes the object present to consciousness." See also Griffiths, *Marriage of East and West,* 104; and idem, *Universal Wisdom,* 40.

36. Griffiths, *Marriage of East and West,* 167, 31.

37. Griffiths, *Return to the Center,* 80–81. Cf. Langer, *Philosophy in a New Key,* 267–75. Langer writes of a similar weakness in the modern scientific mind in her own defense of the meaning value of symbols, seeking to expose the assumption that facts are the world: "Our world 'divides into facts' because we so divide it" (273).

38. Griffiths, *Marriage of East and West,* 171, 198–99; and idem, foreword to *Child and the Serpent,* xiii.

39. Griffiths, *Vedanta and Christian Faith,* 110–14; idem, *New Creation in Christ,* 22.

40. On the principle of *neti, neti* (e.g., *Bṛhadāraṇyaka Upaniṣad* 2.iii.6), see Griffiths, *Golden String,* 172; idem, *Vedanta and Christian Faith,* 106, 113; idem, *Return to the Center,* 120; idem, *Marriage of East and West,* 64, 101; idem, "Mystical Tradition in Indian Theology," 161; idem, "On Poverty and Simplicity," 23; idem, *New Vision of Reality,* 245. On the congruence between the Upaniṣads and Christian theology on this point, see also Griffiths, "Symbolism and Cult," 59; idem, *Vedanta and Christian Faith,* 103–4; and idem, *Marriage of East and West,* 26.

41. Griffiths, *Return to the Center,* 118.

42. Griffiths, "Advaitic Experience and the Personal God in the Upanishads and the Bhagavad Gita," 72; 76–77.

43. Griffiths, "Mystical Dimension in Theology," 244–45; idem, "The Two Theologies," *Tablet* 234/7299 (May 31, 1980): 520. See also idem, "The Search for God," *Tablet* 233/7251 (June 30, 1979): 620–21; idem, *Return to the Center,* 118; and idem, *Marriage of East and West,* 148.

44. Griffiths, "Two Theologies," 520.

45. Griffiths, " Symbolic Theology," 294.

46. Griffiths, *Return to the Center,* 78; idem, *Marriage of East and West,* 175; idem, "The Indian Spiritual Tradition and the Church in India," *Outlook* 15/4 (Winter 1976): 101.

47.   Griffiths, *Marriage of East and West,* 103–104.

48.   Ibid., 69–70. The image of the "uncarved block" is taken from the Chinese classic, the Tao Te Ching where it symbolizes the unmanifest tao or way.

49.   Griffiths identified a similar dual movement in Rahner's account of the relationship between God and the human (Griffiths, "A Meditation on the Mystery of the Trinity," *Monastic Studies* 17 [Christmas 1986]: 71).

50.   Griffiths, "Mystical Dimension in Theology," 244.

51.   Griffiths, "Advaitic Experience and the Personal God in the Upanishads and the Bhagavad Gita," 77.

52.   As examples of Griffiths's discussion and evaluation of diverse Hindu interpretations of *advaita* during the third period, see his *Vedanta and Chrisitian Faith,* chap. 3; "Dialogue with Hinduism"; "Advaitic Experience and the Personal God in the Upanishads and the Bhagavad Gita"; *Cosmic Revelation,* 72ff.; "Mystical Tradition in Indian Theology"; *Marriage of East and West,* 88–94; *New Vision of Reality,* chap. 8.

53.   Griffiths's most sustained treatment of the Trinity is found in "Meditation on the Mystery of the Trinity," 69–79. See also idem, "Interview with a Spiritual Master," 24–31.

54.   Griffiths, "Dialogue with Hinduism," 156. See also idem, *Marriage of East and West,* 35, 98–100; idem, *Vedanta and Christian Faith,* 121; idem, "On Poverty and Simplicity," 26; idem, "Meditation on the Mystery of the Trinity," 73; and idem, "Reincarnation: A Christian View," interview by Wayne Teasdale (Shantivanam, India, December 1986), *Living Prayer* 21/5 (September–October 1988): 25.

55.   Griffiths used different phrases to express the paradoxical nature of the divine mystery in itself and of the relationships between that mystery and the soul and the world. Among these phrases are "identity in relationship," "unity in duality" (both in Griffiths, *Vedanta and Christian Faith,* 141), "unity in distinction" (idem, *River of Compassion,* 126), "unity in relationship" (idem, "On Poverty and Simplicity," 27), "unity in diversity," and "multiplicity in the unity" (both in conversation).

56.   Griffiths, *Return to the Center,* 144; idem, *Cosmic Revelation,* 131; idem, *Marriage of East and West,* 99; idem, "Transcending Dualism," 84.

57.   Griffiths, "Advaitic Experience and the Personal God in the Upanishads and the Bhagavad Gita," 84.

58.   Griffiths, *Cosmic Revelation,* 130. See also idem, "Advaitic Experience and the Personal God in the Upanishads and the Bhagavad Gita," 84. Griffiths cites the school of Śaiva Siddhānta as expressing most clearly the intuition that God (Śiva) is love. Elsewhere he describes this school of Hindu philosophy as the closest to Christian teachings (idem, "Meaning and Purpose of an Ashram," 5). More generally in Hinduism, parallels to the Christian teaching that God is

love are suggested by the imaging of the divine as god and goddess, e.g., Krishna-Radha, Vishna-Śri, Śiva-Śakti.

59. Griffiths, *Marriage of East and West,* 97; idem, "On Poverty and Simplicity," 26.

60. Griffiths, "On Poverty and Simplicity," 26; idem, *Marriage of East and West,* 77–78. See also idem, *Return to the Center,* 144–45.

61. Griffiths, *New Vision of Reality,* 168. Cf. John 10.15; 14.10, 28.

62. Griffiths, "On Poverty and Simplicity," 26–28; idem, *Return to the Center,* 146; idem, "Mystical Tradition in Indian Theology," 163–64.

63. Griffiths, "Meditation on the Mystery of the Trinity," 72. See also idem, "Interview with a Spiritual Master," 26–27. Cf. Aquinas, *Summa Theologiae* 1, q. 15; and Griffiths, *New Vision of Reality,* 249–50.

64. Griffiths, *Marriage of East and West,* 100; see also 93, 190; idem, *Cosmic Revelation,* 130–31; idem, *New Vision of Reality,* 273.

65. Griffiths, "Meditation the Mystery of the Trinity," 71–72. See also idem, *Marriage of East and West,* 273.

66. Griffiths, *Marriage of East and West,* 44; idem, *New Vision of Reality,* 89.

67. Griffiths, *Marriage of East and West,* 84–85; see also 97; idem, "Advaitic Experience and the Personal God in the Upanishads and the Bhagavad Gita," 78; idem, *Return to the Center,* 42–44; idem, *Cosmic Revelation,* 72.

68. Griffiths, "Transcending Dualism," 85.

69. Griffiths, *Return to the Center,* 37–38; idem, *Marriage of East and West,* 92–93; idem, "On Poverty and Simplicity," 24; idem, *River of Compassion,* 169.

70. Griffiths, *New Vision of Reality,* 94, 173, cf. 273. No reference for Teilhard de Chardin is given.

71. Griffiths cites Bohm's *Wholeness and the Implicate Order* in *New Vision of Reality,* 18–19, 93, 149. The implied analogy is between the "implicate order" and the Logos, as the source of all differentiation within the wholeness (universe, Godhead). See Griffiths, *New Vision of Reality,* 269–70; and idem, *Marriage of East and West,* 83–84, citing Aquinas, *Summa Theologiae* 1, q. 8, a.3.

72. Griffiths, *New Vision of Reality,* 55.

73. Ibid., 94–95. See also idem, "Emerging Consciousness and the Mystical Traditions of Asia," 62–63; and idem, *Universal Wisdom,* 42. The quotation is from Capra's *Tao of Physics* (e.g., 124). See also Griffiths, *New Vision of Reality,* 255–75.

74. Griffiths, *Marriage of East and West,* 84–85; idem, *New Vision of Reality,* 254.

75. Griffiths, *New Vision of Reality,* 175.

76. Ibid., 281–82.

77. Griffiths identified a significant parallel on this point between a Christian *advaita* and Kashmir Śaivism, specifically the latter's discussion of the *spanda* or "stir of energy" that exists between the two poles within the ultimate reality, Śiva and Śakti. The presence of this principle in Kashmir Śaivism leads it to a fuller valuation of the cosmos than is found in Vedānta. See ibid., 156–61, 171. See also his analysis of the Buddhist concept of *śūnyatā* (158–59).

78. See Jesu Rajan, *Bede Griffiths and Sannyāsa* (Bangalore, India: Asian Trading Corp., 1989), 187–88.

79. Griffiths, "Interview with a Spiritual Master," 25.

80. Griffiths, *River of Compassion*, 272; idem, "Meditation on the Mystery of the Trinity, 73; idem, *Cosmic Revelation*, 105.

81. Griffiths, *New Vision of Reality*, 249. Cf. *John Ruusbroec: The Spiritual Espousals and Other Works*, trans. James A. Wiseman (New York: Paulist Press, 1985), 148–50 (*Spiritual Espousals* 3.3).

82. Griffiths, *New Vision of Reality*, 250, cf. 172, 254. See also idem, *Return to the Center*, 57–67.

83. This flowing out in love on the basis of the contemplative experience of union with God is described by Ruusbroec as the "common life." See the conclusion to his *Sparkling Stone* (Ruusbroec, *John Ruusbroec*, 184). Cf. Griffiths, *River of Compassion*, 101–103.

84. Griffiths, "Contemplative Community and the Transformation of the World," interview by Wayne Teasdale (Shantivanam, India, December 1986), *Living Prayer* 22/1 (January–February 1989): 12. See also idem, *River of Compassion*, 94, 103, 272, 273.

85. Griffiths, *New Vision of Reality*, 55. See also Griffiths's discussion of the tenth Oxherding Picture in Zen Buddhism ("Plenary Discussions," side 3, *Christian Meditation*).

86. Nasr, *Knowledge and the Sacred*, 200–201. Cf. Griffiths, *New Vision of Reality*, 273. Cf. James Robertson Price III, "Transcendence and Images: The Apophatic and Kataphatic Reconsidered," *Studies in Formative Spirituality* 11 (May 1990): 198–99.

87. Rajan defines *sannyāsa* as "a state of life in which a person is totally detached from everything in the universe and at the same time intensely attached to the Ultimate Reality" (Rajan, *Bede Griffiths and Sannyāsa*, 11). See also Teasdale, *Toward a Christian Vedanta*, 152–65.

88. Griffiths, *Marriage of East and West*, 42; idem, *Christ in India*, 24; idem, "Contemplative Community and the Transformation of the World," 12.

89. Griffiths, *Marriage of East and West*, 42; see also 203.

90. Ibid., 43; see also 199.

91. E.g., Avery Dulles, Susanne Langer, and Paul Ricoeur. See the author's "Mutual Transformation of Self and Symbol," *Horizons* 23/2 (Fall 1996): 215–41.

92. "My emphasis before was on symbolism, to see the nondual reality in the symbol, in the word, in the sign; and, of course, that's valid. But now it's rather the other way around: to see through the symbol to the nondual reality. It's going beyond all the time now; that's my movement now. . . . I see *advaita* as the end toward which all religions are moving, Hindu, Buddhist, Taoist, Sikh, Muslim, Jewish, Christian." In the same interview, he identified the centrality of Trinity as follows: "Trinity more and more is the focus for everything for me"; and, "to me the Trinity is the heart of the whole reality" (Interview by the author, August 1991).

93. Griffiths, "The Ideal of Monastic Life in John Main's Teaching," in *Christian Meditation*. Cf. idem, *New Creation in Christ*, 23.

94. Griffiths, *New Creation in Christ*, 35, 55. Cf. idem, *Universal Wisdom*, 33–35.

95. Griffiths, *New Creation in Christ*, 105. "When on the cross he said, '*Eloi, Eloi, lama sabachthani,*' I wonder if he didn't lose the personal God and go into the infinite . . . a total detachment, a radical detachment. . . . In every tradition there's a death; you die to the whole world, . . . and then it opens up, the whole reality. And the Resurrection is simply the passing beyond" (Interview by the author, January 1989). "And we have to go through all these limited cultural forms of the New Testament, the Church . . . and language, to the mystery of Jesus himself. That *is* the reality, the mystery beyond. And any form or image we make is a projection; it's useful; we have to project in some way. But always we end in this *śūnyatā,* in the void, total emptiness. It sounds terrible, but that emptiness is total fullness; it's the *pleroma.* So that's where I am now" (Interview by the author, August 1991).

96. Griffiths, *New Creation in Christ*, 55.

97. Ibid., 69, 77–78; idem, "Meaning and Purpose of an Ashram," 7–8. See also du Boulay, *Beyond the Darkness,* 214–16.

98. Griffiths, *New Creation in Christ*, 23.

99. Ibid., 78–79.

100. In an interview by the author, Griffiths states:

I feel I'm led to the pure awareness where you don't lose nature or humanity, and so on, but they're taken up into something totally transcendent. And that's where the Upaniṣads come to mean more and more. . . . [Y]ou know the one I'm so fond of, "In the castle of the body there is this shrine, and this shrine is [in the form of] the lotus, and in the lotus is this little space; and in that little space the whole universe is present." And that's where I am now really, in that little space in the heart of the lotus. Everything and everybody is present in a total oneness. . . . The multiplicity is in the unity. You don't lose the multiplicity. You don't lose the beauty of the universe, all of human nature and so on. But it's transcended and experienced in a new way. And that's what I feel, that's what I feel we've got to find. (August 1991)

The scriptural passage paraphrased by Griffiths is from the *Chāṇḍogya Upaniṣad* 8.i.1–3. Cf. idem, *Golden String*, 171–72.

101. Griffiths, "Plenary Discussions," side 4, *Christian Meditation*. Griffiths's sources for this interpretation of *śūnyatā* included Lama Anagarika Govinda's *Creative Meditation and Multi-Dimensional Consciousness* (Wheaton, IL: Theosophical Publishing House, 1976); Michael von Bruck (e.g., "Buddhist Shunyata and the Christian Trinity: The Emerging Holistic Paradigm," in *Buddhist Emptiness and Christian Trinity*, eds. Roger Corless and Paul F. Knitter [New York: Paulist Press, 1990], 44–66); and D. T. Suzuki.

102. Griffiths anticipates the resistance caused for many by the relativizing of religious forms: "I feel we have now to interpret the whole of the Bible, including the New Testament, in the context of *advaita*. . . . And that's where the Church is moving today in India. And it's very demanding because people cling to the forms; it's their security—your faith, your creed, your doctrine. And you won't let it go. But we have to let it go. And as you let go, you don't lose your faith, but you get a deeper perspective on it. You see it in a new light, in a more total reality" (Interview by the author, August 1991).

103. Cf. Abhishiktānanda, *Further Shore*, 25; Griffiths, "One Mystery," 223; and idem, "On Poverty and Simplicity," 25.

104. "*[A]dvaita* is the final emptying. . . . *Sannyāsa* and *advaita* actually come together. You detach from everybody and everything, and then you're open to *be* reality, the total reality" (Interview by the author, January 1989). Cf. Abhishiktānanda, *Further Shore*, 27.

105. See the author's "Two Models of Christian Dialogue with Hinduism," 101–10, 183–91, 243–54; and idem, "The Comparative Study of Religious Experience: Implications for Dialogue," *Dialogue & Alliance* 11/2 (Fall–Winter 1997): 59–87. For a general treatment of the challenge of cross-cultural spirituality among Christians in dialogue with other religions, see Tosh Arai and Wesley Ariarajah, eds., *Spirituality in Interfaith Dialogue* (Maryknoll, NY: Orbis, 1989).

106. For an assessment of how orthodox Abhishiktānanda remained, see James A. Wiseman, "'Enveloped by Mystery': The Spiritual Journey of Henri Le Saux/Abhishiktānanda," *Eglise et Theologie* 23/2 (1992): 241–60.

107. Vandana, ed., *Swami Abhishiktānanda: The Man and His Writings* (Delhi: ISPCK, 1986), 12–13.

Through Dialogue

1.   See Griffiths, *Universal Wisdom*, 26.

2.   Griffiths, "Meeting of Religions," 856.

3.   Griffiths, "Indian Christian Contemplation," 278; idem, "Eastern Religious Experience," 153.

4.   Griffiths, *Vedanta and Christian Faith* (1973 edition, "Author's Preface"), vii–viii. Griffiths has written: "At the time of writing *Golden String*, I accepted the 'fulfillment' theory of religion—Christ as the fulfillment of all religion. By the time I came to write *Return to the Centre* I had come round to the theory of 'complementarity' which is what I hold now" (Shantivanam, India, to the author, May 31, 1988). See also Rajan, *Bede Griffiths and Sannyāsa*, 226.

5.   Griffiths, *Vedanta and Christian Faith*, 163.

6.   Griffiths, "Where World Religions Meet," *Tablet* 226/6877 (April 1, 1972): 315; see also idem, *Return to the Center*, 71; idem, "Meeting of Religions," 856; idem, "Catholicism and the East," in *Christ in India*, 100.

7.   From a letter from Griffiths to John Moffitt, quoted in the latter's *Journey to Gorakhpur*, 264.

8.   Griffiths, "Mission Is Dialogue: An Interview with Fr. Bede Griffiths," *Indian Missiological Review* 3 (January 1981): 47.

9.   Griffiths, "Dialogue with Hinduism," 152–57.

10.   Griffiths, "Erroneous Beliefs and Unauthorised Rites," 356.

11.   Griffiths, "Revelation and Experience," *Tablet* 229/7023 (February 8, 1975): 136–37. See also idem, "Universal Truth," 101–102.

12.   See letters to the editor in *Tablet* 229/7026 (March 1, 1975): 208–209; and Griffiths's response to them (229/7032 [April 12, 1975]: 347). See also Griffiths, "Unity and Diversity," *Tablet* 229/7047a (July 26, 1975): 702, for his controversial letter; 229/7050 (August 16, 1975): 775–76, for positive and negative responses to it; and 229/7053 (September 6, 1975): 847–48, for Griffiths's reply. Indian Catholics also engaged Griffiths through criticism of his ashram and its life of dialogue with Hinduism at this time. See three articles by Griffiths: "Christian Ashram," 14–20; "Shantivanam," 44–48; and "An Open Letter to Father Anastasius Gomes," 67–70.

13.   Griffiths, "One Mystery," 223. See also idem, "Mission Is Dialogue," 47–49. In a 1981 letter to Martyn Skinner, Griffiths wrote: "Theology only advances through conflicting views. Perhaps the human mind is so made that it can only obtain a partial view of reality, and every view has to be corrected by another. . . . All opposites are eventually reconciled in the universal truth, since all are partial expression of the one reality" (quoted in du Boulay, *Beyond the Darkness*, 176).

14. Griffiths, "Indian Spiritual Tradition and the Church in India," 99.

15. Griffiths, "A Christian Ashram," *Vaidikamitram* 9 (1976): 16; idem, "Monastic Order and the Ashram," 140.

16. Griffiths, "Mystical Tradition in Indian Theology," 159; idem, "Indian Spiritual Tradition and the Church in India," 104.

17. See the following sections of *Return to the Center* for Griffiths's position paraphrased in this paragraph: "Sacred Mystery," 16–25; "One Spirit in All Religion," 71–75; and "The Eternal Religion," 98–112. Cf. idem, *Universal Wisdom*, 10–11; and idem, *Marriage of East and West*, 174–75.

18. Griffiths, "On Poverty and Simplicity," 25. See also idem, "Benedictine Ashram," 37; idem, "Transcending Dualism," 87; and idem, "Walking with Vinoba," in *Christ in India*, 131.

19. Griffiths, "On Poverty and Simplicity," 21.

20. Griffiths, "Mission Is Dialogue," 51.

21. Griffiths, *River of Compassion*, 290. Cf. Panikkar, *Intrareligious Dialogue*, xix–xxi. As already noted in chap. 7, two Catholic theologians have accused Griffiths of taking a theosophical rather than a Christian position with regard to non-Christian religions. Robert Fastiggi and Jose Pereira define the theosophical view by three characteristics: the posting of a "transcendental unity behind all religions" in relation to which doctrines are "accidental"; the use of Western European rather than Asian languages to describe in vague fashion so-called "Oriental" religions; and an ambivalence toward "dualism" (Fastiggi and Pereira, "Swami from Oxford," 25). (The same critique of Griffiths is made by Pereira in "Christian Theosophists?") Griffiths's response is implicit in these two analogies. First, Griffiths clearly affirms a transcendental unity or common ground underlying the various religions, including Christianity. But he emphatically denies that the doctrinal or "symbolic" features are merely accidental. The diversity of faiths, cultures, and symbolic forms is affirmed as the indispensable means through which the divine mystery expresses itself and through which the human experiences that mystery. Second, Griffiths does use English almost exclusively in his writing because this is the language of his primary audience. Contradictory to the criticism of Fastiggi and Pereira, Griffiths did have some knowledge of Sanskrit, as shown especially in his *Gītā* commentary. Third, Griffiths's emphasis upon "transcending dualism" reflects his belief, not that dualism or the dualistic mind is wrong or less perfect or evil in itself, but that Western culture is overly identified with this one way of experiencing the world.

22. E.g., an interreligious conference in Madras in 1985, reported upon by Griffiths in "Emerging Consciousness for a New Humankind," 125, 128 (also published as "Reflections and Prospects," in *Emerging Consciousness for a New Humankind: Asian Interreligious Concern*, ed. Michael von Bruck [Bangalore, India: Asian Trading Corp., 1985], 122–25).

23. Griffiths, "Transcending Dualism," 73.

24. Ibid., 87.

25. In response to the sluggish progress of interreligious dialogue as a whole, Griffiths emphasizes the importance of respecting the uniqueness of each religion and thus the value of religious differences:

> I always now maintain the idea of ecumenism, that we see that each religion has its own absolutely unique insight and value. We recognize that our own religion has its own unique insight and value and allow that the other has its own. And we try to understand their perspective as different than our own. But how we reconcile them, I don't know. I think that's probably as far as we can go now really. Each one should recognize the unique insight of the other . . . knowing that the unity is beyond all your formulations, everything you can say. That I find satisfactory for now, because we're all pilgrims on a journey to the beyond. . . . Mind you, some might call that too relative. . . . But it's very subtle. (Interview by the author, Waitsfield, VT, tape recording, August 1992)

26. Griffiths, *New Vision of Reality*, 106, 226; idem, *Universal Wisdom*, 41–42. Griffiths in a letter summarized his conclusions in the latter text as follows:

> The conclusion I have reached is that in each religion there is a movement which culminates in advaita. In Hinduism and Buddhism it is obvious, but it is equally true of Taoism and Sikhism. Islam and Judaism are the main problem. They are both deeply dualistic—God separate from the world and humanity, good and evil, heaven and hell. But in both religions the mystical tradition—in Sufism and the Kabbala—transcends the dualism and reaches pure advaita. In Christianity I see a gradual movement from the dualism of its Jewish origins to the non-duality of the Fourth Gospel, where Jesus prays "that they all may be one, as thou, Father, in me and I in thee—that they may be perfectly one"—in other words a pure advaita sharing in the inner life of God. (Berkeley, to the author, June 21, 1991)

27. Griffiths, *Marriage of East and West*, 177.

28. Griffiths, "Transcending Dualism," 84; see also 81. See also idem, "Advaitic Experience and the Personal God in the Upanishads and the Bhagavad Gita," 71–86; idem, *New Creation in Christ*, 65–67; and idem, *River of Compassion*, 130. In the 1980s, Griffiths began to speak more specifically about the experience and philosophy of nonduality that he found in the mystical teachings of what he calls "the five great religions," Hinduism, Buddhism, Judaism, Christianity, and Islam. In the 1990s he considered as well Taoism, Sikhism, and the so-called primitive religions of the Native Americans and Australian aborigines. Griffiths did not presume to have conducted exhaustive research; his approach is to focus on a key mystical thinker or community within a tradition in which the theme of nonduality is apparent to indicate an important trend or dimension within the religion itself. Thus, in Hinduism he discusses not only possible reinterpretations of Śankara but also Abhinava Gupta and Kashmir Śaivism; in Mahāyāṇa Buddhism, Nagarjuna and the

Tibetan schools; in Judaism, the Kabbalist tradition; in Christianity, the several mystical theologians already mentioned, namely, John the Apostle, Gregory of Nyssa, Dionysius, Aquinas, Eckhart, Ruusbroec, and John of the Cross; and in Islam, Ibn 'Arabi and Sufism. Given Griffiths's methodology of focusing primarily on the mystical dimension, there are problems in substantiating some of his broader claims concerning entire traditions. Such difficulties did not seem to trouble him and were outweighed by the strength of convictions arising from his own nondual experiences. Some of the specific directions he explored in his later writings include the common role of the cosmic person as symbolizing a principle of differentiation within ultimate Reality in various religions, the possible parallels to the Christian Trinity (e.g., *saccidānanda, trimūrti,* and *trikāya*), and the common dynamic of self-transcendence. Key references on these points are Griffiths, *New Vision of Reality,* chaps. 6 and 7; idem, "Transcending Dualism"; and idem, "Meditation on the Mystery of the Trinity."

29.   Griffiths, *Universal Wisdom,* 41–42.

30.   Griffiths, "Transcending Dualism," 87. The most important contemporary interpreters of nonduality for Griffiths were Michael von Bruck (e.g., his *The Unity of Reality: God, God-Experience, and Meditation in the Hindu-Christian Dialogue,* trans. James V. Zeitz [New York: Paulist, 1991]) and Lama Anagarika Govinda *(Creative Meditation and Multi-Dimensional Consciousness).*

31.   Griffiths, *Universal Wisdom,* 40. (Gospel quotation is John 14.23.) See also idem, *Return to the Center,* 59–60.

32.   Griffiths, *New Vision of Reality,* 103–104.

33.   The term *unitive pluralism,* not used by Griffiths, is discussed in Knitter's *No Other Name?* (7–16). After distinguishing this position from syncretism, religious imperialism, and a "lazy tolerance," Knitter writes: "[U]nitive pluralism is a unity in which each religion, although losing some of its individualism (its separate ego), will intensify its personality (its self-awareness through relationship). Each religion will retain its own uniqueness, but this uniqueness will develop and take on new depths by relating to other religions in mutual dependence" (9).

34.   Griffiths, *New Vision of Reality,* 286; see also idem, *Universal Wisdom,* 10. In response to the suggestion that he had moved beyond a theory of complementarity, Griffiths summarized his theology of religions as follows:

I see the one Mystery is manifesting in all its complements, but it's totally in the all. It's not the parts come together to make the whole, it's present in all the parts. The divine Mystery is present under these limiting signs. But the whole Mystery is present everywhere. And that's why I can say that the Australian Aborigine or American Indian experiences Christ. It's not part of him, but the whole Christ is present under these limiting signs. And in the Christian tradition itself, again it's still under limiting signs. So they're all taking us to the one Christ, to the One . . . whatever you like to call it. (Interview by the author, August 1991)

Compare to Griffiths's *Golden String*, 187, and contrast to his *Return to the Center*, 71.

35.   In an interview by the author, Griffiths states:

> I think we all have our human, cultural, historical limitations. And we all come towards the supreme with all these cultural differences and they narrow down. But I don't think in this life we ever lose the differences. It's not the same experience. It's the one Reality experienced *in* these different traditions. We don't lose our cultural limitations; the *advaitin*, whatever he likes to say, *is* a Hindu in the Hindu tradition. And a Christian *advaitin* is a Christian. (August 1991)

36.   Griffiths, Waitsfield, VT, to the author, October 8, 1990; and idem, interview by the author, November 1990. In the same context he agreed again that this third stage had begun with the move to Shantivanam. From then on he was "working towards *advaita*."

37.   Griffiths, *Universal Wisdom*, 39; cf. idem, *Golden String*, 188.

Conclusion

1.   Griffiths, "The Ashram as a Way of Transcendence," in *Christian Ashrams: A Movement with a Future*, ed. by Vandana Mataji (New Delhi: ISPCK, 1993), 33.

2.   See Andrew Harvey's firsthand account of Griffiths's dying as birthing, quoted in du Boulay, *Beyond the Darkness*, 259.

3.   This remark was made at a Memorial Service for Griffiths, 1993 Parliament of the World's Religions, Chicago (tape recording).

4.   In 1992, Griffiths described the importance of orthodoxy in theology as follows: "Trinitarian theology to me is *the* test of Christian orthodoxy. And with that comes incarnation, redemption. . . . I think this orthodoxy is extremely important. It's got an insight you won't find anywhere else, I'm convinced" (Interview by the author, August 1992). He went on to justify the importance of orthodoxy in an interreligious context by stating that adhering to it ensures that the uniqueness of one's tradition is sustained, just as one desires that the uniqueness of the other's tradition also be maintained. Blurring the differences between traditions, he said, is not productive for dialogue—a tendency he found among some Hindus. Nonetheless, the Vatican's Congregation for the Doctrine of the Faith's document "Dominus Iesus" (September 2000) explicitly attacks the assertion that other religions are complementary to Christianity in a way to which Griffiths would likely have objected.

5.   Griffiths, "An Open Letter to Father Anastasius Gomes," *Vaidikamitram* 9 (1976): 69–70. Cf. Wiseman's conclusion that some key aspects of Abhishiktānanda's theology are heterodox, such as his dichotomizing the cosmic Christ and the historical Jesus and his sharp criticism of the mislead-

ing effect of some Christian doctrines if disconnected from direct experience—distinctions that Griffiths also made but less absolutely (Wiseman, "'Enveloped by Mystery,'" 256–57).

6.   Griffiths, "Open Letter to Father Anastasius Gomes," 70.

7.   Du Boulay, *Beyond the Darkness,* 207. She quotes Ursula King's critical review of Griffiths's *Marriage of East and West* in *Clergy Review* (September 1983) as an example of such objections to his conclusions (209). Note that Felicity Edwards, a South African scholar sympathetic with Griffiths's writings, concludes that he is not a theologian, just as she would not characterize Jesus as one (du Boulay, *Beyond the Darkness,* 209). However, according to Griffiths's own sense of what theology entails (as developed in chap. 9), which admittedly is not the conventional sense of the term, it is indeed appropriate to claim the role of theologian for him.

8.   For a critical assessment of the implications of Griffiths's comparative methods for interreligious dialogue, see the author's "Comparative Study of Religious Experience: Implications for Dialogue," 59–87.

9.   Panikkar, whose own journey has been more closely aligned with the academy but nonetheless risky in "trespassing" accepted standards of cultural and religious orthodoxy, made the following candid assessment of Griffiths: "In my opinion, his witness is not a deep knowledge of Vedānta, is not a deep knowledge of all the intricacies of Hindu theology or even of Christian theology. We can find fault with many of his ideas in which his presentation from the scholarly point of view was not up to the point. That was not his forte. That was not his mission. The importance of Fr. Bede which we should never forget, for us, was his person . . . not his ideas . . . was his being there. Praxis before theory. . . ." (Memorial Service for Bede Griffiths, 1993 Parliament of the World's Religions, Chicago). See also du Boulay, *Beyond the Darkness,* 205–209; and Teasdale, "Bede Griffiths's As Mystic and Icon of Reversal," 23.

10.   Cf. Griffiths, *New Vision of Reality,* 266. If the "ordinary, rational level of mind" cannot grasp or even enter the realms of contemplative experience, then is it wishful thinking to believe that insights from this realm can be understood, related, and systematized by reason without distorting them? Griffiths would respond that, while it is true that the rational mind cannot grasp the fullness of knowledge experienced in contemplation or express it completely, the admittedly imperfect tool of reason can recognize distortions and confusions, shed light on the often paradoxical nature of intuitive wisdom, and articulate the need for the mind to transcend reason in order to grasp this wisdom.

11.   Griffiths, *Golden String,* unpaginated 1980 foreword.

12.   Griffiths, *Marriage of East and West,* 43.

13.   Contrast Griffiths's synthetic statements on the power of the symbols in all traditions in *Return to the Center* (71) with the following reflection upon his preference for Christian symbols: "[P]erhaps one could say that the Christian symbols are not only more adequate for a Christian but probably have, I would

think, power for others. There's something fuller. I often say there's a fullness and finality in Christ. But I have to be careful, I know" (Interview by the author, August 1992). In the same interview, he remarked: "I'm very Christocentric actually. I'm always tending to it. But then I begin to check myself and say that this is from our point of view. St. Thomas Aquinas is so wonderful [on this]. He says that no individual concept of God is remotely adequate. . . . All our theology is a symbolic structure that points to something beyond."

The question raised here does not concern Griffiths's continuing use of Christian symbols for, as his own interpretation of this calling specifies, the *sannyāsi* does not reject all religious symbols; he or she may in fact still participate in symbolic acts (cf. idem, *Marriage of East and West*, 43). The issue here is whether Griffiths's use of Christian symbols exhibits the detachment characteristic of one who has "gone beyond."

On Griffiths's continued inclusivist use of Christian symbols in an interreligious context, compare Diana Eck's discussion of a similar limitation in her own writing in her *Encountering God: A Spiritual Journey from Bozeman to Banaras* (Boston: Beacon, 1993), 170. See also the author's "Indian Sources on the Possibility of a Pluralist View of Religions," *Journal of Ecumenical Studies* 35/2 (Spring 1998): 210–34.

14. As Wach's criteria for "integral understanding" suggest, comprehension of a life necessarily includes elements that can be easily analyzed ("information") and those that cannot because they arise from "an engagement of feeling . . . or participation." Appeal to both types of evidence is being made in coming to this judgment about Griffiths's relationship to his culture and religion. See Wach, *Comparative Study of Religions*, 11.

15. Cf. James Conner, OCSO's use of the same image in his "The Monk As a Bridge between East and West," in *The Other Half of My Soul: Bede Griffiths and the Hindu-Christian Dialogue*, ed. Beatrice Bruteau (Wheaton, IL: Theosophical Publishing House, 1996), 80–97.

16. See Cenkner, "Understanding the Religious Personality," 4–5.

17. Recall the contrast between the missions of Abhishiktānanda and Griffiths.

18. In conversation, Griffiths maintained both that a hierarchy of symbols exists and yet that every symbol in the hierarchy potentially discloses the whole mystery.

19. Griffiths, "Mystical Dimension in Theology," 243.

20. John A. T. Robinson, *Truth Is Two-Eyed* (Philadelphia: Westminster, 1979), 39–40.

21. Griffiths, *New Vision of Reality*, 254.

22. Interview by the author, August 1991. Griffiths is quoting Maximus the Confessor.

Bibliography

For a complete bibliography of sources by and about Bede Griffiths, contact the Graduate Theological Union in Berkeley, where his archives are housed, or the Bede Griffiths Trust, c/o New Camaldoli Hermitage, Big Sur, CA 93920.

Primary Sources

Books

Griffiths, Bede. *The Golden String: An Autobiography*. Springfield, IL: Templegate Publishers, 1954, 1980.

———. *Christ in India: Essays Towards a Hindu-Christian Dialogue*. Springfield, IL: Templegate Publishers, 1966, 1984.

———. *Vedanta and Christian Faith*. Clearlake, CA: Dawn Horse Press, 1973, 1991.

———. *Return to the Center*. Springfield, IL: Templegate Publishers, 1976.

———. *The Marriage of East and West: A Sequel to the Golden String*. Springfield, IL: Templegate Publishers, 1982.

———. *The Cosmic Revelation: The Hindu Way to God*. Springfield, IL: Templegate Publishers, 1983.

———. *River of Compassion: A Christian Commentary on the Bhagavad Gītā*. Warwick, NY: Amity House, 1987. (Reprinted in New York: Continuum, 1995.)

———. *A New Vision of Reality: Western Science, Eastern Mysticism and Christian Faith*. Edited by Felicity Edwards. Springfield, IL: Templegate Publishers, 1990.

———. *The New Creation in Christ: Christian Meditation and Community*. Edited by Robert Kiely and Laurence Freeman. Springfield, IL: Templegate Publishers, 1994.

——. *Universal Wisdom: A Journey through the Sacred Wisdom of the World.* Edited by Roland Ropers. San Francisco: HarperCollins, 1994.

——. *Pathways to the Supreme: The Personal Notebook of Bede Griffiths.* Edited by Roland Ropers. London: HarperCollins, 1995.

——. *Psalms for Christian Prayer.* Edited by Roland Ropers. London: HarperCollins, 1995.

——. *A Human Search: Bede Griffiths Reflects on His Life.* Edited by John Swindells. Liguori, MO: Triumph Books, 1997.

Articles and Published Lectures

Griffiths, Bede. "The Power of the Imagination." 1930s. (Photocopy from Griffiths's typewritten unpublished manuscript.)

——. "The Power of Intuition." 1930s. (Photocopy from Griffiths's typewritten unpublished manuscript.)

——. "The Process of Knowledge." 1930s. (Photocopy from Griffiths's typewritten unpublished manuscript.)

——. "St. Justin's 'Apology.'" *Pax* 27 (March 1937): 289–93.

——. "A Pilgrim to Jerusalem." *Pax* 28 (1938): 7–11, 30–35.

——. "The Mysticism of Mary Webb." *Pax* 28 (October 1938): 161–65.

——. "The Platonic Tradition and the Liturgy." *Eastern Churches Quarterly* 4/1 (January 1940): 5–8.

—— "The Priesthood and Contemplation." *Life of the Spirit* 5 (April 1951): 439–46. (Reprinted in *Orate Fratres* 25/8 [July 1951]: 347–55.)

——. "The Divine Office as a Method of Prayer." *Life of the Spirit* 6/62–63 (August–September 1951): 77–85.

——. "Liturgical Formation in the Spiritual Life." *Life of the Spirit* 6/69 (March 1952): 361–68.

——. "The Mystery of the Scriptures." *Life of the Spirit* 7/74–75 (August–September 1952): 67–75.

——. "Christian Existentialism." *Pax* 43 (1953): 141–45.

——. "The Cloud on the Tabernacle." *Life of the Spirit* 7/83 (May 1953): 478–86.

——. "The Enigma of Simone Weil." *Blackfriars* 34/398 (May 1953): 232–36.

——. "The Transcendent Unity of Religions." *Downside Review* 72/229 (July 1954): 264–75.

——. "For a Hindu Catholicism." *Tablet* 205/6000 (May 21, 1955): 494–95.

——. "Vinoba Bhave." *Blackfriars* 38/443 (February 1957): 66–71.

——. "Symbolism and Cult." In *Indian Culture and the Fullness of Christ.* Madras, India: Madras Cultural Academy, 1957, 52–61.

——. "Experiment in Monastic Life." *Commonweal* 68/26 (September 26, 1958): 634–36.

——. "Kurisumala Ashram." *Pax* 48 (1958): 128–33.

——. "The Language of a Mission." *Blackfriars* 41/478 (January–February 1960): 20–27.

——. "A Letter from India." *Life of the Spirit* 15/172 (October 1960): 178–82.

——. "Liturgy and the Missions." *Asia* 12 (1960): 148–54.

———. "The Ecumenical Approach to Non-Christian Religions." *Catholic World* 193/1157 (August 1961): 304–10.

———. "Christian Witness in India: Ways of Knowing God." Transcript of "The Catholic Hour" radio program (November 10, 1963). Washington, DC: NCCM, 1963.

———. "Placing Indian Religion." *Blackfriars* 44/521 (November 1963): 477–81.

———. "Liturgy and Culture." *Tablet* 218/6471 (May 30, 1964): 602–603.

———. "Background to Bombay." *Month* 32/6 (December 1964): 313–18.

———. "Kurisumala Ashram." *Eastern Churches Quarterly* 16/3 (1964): 226–31. (Reprinted in *Christ in India* [41–47]).

———. "The Vatican Council." *Star of the East* 25 (1964): 9–12.

———. "Indian Spirituality and the Eucharist." In *India and the Eucharist*, ed. Bede Griffiths and Co., 9–18. Ernakulam, India: Lumen Institute, 1964.

———. "India after the Pope." *Commonweal* 81/20 (February 12, 1965): 641–42.

———. "The Dialogue with Hinduism." *New Blackfriars* 46/538 (April 1965): 404–10. (Reprinted in *Catholic Mind* 63 [1965]: 36–42.)

———. "The Church and Non-Christian Religions: Salvation Outside the Church." *Tablet* 219/6552 (December 18, 1965): 1409–10.

———. "Light on C. S. Lewis." *Month* 35/6 (June 1966): 337–41.

———. "Monastic Life in India Today." *Monastic Studies* 4 (Advent 1966): 117–35.

———. "The Declaration on the Church and Non-Christian Religions." *Examiner* 117 (1966): 117, 122.

———. "The Sacred Cow." *Commonweal* 85/17 (February 3, 1967): 483–84.

———. "The Christian Doctrine of Grace and Freewill." *Mountain Path* (April 1967): 124–28.

———. "Forest of Peace in South India." *Tablet* 223/6716 (February 8, 1969): 130–32.

———. "The Meeting of Religions." *Tablet* 223/6745 (August 30, 1969): 856.

———. "St. Benedict in the Modern World." *Pax* 59 (1969): 77–79. (Reprinted from *Church and People* "nearly twenty years ago," according to the editors.)

———. "Indian Christian Contemplation." *Clergy Monthly* 35/7 (August 1971): 277–81.

———. "Where World Religions Meet." *Tablet* 226/6877 (April 1, 1972): 314–15.

———. "Eastern Religious Experience." *Monastic Studies* 9 (Autumn 1972): 153–60.

———. "Erroneous Beliefs and Unauthorised Rites." *Tablet* 227/6928 (April 14, 1973): 356, 521.

———. "The One Mystery." *Tablet* 228/6975 (March 9, 1974): 223.

———. "Shantivanam: A New Beginning." In *Kurisumala: A Symposium on Ashram Life*, ed. Francis Mahieu. Bangalore, India: Asian Trading Corp., 1974, 75–76.

———. "The Universal Truth." *Tablet* 229/7022 (February 1, 1975): 101–102, 347.

———. "Revelation and Experience." *Tablet* 229/7023 (February 8, 1975): 136–37.

———. Letter to the Editor. *Tablet* 229/7032 (April 12, 1975): 347.

———. "Indianisation." *Examiner* 126/19 (May 10, 1975): 233.

———. "Unity and Diversity." *Tablet* 229/7047a (July 26, 1975): 702, 847–48.

————. "Shantivanam." *Spirit and Life* 70 (1975): 24–27.

————. "Dialogue with Hinduism." *Impact* 11 (May 1976): 152–57.

————. "Village Religion in India." *Tablet* 230/7098 (July 24, 1976): 726–27.

————. "The Indian Spiritual Tradition and the Church in India." *Outlook* 15/4 (Winter 1976): 98–104.

————. "A Christian Ashram." *Vaidikamitram* 9 (1976): 14–20.

————. "Shantivanam: An Explanation." *Vaidikamitram* 9 (1976): 44–48.

————. "An Open Letter to Father Anastasius Gomes." *Vaidikamitram* 9 (1976): 67–70.

————. "The Vedic Revelation." *Tablet* 231/7165 (November 5, 1977): 1053–54.

————. "The Mystical Dimension in Theology." *Indian Theological Studies* 14 (1977): 229–46.

————. "Christian Monastic Life in India." *Journal of Dharma* 3/2 (April–June 1978): 123–35. (Reprint, with revisions, of "Monastic Life in India Today.")

————. "The Advaitic Experience and the Personal God in the Upanishads and the Bhagavad Gita." *Indian Theological Studies* 15 (1978): 71–86.

————. "The Monastic Order and the Ashram." *American Benedictine Review* 30/2 (June 1979): 134–45.

————. "The Search for God." *Tablet* 233/7251 (June 30, 1979): 620–21.

————. "The Two Theologies." *Tablet* 234/7299 (May 31, 1980): 520–21, 677.

————. Foreword to *The Child and the Serpent: Reflections on Popular Indian Symbols*, by Jyoti Sahi. London: Routledge and Kegan Paul, 1980.

————. "The Church of the Future." *Tablet* 236/7396–97 (April 10, 17, 1982): 364–66.

————. "The Mystical Tradition in Indian Theology." *Monastic Studies* 13 (Autumn 1982): 159–73.

————. "The Ashram and Monastic Life." *Monastic Studies* 15 (Advent 1984): 117–23. (Reprinted in *In Christo* 22 [1984]: 217–22.)

————. "Christian Ashrams." *Word and Worship* 17 (1984): 150–52.

————. "Emerging Consciousness for a New Humankind." *Examiner* 136 (February 9, 1985): 125, 128.

————. "Emerging Consciousness and the Mystical Traditions of Asia," 48–64; and "Reflections and Prospects," 122–25. In *Emerging Consciousness for a New Humankind: Asian Interreligious Concern*, ed. Michael von Bruck, 48–64. Bangalore, India: Asian Trading Corp., 1985.

————. "The Church of Rome and Reunion." *New Blackfriars* 66/783 (September 1985): 389–92.

————. "Transcending Dualism: An Eastern Approach to the Semitic Religions," ed. Wayne Teasdale. *Cistercian Studies* 20/2 (1985): 73–87. (Reprinted in Griffiths, *Vedanta and Christian Faith* [1991 edition], 73–93.)

————. "Dialogue and Inculturation." *Examiner* 137/33 (August 16, 1986): 777–78.

————. "A Meditation on the Mystery of the Trinity." *Monastic Studies* 17 (Christmas 1986): 69–79.

————. "A Symbolic Theology." *New Blackfriars* 69/817 (June 1988): 289–94.

————. "The Christian Ashram." *Examiner* 139 (December, 17, 1988): 1235.

———. "The Meaning and Purpose of an Ashram." In *Saccidananda Ashram: A Garland of Letters*, 4–9. Tiruchchirappalli, India: Saccidananda Ashram, 1988.

———. "A Benedictine Ashram." In *Saccidananda Ashram: A Garland of Letters*, 3–5. Tiruchchirappalli, India: Saccidananda Ashram, 1989.

———. "The M-word." *Tablet* 244/7830 (August 11, 1990): 1002.

———. "Monk's Response to the Document on Christian Prayer from the Congregation for the Doctrine of the Faith." *NABEWD Bulletin* (Trappist, KY: Abbey of Gethsemani, 1990): 11.

———. "For Those Without Sin." *National Catholic Reporter* 28/36 (August 14, 1992): 20.

———. "In Jesus' Name." *Tablet* 246/7915–16 (April 18, 25, 1992): 498–99.

———. "The Ashram as a Way of Transcendence." In *Christian Ashrams: A Movement with a Future?* ed. Vandana Mataji, 30–33. New Dehli: ISPCK, 1993.

Griffiths, Bede, and A. K. Saran. "Further Towards a Hindu-Christian Dialogue." *Clergy Monthly* 32/5 (May 1968): 213–20. (A response by A. K. Saran to *Christ in India*, followed by Griffiths's reply.)

Recorded Lectures

Griffiths, Bede. *Christian Meditation: The Evolving Tradition.* John Main Seminar, New Harmony, IN, 1991. Chevy Chase, MD: John Main Institute, 1991. (These lecturers and discussions have been edited and published as *The New Creation in Christ: Christian Meditation and Community*.)

Interviews

Griffiths, Bede. "Mission Is Dialogue: An Interview with Fr. Bede Griffiths." *Indian Missiological Review* 3 (January 1981): 43–53.

———. "On Poverty and Simplicity: Views of a Post-Industrial Christian Sage." Interview by Renee Weber. *ReVision* 6/2 (Fall 1983): 16–30. (Reprinted in Renee Weber, *Dialogues with Scientists and Sages: The Search for Unity* [New York: Routledge and Kegan Paul, 1986], 157–80.)

———. "Benedictine Ashram: An Experiment in Hindu-Christian Community." Interview by Fred Rohe and Ty Koontz (California, 1984). *Laughing Man* 5/3 (1984): 34–37.

———. "Interview: Father Bede Griffiths, O.S.B." Interview by Johannes Agaard and Neil Duddy (Europe, Summer 1984). *Update* 9 (1985): 22–36.

———. "Interview with a Spiritual Master: The Trinity." Interview by Wayne Teasdale (Shantivanam, India, December 1986). *Living Prayer* 21/3 (May–June 1988): 24–31.

———. "Reincarnation: A Christian View." Interview by Wayne Teasdale (Shantivanam, India, December 1986). *Living Prayer* 21/5 (September–October 1988): 22–28.

————. "Contemplative Community and the Transformation of the World." Interview by Wayne Teasdale (Shantivanam, India, December 1986). *Living Prayer* 22/1 (January–February 1989): 11–15.

————. "Father Bede Griffiths." Interview by Malcolm Tillis (January 27, 1981, Shantivanam, India). In *Turning East: New Lives in India: Twenty Westerners and Their Spiritual Quests,* eds. Malcolm Tillis and Cynthia Giles, 119–26. New York: Paragon House, 1989.

Secondary Sources on Bede Griffiths

Bruteau, Beatrice, ed. *The Other Half of My Soul: Bede Griffiths and the Hindu-Christian Dialogue.* Wheaton, IL: Theosophical Publishing House, 1996.

Du Boulay, Shirley. *Beyond the Darkness: A Biography of Bede Griffiths.* New York: Doubleday, 1998.

Fastiggi, Robert, and Pereira, Jose. "The Swami from Oxford." *Crisis* (March 1991): 22–25. (A revision of Pereira, "Christian Theosophists?")

Fernandes, Albano. "The Hindu Mystical Experience according to R. C. Zaehner and Bede Griffiths: A Philosophical Study." Ph.D. diss., Gregorian Pontifical University, 1993.

Goel, Sita Ram, ed. *Catholic Ashrams: Sannyasins or Swindlers?* New Delhi: Voice of India, 1988, 1994.

Kalliath, Antony. "Inward Transcendence: A Study on the Encounter of Western Consciousness with Indian Interiority Based on the Works of Fr. Bede Griffiths." Master's thesis, Dharmaram Pontifical Institute, 1986.

Panikkar, Raimon (Raimundo). "The Wider Ecumenism: An Explorer Crosses the Borders." Review of *River of Compassion,* by Bede Griffiths. In *Tablet* 246/7938 (September 26, 1992): 1192–93.

————. "A New Vision of Reality: A Tribute to Fr. Bede Griffiths." *Journal of Dharma* 18/3 (July–September 1993): 285–93.

Pereira, Jose. "Christian Theosophists?" *Dilip* (November–December 1990): 11–19.

Rajan, Jesu. *Bede Griffiths and Sannyāsa.* Bangalore, India: Asian Trading Corp., 1989.

————. *Bede's Journey to the Beyond.* Bangalore, India: Asian Trading Corp., 1997.

Savio, Samuel. "The Principle of Relatedness in the Ecological Ethic of Bede Griffiths." Doctor of Sacred Theology diss., Catholic University of America, 2000.

Spink, Kathryn. *A Sense of the Sacred: A Biography of Bede Griffiths.* Maryknoll, NY: Orbis Books, 1989.

Teasdale, Wayne Robert. "Bede Griffiths and the Uniqueness of Christianity." *Communio* 9/2 (Spring 1984): 177–86.

————. *Towards a Christian Vedanta: The Encounter of Hinduism and Christianity According to Bede Griffiths.* Bangalore, India: Asian Trading Corp., 1987.

————. "Bede Griffiths as Mystic and Icon of Reversal." *America* 173/9 (September 30, 1995): 22–23.

Trapnell, Judson B. "Bede Griffiths' Theory of Religious Symbol and Practice of Dialogue: Towards Interreligious Understanding." Ph.D. diss., Catholic University of America, 1992.

———. "Bede Griffiths, Mystical Knowing, and the Unity of Religions." *Philosophy & Theology* 7/4 (Summer 1993): 355–79. (Reprinted in revised form as "Multireligious Experience and the Study of Mysticism." In *The Other Half of My Soul: Bede Griffiths and the Hindu-Christian Dialogue,* ed. Beatrice Bruteau, 198–222 [Wheaton, IL: Theosophical Publishing House, 1996].)

———. "Bede Griffiths as a Culture Bearer: An Exploration of the Relationship between Spiritual Transformation and Cultural Change." *American Benedictine Review* 47/3 (September 1996): 260–83.

———. "Two Models of Christian Dialogue with Hinduism: Bede Griffiths and Abhishiktānanda." *Vidyajyoti* 60/2–4 (February–April 1996): 101–10, 183–91, 243–54.

———. "The Mutual Transformation of Self and Symbol: Bede Griffiths and the Jesus Prayer." *Horizons* 23/2 (Fall 1996): 215–41.

———. "The Comparative Study of Religious Experience: Implications for Dialogue." *Dialogue & Alliance* 11/2 (Fall/Winter 1997): 59–87.

Other Secondary Sources

Abhishiktananda. *The Further Shore.* Delhi: ISPCK, 1975.

———. *Hindu-Christian Meeting Point: Within the Cave of the Heart.* Rev. ed. Delhi: ISPCK, 1976.

Aquinas, Thomas. *Summa Theologiae.* New York: McGraw-Hill, 1964–76.

Arai, Tosh, and Wesley Ariarajah, eds. *Spirituality in Interfaith Dialogue.* Maryknoll, NY: Orbis Books, 1989.

Barfield, Owen. *Poetic Diction.* 3rd ed. Middletown, CT: Wesleyan University Press, 1973.

Bohm, David. *Wholeness and the Implicate Order.* London: Ark Paperbacks, 1980.

Capra, Fritjof. *The Tao of Physics: An Exploration of the Parallels between Modern Physics and Eastern Mysticism.* New York: Bantam Books, 1975.

Cenkner, William. "Understanding the Religious Personality." Horizons 5/1 (1978): 1–16.

Coleridge, Samuel Taylor. *The Collected Works of Samuel Taylor Coleridge.* No. 4, *Friend;* no. 7, *Biographia Literaria,* vol. 1; and no. 9, *Aids to Reflection.* Princeton: Princeton University Press, 1969–90.

Corless, Roger, and Paul F. Knitter, eds. *Buddhist Emptiness and Christian Trinity.* New York: Paulist Press, 1990.

Cornille, Catherine. *The Guru in Indian Catholicism: Ambiguity or Opportunity for Inculturation?* Louvain, Belgium: Peeters Press, 1991.

Dulles, Avery. *Models of Revelation.* Garden City, NY: Doubleday and Co., 1985.

Eck, Diana. *Encountering God: A Spiritual Journey from Bozeman to Banaras.* Boston: Beacon, 1993.

Govinda, Lama Anagarika. *Creative Meditation and Multi-Dimensional Consciousness*. Wheaton, IL: Theosophical Publishing House, 1976.

James, William. *The Varieties of Religious Experience: A Study in Human Nature*. New York: Collier Books, 1961.

Joyce, Kevin. "A Study of the Higher States of Consciousness and Their Interpretation According to Teresa of Avila and Maharishi Mahesh Yogi." Ph.D. diss., Catholic University of America, 1991.

Knitter, Paul. *No Other Name? A Critical Survey of Christian Attitudes Toward the World Religions*. Maryknoll, NY: Orbis Books, 1985.

Langer, Susanne. *Philosophy in a New Key: A Study in the Symbolism of Reason, Rite, and Art*. Cambridge: Harvard University Press, 1942.

Lewis, C. S. (Clive Staples). *Surprised by Joy: The Shape of My Early Life*. New York: Harcourt, Brace & World, 1955.

Maritain, Jacques. *Creative Intuition in Art and Poetry*. New York: Pantheon Books, 1953.

———. *Distinguish to Unite, or the Degrees of Knowledge*. New York: Scribner, 1959.

Maritain, Jacques, and Raissa Maritain. *The Situation of Poetry: Four Essays on the Relations Between Poetry, Mysticism, Magic, and Knowledge*. Translated by Marshall Suther. New York: Philosophical Library, 1955.

Mascaro, Juan, trans. *The Upanishads*. New York: Viking Penguin, 1965.

Moffitt, John. *Journey to Gorakhpur: An Encounter with Christ beyond Christianity*. New York: Holt, Rinehart and Winston, 1972.

Nasr, Seyyed Hossein. *Knowledge and the Sacred*. New York: Crossroad, 1981.

Panikkar, Raimundo. *The Trinity and the Religious Experience of Man*. Maryknoll, NY: Orbis Books, 1973.

———. *The Intrareligious Dialogue*. New York: Paulist Press, 1978.

Price, James Robertson III. "Transcendence and Images: The Apophatic and Kataphatic Reconsidered." *Studies in Formative Spirituality* 11 (May 1990): 195–201.

Rahner, Karl. "The Theology of the Symbol." In *Theological Investigations*. Vol. 4. Translated by Kevin Smyth. Baltimore: Helicon Press, 1966.

———. *Foundations of Christian Faith: An Introduction to the Idea of Christianity*. New York: Crossroad, 1986.

Ratzinger, Joseph. "Some Aspects of Christian Meditation." *Origins* 19/30 (1989): 492–98.

Redington, James. "The Hindu-Christian Dialogue and the Interior Dialogue." *Theological Studies* 44 (1983): 587–603.

Reynolds, Frank E., and Capps, Donald, eds.. *The Biographical Process: Studies in the History and Psychology of Religion*. The Hague: Mouton, 1976.

Richard, Lucien. *What Are They Saying about Christ and the World Religions?* New York: Paulist Press, 1981.

Robinson, John A. T. *Truth Is Two-Eyed*. Philadelphia: Westminster Press, 1979.

Ruusbroec, John. *John Ruusbroec: The Spiritual Espousals and Other Works*. Translated by James A. Wiseman. New York: Paulist Press, 1985.

Schuon, M. Frithjof. *The Transcendent Unity of Religions*. Wheaton, IL: Theosophical Publishing House, 1984.

Sheldrake, Rupert. *A New Science of Life: The Hypothesis of Formative Causation*. Los Angeles: Jeremy Tharcher, Inc., 1981.

Spinoza, Benedict de. *Ethics*. Vol. 2, *The Chief Works of Benedict de Spinoza*. Translated by R. H. M. Elwes. New York: Dover Publications, 1951.

Stuart, James. *Swami Abhishiktānanda: His Life Told through His Letters*. Delhi: ISPCK, 1989.

Trapnell, Judson B. "Indian Sources on the Possibility of a Pluralist View of Religions." *Journal of Ecumenical Studies* 35/2 (Spring 1998): 210–34.

Urubshurow, Victoria Kennick. "Hierophanic History and the Symbolic Process: A Response to Ricoeur's Call for a 'Generative Poetics.'" *Religious Traditions* 13 (1990): 23–67.

Vandana, ed. *Swami Abhishiktānanda: The Man and His Writings*. Delhi: ISPCK, 1986.

von Bruck, Michael. *The Unity of Reality: God, God-Experience, and Meditation in the Hindu-Christian Dialogue*. Translated by James V. Zeitz. New York: Paulist Press, 1991.

Wach, Joachim. *The Comparative Study of Religions*. New York: Columbia University Press, 1958.

Weber, Joseph G., ed. and trans. *In Quest of the Absolute: The Life and Works of Jules Monchanin*. Kalamazoo, MI: Cistercian Publications, 1977.

Weintraub, Karl Joachim. *The Value of the Individual: Self and Circumstance in Autobiography*. Chicago: University of Chicago Press, 1978.

Wilber, Ken. *The Spectrum of Consciousness*. Wheaton, IL: Theosophical Publishing House, 1977.

———. *Up From Eden: A Transpersonal View of Human Evolution*. Boston: Shambhala, 1981.

———. *The Holographic Paradigm and Other Paradoxes: Exploring the Leading Edge of Science*. Boston: Shambhala, 1985.

———. *Eye to Eye: The Quest for the New Paradigm*. Expanded ed. Boston: Shambhala, 1990.

Wiseman, James A. "'Enveloped by Mystery': The Spiritual Journey of Henri Le Saux/Abhishiktānanda." *Eglise et Theologie* 23/2 (1992): 241–60.

Wong, Joseph H. P. *Logos-Symbol in the Christology of Karl Rahner*. Rome: Libreria Ateneo Salesiano, 1984.

Index

—

Abhishiktānanda, *see* Le Saux, Henri
advaita (nonduality)
  as characteristic of God or divine
    mystery, 40, 120, 129–31, 144
  Christian, xi, 92, 94–100, 153–54,
    163–71, 176–81, 197, 202
  as common principle in the reli-
    gions, 188, 190–92, 255n. 26
  as epistemological principle, 91–92,
    132–35
  as experience of soul's relation to
    God, 32–33, 35, 92–100, 129–31,
    140–41, 144, 147–50, 204, 216n.
    18. *See also* God
  as experience of transcending dual-
    istic mind, 162, 192–93, 204
  Hindu, 92–100, 167, 169, 171, 178,
    197–98, 239n. 4
  and interpersonal relationships,
    120
  as mystical experience of reality,
    32–33, 130–31, 183–84, 187–88
Alapatt, Benedict, xvi, 49–51, 54
Amaldass, xvi, 3, 114, 236n. 7
anthropology (relation of body, mind,
    and spirit), 6
  and contemplative experience,
    27–35, 56, 71–72, 92–93, 99,
    131–34, 140
  and origin of symbols, 80, 156–59
Aquinas, Thomas, x, 41, 44

on faculties of the soul, 21
on God, 160
Griffiths's reading of, 47, 196,
    216n. 22
on knowledge by connaturality or
    intuition, 59–67, 97–98,
    238n. 38, 239n. 4
on role of symbols in intuition,
    72–73, 99, 158
on *sacramentum* and *res*, distinction
    between, 77–79, 174–75
Sankara, compared to, 129
Augustine, 8, 18, 181, 202, 205
Aurobindo (Aurobindo Ghose), 94,
    141, 189
avatāra ("descent," or incarnation of
    God), 90, 96, 230n. 61

Barfield, Owen, 28–30
Bede, the Venerable, 43, 47, 163
Benedictine life
  Griffiths's experience of in
    England, 47–49, 107–108, 194,
    218n. 8
  Griffiths's experience of in India,
    49–55, 70, 107–108, 115, 194
  sacramentality of, 67, 75, 78, 99
Bhagavad Gītā, x, 18, 117, 134, 142,
    171, 191
Bhave, Vinoba, 52, 106, 220–
    221n. 24

271

Bible
  and *advaita*, 252n. 102
  and faith as way of knowing, 65
  Griffiths's mature reading of,
    176–77, 196, 252n. 102
  Griffiths's pre-conversion reading
    of, 18, 25–26, 33–34, 40, 56
  symbolic quality and worldview
    of, 52, 68, 72, 76–80, 161
  See also John, Gospel of
Blake, William, x, 54
Bohm, David, x, 125, 141–42, 165, 168,
    205–206, 216n. 12
Buddhism
  the Buddha, 151
  and experience of nonduality, 93,
    95, 251n. 92
  and "hidden" Christ, 105
  meditation, 131–32, 144
  Oxherding pictures, 250n. 85
  relation to Christianity and other
    religions, 188, 190–91, 251n. 92
  śūnyatā (emptiness), 178–79,
    190–91, 250n. 77, 251n. 95

Camaldolese order, 116, 236n. 7
Capra, Fritjof, x, 125, 141–42, 144–46,
    192, 205–206
Cenkner, William, 209n. 2, 259n. 16
Christ, Jesus
  as complementary to other revela-
    tions, 151–52, 190
  and the cross, 47, 71, 251n. 95
  as fulfillment of other religions,
    89–90, 102, 105–107, 244n. 13,
    245n. 16
  Griffiths's mature experience of,
    152–53, 161, 251n. 95
  humanity of, 83–84, 151, 154–55,
    174
  images in meditation and prayer,
    44, 47, 71, 132, 177, 245n. 22,
    251n. 95
  Incarnation, 80–81, 90, 96, 161, 162,
    163, 173
  knowledge of, 185–86
  love of, 134

  mystical body of, 166–67
  pre-conversion respect for, 38
  as real symbol of God, 81–84,
    99–100, 151–55, 162, 170, 174
  relationship to the Father, 96–98,
    151, 153, 157, 165–66, 169, 173,
    176–77
  universal Christology, 152–53, 186,
    244n. 13, 256n. 34
  See also Trinity
Christianity
  and "the East," 93, 103–104
  Griffiths's early views of, 15–19,
    25–26, 121
  Griffiths's reassessment of, 46, 48,
    56–59
  in India, 52–54, 66, 197, 230n. 62
  in relation to the perennial philoso-
    phy, 62–64
  orthodoxy, importance of, 196,
    200–201, 257n. 4
  See also Griffiths, criticisms of
  See also advaita, Christian; God; in-
    culturation; Christ, Jesus;
    liturgy; Second Vatican
    Council; theology of religions;
    Trinity
Christudas, xvi, 3, 114, 236n. 7
Coleridge, Samuel Taylor
  Griffiths's reading of, x, 15, 22, 28,
    139, 210n. 23
  on imagination, 22–24, 29, 38, 59,
    65, 214n. 15
comparative religious studies, 88–90,
    151–55, 198–99
contemplation (meditation)
  and *advaita*, 92–93, 128–32, 202
  Christian symbols as mediators
    of, 74–81, 84, 99, 131–32,
    155–57
  as common in the religions, 185,
    187, 242n. 52
  defined, 239n. 6
  Griffiths's practice and experience
    of, 53, 112, 115, 129–32, 149,
    184, 200, 245n. 21
  See also Jesus Prayer

and Indian spirituality, 85, 88,
    92–93, 133–35
and interreligious dialogue, 105,
    107, 184, 225n. 36
as perfection of the Christian life,
    75–76, 88, 177–78, 242n. 52
as state of knowledge, 58–62,
    64–67, 69, 72–74, 132–33,
    135–36, 140–42, 144–47,
    242n. 51
and theology, 156–57, 163
as union with God, 172, 245n. 21
See also Hinduism; intuition; mysti-
    cism; reason

Dante Aligheri, 18, 25, 139
Dawson, Christopher, 212n. 14
De Lubac, Henri, x, xi, 103, 155, 161
De Nobili, Roberto, x, 51, 219–20n. 19
De Smet, Richard, 239n. 1
Dhammapada, 18
Dionysius the Areopagite, 133, 144,
    160, 229n. 42
D'Silva, Russill Paul, 4, 120, 238n. 20
Du Boulay, 199, 222n. 29, 238n. 20
Dulles, Avery, 196, 230–31n. 63,
    244n. 13

"East" and "West"
    critique of both, 51, 86–88, 123–27,
        188
    dialogue between, 103–105, 115–17,
        146, 183, 189, 194
    Griffiths's turn from West to East,
        8, 30, 55, 103–105, 119, 206
    on knowledge, 63–66, 69–70, 133,
        141–42
    and liturgy, 52, 68
    marriage of, 49, 105, 136, 141, 194
    on nature, 22, 49
    use of terms, 147, 199, 218n. 11
Eckhart, Meister, 97–98
Eliade, Mircea, 216n. 12, 228n. 33
Eliot, T. S., x, 17, 123
emotions and feelings as type of
        knowledge, 132, 137–38, 140,
        141, 168, 189

Erikson, Erik, 211n. 29
experience in relation to ideas, 5–6,
        14, 17, 18, 20–21, 22–23, 25

faith
    Christian, 77–78, 87, 157, 161–62,
        174–75
    in debate with perennial philoso-
        phy, 224–25n. 29
    defined, 25–26, 222n. 4, 226n. 42
    Griffiths's, 180
    as openness to divine mystery, 149,
        174–75, 185–86, 226n. 42
    as type of knowledge, 24–26, 57–70,
        99, 102, 104, 132–33, 139–40,
        188–89, 223n. 7
Fastiggi, Robert, 118–19, 254n. 21
feminine and masculine
    East and West, 105, 136, 199
    in Griffiths's psyche, 2–3, 7, 146–47,
        192, 243n. 58
    intuitive and rational, 7, 105, 136, 199
Fernandes, Albano, 231n. 66
Freud, Sigmund, 241n. 24

Gandhi, M. K., 52, 198
God or divine mystery
    in the darkness, 9, 44–45, 57, 79,
        157, 162, 185, 229n. 42
    knowledge of, 57–64, 66, 68, 75,
        79–80, 95, 97, 107, 129, 133–34,
        187, 207, 239n. 4
    as love, 5, 58, 95, 100, 120, 146,
        163–66, 168–73, 176–78,
        190–92, 206, 217–18n. 3
    love of, 58, 92, 97, 98–100, 147
    in nature
        and divine immanence, 134, 184,
            235n. 4
        Griffiths's experience of, 5,
            13–14, 16, 18–19, 20–21, 40,
            235n. 4
        in Indian spirituality, 85, 122
        limitations of, 25–27, 34, 48, 57,
            71, 218n. 6
        reflection upon experience of,
            21–23, 28

God or divine mystery (*continued*)
  in nature
    as symbol, 29, 31–32
    in tension with God in the
      Church and Christ, 48, 78,
      122–23
  as nondual reality in relation to
    world and soul, 94–100, 129,
    163–73, 178–81
    See also advaita
  as an outdated idea, 17
  and symbols of, 8, 79, 149–70
    See also symbols, real
  as Trinity
    in Christian *advaita*, 163–65, 202
    as communion of love, 134,
      163–66, 170–73, 176
    Eckhart on, 97
    Griffiths's focus on, 176, 251n. 92
    nondual relation of Father, Word,
      Spirit, 81–82, 97–98, 163–66,
      172
    in other religions, 50–51, 118,
      190–91, 255–56n. 28
    parallel nonduality in human re-
      lations, 120
    as symbol for Jesus's experience
      of God, 153–54, 161, 178
Goel, Sita Ram, 119
Grant, Sara, 239n. 1
Gregory of Nyssa, 62–64, 67, 229n. 42
Griffiths, Bede
  conversion to Christianity, 43–47,
    56–57, 68–69, 71, 74–75, 98–99,
    102, 122–23, 213n. 21
  criticisms of, xii, 117–19, 124, 150,
    186, 195–200, 203, 218n. 11,
    258n. 9
  as culture bearer, xi, 7–8, 37–40,
    54–55, 126–27, 148, 181, 195,
    200–207
  early years in India, 49–51, 65–67
  final illness, 2–4, 9, 120, 193–95,
    257n. 2
  at Kurisumala Ashram, 51–54,
    67–69, 107, 114–15, 221n. 24
  his life as symbol, 1, 207

  as monk in England, 48–49, 58–65,
    74–84, 149, 161
  as pioneer of interreligious dia-
    logue, ix, x, 195
  relationship to the Mother, 2–3, 9,
    15, 32, 120, 146, 193, 243n. 58
  Shantivanam (Saccidananda
    Ashram), xvi, 50–51, 91, 100,
    111–20, 128–33, 149–51, 184,
    187, 235–36n. 5, 240n. 16
  stages of his life, 5, 54–55, 68–69,
    71, 75, 99–102, 107, 119–20, 148,
    183, 192, 257n. 36
  stroke (1990), 2, 119–20, 146–47,
    175–76, 178, 179, 192–93, 206,
    243n. 57, 58
  youth and education, 15–19, 20–35,
    39, 56–57, 138–39
  See various topics for his ideas

Hinduism
  Christian dialogue with, 87–89,
    105, 169, 188
  comparison to Christianity and
    other religions, 88–100, 102,
    133–36, 160, 184, 190–91
  critique of, 90–100, 164, 167, 188,
    197–98, 197–99, 230n. 61
  on nature of God, 135, 140, 167,
    248–49n. 58, 250n. 77
  Griffiths's experience of, 49–54, 85,
    108, 180
  Kashmir Śaivism, 250n. 77,
    255n. 28
  meditation or contemplation,
    131–36, 184
  on nature, 122, 154
  Śaiva Siddhānta, 248n. 58
  sense of time, 230n. 61
  on symbols, 160, 198
  See also advaita, Hindu; *avatāra;*
    Vedānta
history
  axial period, 143
  Christian symbols as grounded in,
    78–79, 83, 90, 103, 153, 162,
    177, 188, 228n. 24

God in, 184
Griffiths's identification with the
   past, 124
Hindu *avatāras* as semihistorical,
   90, 96
revelation in historical context,
   151–52, 187

imagination
   as faculty of soul, 21, 72, 80, 92, 141
   and faith, 25–26, 57–58
   imaginative intuition, 138–40
   poetic, 17, 28, 34, 60–61
   and reason, 23–24, 27, 56–57, 65,
      145, 159
   and symbols, 73, 81, 158
   as way of knowing, 5–6, 17, 60–61,
      65, 132, 143, 162, 168
   See also Coleridge; faith; poetry;
      reason; symbols
Incarnation. *See* Christ, Jesus
inculturation, xi, 88, 90–91, 117–19,
   150–51, 195–97, 230n. 62
India
   and Christian missions, 197, 200
   dialogue with, 8, 102, 108, 136
   Griffiths's experience of, 49–54,
      65–66, 206, 221n. 24
   impact of Griffiths's move, 69,
      84–88, 219n. 16
intellect (active and passive), 21, 28,
   137, 139, 241n. 26
   See also reason
interreligious dialogue, ix
   defined, 7
   Griffiths's practice of, 8
      during first period, 38
      during second period, 50, 52–54,
         68–69, 101–108
      during third period, 115–19,
         184–93, 197–99, 200–205
   See also Hinduism
intuition
   Aquinas, Thomas, on, 59–60
   Coleridge, Samuel Taylor, on, 24
   defined, 136–37
   as faculty of the soul, 21

and the feminine, 192, 199
levels of, 136–41, 147
Lawrence, D. H. on, 213–14n. 7
Maritain, Jacques and Raissa, on,
   60–62, 72–74, 224n. 24
meditation and contemplation as,
   130, 133–36, 194
in "new science," 141–46, 200
perennial philosophy on, 62–64,
   66–67
and reason, 64–68, 132–33, 135, 136,
   141–42, 144–45, 147, 187, 202,
   204
Schuon, Frithjof, on, 62–64
and self-transcendence, 158–59,
   162
Spinoza, Benedict de, on, 23
and symbols, 30, 158–59
West's need for, 105, 125, 127,
   194
Islam, 95, 105, 164, 190–91, 255n. 26
   dialogue with, 188
   Sufism, 131–32, 144, 190–91

James, William, 211n. 29
Jesus Prayer, 48, 53, 69, 99, 131, 152,
   180, 218n. 9, 239n. 6, 239–
   40n. 9
Johanns, Pierre, x, 96, 102, 231n. 69,
   233n. 4
John, Gospel of, 4, 25, 109, 164, 165,
   177, 255n. 26
Joyce, Kevin Patrick, 243n. 59
Judaism, 177, 190–91, 255n. 26
Jung, Carl, x, 218n. 10, 241n. 24,
   246nn. 31, 34
Justin Martyr, 102, 104–105, 152

Kalliath, Antony, 222n. 33
Kant, Immanuel, 18, 24, 29
Keats, John, 15, 22, 28, 34, 210n. 23
Kurisumala Ashram. *See* Griffiths;
   Mahieu

Langer, Susanne, x, 245–46n. 26,
   247nn. 35, 37
Lawrence, D. H., 213–14n. 7, 214n. 8

Le Saux, Henri (Abhishiktānanda)
    as Christian *sannyāsi*, x, 50–51, 114,
        195, 219–20n. 19
    comparison to Griffiths, 115, 126,
        180–81
    Griffiths's critique of, 179–80
    orthodoxy of, 257–58n. 5
    on *sannyāsa*, 120, 126, 180
Lewis, C. S., x, xv, 18–19, 23, 25, 37,
        212n. 16, 213n. 21
liturgy
    and contemplation, 59–62, 66,
        72–81
    in England, 48
    in India, 52, 67–69, 88–91, 115,
        117–19, 150, 196
    as symbolic, 72–81, 87–88
    See also inculturation

Madhva, 94, 231n. 70
Mahieu, Francis, xvi, 51–54, 68, 107,
        114, 222n. 29
Main, John, 131, 178
Maritain, Jacques, x, 139, 196
    on *advaita*, 92
    on degrees of knowledge, 58,
        60–65, 72–74, 223n. 7, 224n. 24
    and the unconscious, 241n. 24
Maritain, Raissa, x, 60–65, 72–74, 139,
        196
Martin, John, 3
Maximus the Confessor, 166, 207,
        259n. 22
meditation. *See* contemplation
missions, xi, 106, 119, 123, 186,
        196–97, 234n. 15
modern Western culture, critique of
    in Griffiths's first period, 16–19,
        22–25, 30–31, 40, 123
    in Griffiths's second period, 48,
        61–62, 64, 86–88, 221n. 25
    in Griffiths's third period, 116, 119,
        146
    and Griffiths's role of culture
        bearer, 54–55, 200–202
    as necessary stage in cultural evo-
        lution, 39–40, 124–25, 175

possibilities for change, 125–26,
        146, 169, 206
reason and science, overreliance
    upon, 17, 22–25, 30, 61–62, 65,
        76, 86–87, 116, 123–25, 138–39,
        143–44, 159–61
sense of sacred and symbols, loss
    of, 81, 86–88, 175
    See also culture bearer; "East" and
        West"; reason; science
Monchanin, Jules, x, xi, xvi, 50–51,
        112, 114–15, 155, 195, 219–
        20n. 19
mysticism
    and center of the soul or spirit, 27,
        134, 140
    as common ground in the religions,
        149, 154, 187, 190, 255n. 26,
        255–56n. 28
    as conditioned and unconditioned,
        154–55, 204
    and contemplative knowledge,
        58–62, 66, 75, 140, 144
    cross-cultural, possibility of, 9,
        108
    Eastern, 69, 144
    Griffiths as mystic, 199
    Hindu, 50, 86, 88, 92
    and intuition, 137, 141
    nature mysticism, 21, 29, 46, 50, 71,
        107, 224n. 20
    and Shantivanam, 115, 149,
        235–36n. 5
    and symbols, 73, 149, 154–63
    and theology, 155–63
    as union with God, 98, 154–55

Nasr, Seyyed Hossein, 173, 245n. 17
Newman, John Henry, 47
"new science." *See* science

Panikkar, Raimundo (Raimon), xii, 8,
        195, 211n. 25, 218–19n. 13,
        237n. 19, 258n. 9
Pereira, Jose, 118–19, 254n. 21
perennial philosophy, 62–64, 66–67,
        69, 103

Plato and Platonism, 24, 25, 29, 62, 74, 166, 167
poetry
  Bible as, 25, 34, 68–69
  in comparison to philosophy, 28–29, 62–64
  poetic knowledge, 29, 59–64, 72–73, 138–39
  Romantic, x, 15, 22–23, 27, 28, 34, 50, 88, 215n. 4, 219n. 16
    See also Coleridge; Keats; Shelley; Swinburne; Wordsworth
  symbols in, 29–30, 34–35, 72–73, 80, 139, 150, 158–59
  See also Eliot; imagination
Price, James Robertson III, 250n. 86

Rahner, Karl, x, 149, 196, 228n. 33, 229n. 42
  on humanity of Jesus, 82, 151, 229n. 42
  on "mediated immediacy," 83–84, 155, 245n. 22
  on real symbols, 81–84, 99–100, 151–52, 170, 173, 203–204, 230n. 55
  on relation of God and humanity, 171, 248n. 49
  on theology, 161
Rajan, Jesu, 250nn. 78, 87; 253n. 4
Rāmānuja, 94, 231n. 70
reason (rational mind)
  as analytical, 30, 158, 184, 187, 204
  Aquinas on, 21, 59, 72–73, 224n. 24
  Capra on, 141–42
  and contemplation (meditation), 66, 130, 132–36, 185, 200
  defined, 213–14n. 7
  as discursive, 24, 62, 68
  as dualistic, 142–44, 147, 162, 168, 192–93, 200, 204, 242n. 51, 254n. 21
  as faculty of the soul, 21–22, 57
  and faith, 25–26, 57–59, 64–65, 183
  and Griffiths's conversion, 44–47, 57

and Griffiths's critique of West, 22–25, 31, 57, 76, 88, 105, 125, 127, 139, 159, 199, 206
and Griffiths's stroke (1990), 192–93
and imagination, 22–28, 143, 159
and intuition, 59–62, 127, 132–47, 194, 202, 213–14n. 7, 258n. 10
as level of consciousness, 168
limits of, 29, 62, 66, 87, 132–36, 258n. 10
Maritains on, 61–62, 72–73, 224n. 24
Spinoza on, 23
and symbols, 72–74, 160–61
Wilber on, 142
See also intellect; imagination; intuition; modern Western culture; science
Ricoeur, Paul, x, 217n. 5
Robinson, John A. T., 204–205
Ruusbroec, John, 144, 171–72, 250n. 83

Śankara, 86, 93–97, 128–29, 133, 216n. 18, 231n. 69, 232n. 73
  See also Vedānta
sannyāsa (renunciation)
  and *advaita*, 252n. 104
  Christian appropriation of, 51, 52, 106, 126, 194
  as spiritual ideal, 120, 126, 162, 172–73
  and transcending of symbols, 174–75, 180–81, 200–201, 205
  See also surrender
Sarvodaya movement, 52–53, 220–21n. 24
Savio, J. Samuel, 216n. 21
science
  in Griffiths's critique of modern Western culture, 25, 76, 86–87, 116, 123, 146, 159
  and levels of knowledge, 135–36, 139
  "new science," 116, 125–26, 141–46, 165, 168–69, 189, 200–201, 205–206, 236n. 8

science (*continued*)
  and symbols, 34
  See also modern Western culture
Schuon, Frithjof, 62–64, 224–25n. 29
Second Vatican Council, 115, 117–18,
    124, 185, 195–96, 197, 198
self-transcendence. *See* surrender;
    symbols
senses
  as faculty of the soul, 21, 57, 58
  and intuition, 138, 140–41
  in liturgy, 75
  in relation to ideas, reason, 5–6,
    22–23, 144
  as source of knowledge, 5–6,
    132–33, 138, 140, 189
  transcended in contemplation
    (meditation), 128–29, 131, 135,
    137, 162, 168
Shantivanam. *See* Griffiths
Shaw, George Bernard, 123
Sheldrake, Rupert, x, 125, 141,
    205–206
Shelley, Percy, 15, 34
Skinner, Martyn, xv, 17–19, 37
Spengler, Oswald, 123, 212n. 14
Spink, Kathryn, 212n. 16, 213n. 21,
    222n. 29, 236n. 7
Spinoza, Benedict de, 18, 23, 38, 59,
    214nn. 13, 15
surrender
  and *advaita*, 148
  to Christ and Church, 47, 71, 75,
    112
  and the cross, 100, 177, 251n. 95
  through dialogue, 4–9, 40
  in Griffiths's life, 46, 47, 49, 54, 55,
    100, 114, 120, 125–26, 194, 207,
    217–18n. 3
  and love, 32, 92, 100, 120, 176, 194
  to the Mother, 2, 120, 193
  of reason, 57
  and *sannyāsa*, 172–75, 179–81,
    210n. 17
  as self-transcendence, 32, 100, 148,
    179–80, 205
  and symbols, 28, 173–75, 180, 207

and Trinity, 164, 176
and union with God, 112, 193
Swinburne, Algernon Charles, 15
symbols
  and *advaita*, 251n. 92
  in Christian liturgy, 67–68, 72–81,
    87–91, 150
  as common feature of the religions,
    35, 191, 204, 254n. 21, 256n. 34
  and contemplation, 76–81, 84, 149,
    156, 190, 226n. 14
  and the culture bearer, 200–207
  defined, 29, 30, 34–35, 158,
    215–16n. 10, 246n. 30
  and demythologization, 161–62
  Griffiths's preference for Christian,
    258–59n. 13
  See also history
  in Hinduism, 85–88, 198
  and idolatry, 78, 88, 156, 174–75,
    178
  and imagination, 143
  Jesus Christ as, 81–84, 89–90,
    99–100, 133, 151–55, 177, 180,
    200–201, 230n. 55
  and knowledge, mediators of,
    28–30
  nature as, 31–35, 38, 71, 78, 82–84,
    154, 203
  real symbols, 81–84, 99–100, 132,
    151–52, 154–55, 163, 170, 173,
    180, 198, 203–204
  and theology, 155–163, 175, 196,
    253n. 13, 258n. 7
  three movements of love in con-
    sciousness
    symbolization (origins), 156–63,
      170–75, 204, 245–46n. 26,
      246n. 34, 247n. 35
    self-transcendence, 79–80,
      148–49, 156–63, 170–75, 181,
      201, 203
    reintegration, 173–75, 178–81,
      201, 203
  See also Aquinas; Bible; Christ,
    Jesus; contemplation; God;
    Griffiths; Hinduism; history;

imagination; inculturation; intuition; liturgy; modern Western culture; mysticism; poetry; Rahner; reason; *sannyāsa*; science; surrender

Tao Te Ching, Taoism, 18, 162, 190–91, 248n. 48
Teasdale, Wayne Robert, 211n. 28, 237n. 15
Teilhard de Chardin, Pierre, x, 124, 141, 168, 189
theology. *See* symbols
theology of religions (relation of Christianity to other religions)
  convergence in *advaita*, 188, 190, 251n. 92, 255n. 26, 255–56n. 28
  in first period, 38
  in second period (fulfillment theory), 49, 101–108, 253n. 4
  in third period (complementarity, unitive pluralism), 183–93, 234nn. 18, 21; 253n. 4, 256nn. 33, 34; 258–59n. 13
  religious differences, importance of, 106, 186, 188–90, 255n. 25, 257nn. 35, 4
  role of dialogue in, 7, 186–87
  syncretism, rejection of, 106, 186, 188, 190
  See also comparative religious studies; interreligious dialogue
time, 130–31, 228n. 24, 230n. 61
Tolstoy, Leo, 123
Trinity. *See* God

Upadhyay, Brahmabandhab, x, 51, 220n. 19
Upaniṣads
  advaita in, 95, 165, 251–52n. 100
  Griffiths's reading of, 4, 176, 251–52n. 100
  knowledge in, x, 142, 144

ultimate reality in, 109, 135, 160
use in liturgy, 117

Vatican II. *See* Second Vatican Council
Vedanta
  advaita, interpretations of, 92–96, 129, 140, 167, 232n. 73
  Advaita school (associated with Śankara), 93–94, 97, 128–29, 134, 167, 169–70, 216n. 18, 232n. 73
  Christian, 107, 134
  Griffiths's critique of, 93–98, 107, 128–29, 169–70, 199
  on knowledge, 135
  Madhva, 94, 231n. 70
  Rāmānuja, 94, 231n. 70
  See also Śankara

Wach, Joachim, 1, 259n. 14
Waterman, Hugh, xv, 17–19, 37
Webb, Mary, 213n. 4, 224n. 20
Weil, Simone, 80, 227n. 19
Weintraub, Karl Joachim, 8, 37, 54–55, 202, 205
Wilber, Ken
  on evolution of consciousness, 124–25, 142–45, 168, 171, 175, 189, 217n. 5, 238nn. 28, 29
  on knowledge, 142
  as representative of "new science," x, 141, 145–46, 205–206
Wiseman, James A., 252n. 106, 257–58n. 5
Wordsworth, William
  experience of nature, 11, 16–17, 21, 31, 34
  Griffiths's reading of, x, 15, 22, 28, 34, 39, 210n. 23, 213n. 3
  on imagination and intuition, 23, 138

Yoga, 53, 107, 131, 133, 239–40n. 9

Zaehner, R. C., 92–93